To Pat... Colleague, friend, friend! Thanks, Best, Greg Bell

Remaking the
American University

Remaking the American University

Market-Smart and Mission-Centered

ROBERT ZEMSKY
GREGORY R. WEGNER
WILLIAM F. MASSY

RUTGERS UNIVERSITY PRESS
New Brunswick, New Jersey, and London

Library of Congress Cataloging-in-Publication Data

Zemsky, Robert, 1940–
    Remaking the American university : market-smart and mission-centered
/ by Robert Zemsky, Gregory R. Wegner, William F. Massy.
        p. cm.
    Includes bibliographical references and index.
    ISBN 0-8135-3624-3 (hardcover : alk. paper)
    1. Education, Higher—Aims and objectives—United States. 2. Education,
Higher—Economic aspects—United States. 3. Educational change—United
States. I. Wegner, Gregory R., 1950– II. Massy, William F. III. Title.

    LA227.4.Z46 2005
    378.73—dc22

                                                        2004025321

A British Cataloging-in-Publication record for this book is available from the
British Library.

Manufactured in the United States of America

For Tom Langfitt, friend, funder,
fellow traveler

Contents

Acknowledgments

Because our work so often depends upon the insights of the colleagues we entice to join us as participants in our roundtables or as collaborators in research, we have a long list of those to whom we are truly indebted. First, Joan Girgus, Jim Galbally, and Ann Duffield joined us as editors of *Policy Perspectives*. Ann was responsible for the publication's style and format as well as purpose. We have, over the years, had three extraordinary sponsors: The Pew Charitable Trusts—Tom Langfitt, Rebecca Rimel, Susan Stine, and Bob Scwhartz; The John S. and James L. Knight Foundation—Creed Black, Hodding Carter, and Rick Love; and the U.S. Department of Education through its funding of the National Center on the Educational Quality of the Workforce (EQW) and subsequently the National Center on Postsecondary Improvement (NCPI). Peter Cappelli of the University of Pennsylvania and Patti Gumport of Stanford University superintended those projects and frequently joined our roundtables.

The members of the original Pew Roundtable require individual recognition: Pat Cross, Darryl Greer, John Gould, Bruce Johnstone, Hank Levin, Art Levine, Arturo Madrid, Pat McPherson, Dolf Norton, Lew Solomon, Glen Stine, Ursula Wagener, Tim Warner, Marna Whittington. It is always dangerous to single out a few from what was fundamentally a collective endeavor; we would be remiss, however, if we did not acknowledge the particular contributions of a few. Pat Callan taught us the meaning of public policy. Alfredo de los Santos made certain that access remained an integral part of our agenda. Virginia Smith was both sage counselor and our connection to the worlds of policy and action that often swirled around Clark Kerr.

Many of our roundtables—and, given the frequency with which they were drawn upon for this volume, many of our most important— were cosponsored by a variety of national organizations: the National Association of College and University Business Officers, Jay Morley; the Association of Research Libraries, Duane Webster; the Association of American Universities, John Vaughn; the American Association of University Women, Patricia McCabe; the American Council on Education, Bob Atwell and Madeleine Green; the Association of Governing Boards of Universities and Colleges, Tom Ingram. Doug Toma, now of the University of Georgia, was responsible for the special roundtable on intercollegiate athletics.

We have worked with a host of dedicated scholars, colleagues, and graduate students. Peter Ewell helped shape our understanding of learning and assessment. Tom Ehrlich was responsible for our balancing of market forces and public purposes. Martin Meyerson, as always, was both guide and spur. Jim Duderstadt kept after us until we wrote this volume. Sally Vaughn Massy provided valuable insights on higher education as well as an insistence on clear expression. For their insights and assistance on the nature of education quality and the academic audit, we owe a special debt to Nigel French, Steve Graham, David Dill, and Frans van Vught. Dennis Bartels taught us about the nature of distressed liberal arts colleges.

Susan Shaman and Dan Shapiro of the Institute for Research on Higher Education with the support of Greg Dubrow, Liza Herzog, Jesse Lytle, Nichole Rowles, Aimee Tabor, and Jennifer Giancola were responsible for much of the statistical analyses we drew on for this volume. Andrea Wilger played the same role at the Stanford Institute for Higher Education Research. We have always been dependent on skilled editors. In recent years Marc Iannozzi has had that principal responsibility.

Sarah Hardesty Bray of the *Chronicle of Higher Education* worked with Bob on the opinion piece that first laid out the concept of diminishing public purpose, the central theme of this volume. Marlie Wasserman of the Rutgers University Press saw that piece in the *Chronicle* and invited us to expand those ideas into a full-blown book.

We alone are responsible for what we have written, though we trust we have made clear that we were seldom alone.

Bob Zemsky
Greg Wegner
Bill Massy
September 2004

*Remaking the
American University*

1 | Introduction

The Diminishing of Public Purpose

For more than two decades we have been writing about the transformation of the American university—in books, monographs, and a host of essays, many of which first appeared in *Change* magazine, but mostly in the pages of *Policy Perspectives*. By the late 1980s *Policy Perspectives* had become higher education's principal catalog of changing circumstances—the rise of markets, the corresponding diminution of public purpose, the necessary but largely unsuccessful battle to make American universities as diverse and accessible as the communities they serve.

Each essay of *Policy Perspectives* was itself the product of an extended discussion among a roundtable of higher education's movers and shakers, men and women whom we often described as "pooh-bahs in waiting." Some were college and university presidents; others were scholars across a broad range of disciplines; still others were public policy wonks, including on occasion former governors and legislators. From time to time we also attracted members of the working press whose siftings through higher education's laundry had made them unique witnesses to the transformations *Policy Perspectives* was mapping.

No matter who joined us for a particular roundtable, we reminded them and ourselves that we would not become Cassandras. We intended to speak in terms that both those within and outside the academy would readily understand and believe—no easy task given the cultural divide that often separates the one from the other.

We were also in search of a touchstone to make sense of what was happening to American higher education and why. As we write now, in the opening decade of the twenty-first century, we have adopted as that touchstone the quarter-century following the Second World War, a period many consider to have been the golden age of the American university. Not much given to nostalgia, we resist that hallowed portrait. In fact, the 1950s and 1960s were characterized just as frequently by political numbness as by fevered commitment.

Federal Initiatives at Midcentury

In one important respect, however, the twenty-five years following the Second World War were both different and better: during that time, the American university was expected to play a major role in the pursuit of broad societal goals, a role that no one expects the university to now play.

Take, for example, the two major higher-education initiatives that the federal government launched in 1945. The more celebrated, and hence better remembered, was the GI Bill and the educational benefits that it conferred. With its passage, a college education became *the* gateway to middle-class status for the veterans who flocked to American campuses in unprecedented numbers; thus, colleges and universities became prime platforms of economic development.

The second initiative, now largely forgotten but no less seminal, was *Science, The Endless Frontier: A Report to the President,* by Vannevar Bush, then director of the Office of Scientific Research and Development. In his 1945 report, Bush called on the federal government to make a massive and sustaining investment in basic scientific research. The agency of that research, Bush argued, should be the American research university, in part because of the role it had played in the war effort, but mostly because only a university and its research faculty were capable of achieving what the nation required. "It is chiefly in these institutions that scientists may work in an atmosphere which is relatively free from the adverse pressure of convention, prejudice, or commercial necessity," Bush wrote. "At their best they provide the scientific worker with a strong sense of solidarity and security, as well as a substantial degree of personal intellectual freedom. All of these factors are of great importance in the development of new knowledge, since much of new knowledge is certain to arouse opposition because of its tendency to challenge current beliefs or practice."

Most of what Bush recommended, including the chartering of a National Science Foundation, became federal policy, making the federal government the principal funder of a scientific revolution that recast the state of knowledge while giving science departments an often dominant voice in the ordering of their universities. Taken together, the GI Bill and Vannevar Bush's report helped make colleges and universities matter as they had never done before. The responsibilities conferred on these institutions, their faculty and students, made them subjects of controversy, celebration, scrutiny, and sustained public interest.

Throughout the following two decades, academic place and public purpose commingled in a growing number of ventures. Some enterprises focused exclusively on economic development, like the role that universities played in founding North Carolina's Research Triangle Park and Foundation in 1959 and, later, Stanford University's participation in developing what became Silicon Valley.

University leaders became public figures, expected to speak out on issues of public concern as both experts and witnesses. It is interesting to note how easy it is, more than thirty years after the fact, to generate a roll-call of public presidents from the 1960s and 1970s: Father Hesburgh of Notre Dame, Bill Friday of North Carolina, Edwin Levy of Chicago, Clark Kerr of the University of California, Kingman Brewster of Yale all come readily to mind in a way that almost no currently sitting university president does.

In the 1960s colleges and universities were important staging and recruiting grounds for many social and political movements that became the decade's hallmarks: the civil rights marches; the Free Speech Movement at UC–Berkeley; the protests against racism and poverty that linked Yale and the City of New Haven; and the increasingly effective as well as virulent antiwar protest that closed the decade.

Perhaps the most telling change, however, is the recasting of the university in the imagination of the American public. In the 1960s and, to a lesser extent, the 1950s, campuses were public arenas—platforms for political theater, recruiting grounds for social activists, and often the places where public officials sought judicious expertise when sorting out vexing issues. Certainly not every idea discussed in collegiate settings really mattered, but rare was the social, political, or economic movement that did not consider the college campus a critical venue for the airing of viewpoints and perspectives.

In the early twenty-first century, all that social activism is now gone or disappearing. Today colleges and universities are seen principally as gateways to economic security and middle-class status. Except for the occasional bout with political correctness, almost no one worries about higher education institutions leading young people astray. If anything, the lament is that they have, in their pursuit of market advantage, become dispensers of degrees and certificates rather than communities of educators who originate, debate, and promulgate important ideas.

The Drift toward Private Purposes

What happened? In part colleges and universities are what they are today because the 1970s began so badly. The killings at Jackson State and Kent State genuinely frightened most people on college campuses. In the aftermath of those tragedies and a host of lesser ones, a politically destructive and socially dysfunctional retreat ensued. Students as well as faculty turned inward; both became less concerned with societal issues and less willing to wear their values on their sleeves. Students and faculty began asking less about what others were doing or thinking; instead, they focused on their own preferences. It was an age of personal experimentation—with drugs, sex, alternate lifestyles—in which the doing was more important than the explaining or the justifying. Although the terminology would not come into fashion for another two decades, the unofficial motto on most campuses became "Don't ask, don't tell."

A changing economy also led a host of American institutions—universities and hospitals offer the most conspicuous examples—to the understanding that their survival depended on being more responsive to market forces. The growing importance of a college education in obtaining jobs and higher pay played its part as well, signifying to many that the real purpose of a college degree was to confer advantages to individual students. Experiences became more important than ideas.

Yet the principal responsibility for making colleges and universities less places of public purpose belongs to the public itself, or the voters and the officials they have elected to national and state offices. At the federal level, the evolution of financial aid as a subsidy to student "consumers" has reinforced the notion that a college education is principally, if not solely, an investment in personal advancement. It was as if the GI Bill had been designed to aid only individuals and not to help America transfer from a wartime to a peacetime footing. In state capitals, the willingness of legislatures to encourage tuition increases in place of state appropriations—a pattern that now repeats itself every time state tax revenues decrease—has helped privatize public higher education. Legislators and governors everywhere have become accustomed to letting higher education pay its own way; they remind students and parents who balk at ever-higher tuitions that nothing beats a college education from the standpoint of return on investment.

Accompanying the rise of tuitions at public institutions have been sizable leaps in the price of attendance charged by private universities and colleges. While driven by somewhat different causes, the actions of the two sectors, public and private, collectively reinforce the notion that a college education is becoming a private good. Just as the publics have had no discipline from state agencies to contain prices, the privates have shown no restraint. Conceived originally as institutions to serve the public well-being through the creation of educational opportunity, higher education institutions have become instead the thresholds delineating the advantaged from the rest of society. In the nation's 250 most selective private and public institutions, 55 percent of the freshman classes had family incomes in the highest quartile in 2000, up from 46 percent in 1985.

Having left the nation's colleges and universities largely to their own devices, most state policymakers have largely allowed those institutions, again public as well as private, to pursue their own, as opposed to the public's, agenda. A telling reflection of this policy stance is the degree to which higher education institutions, in the face of the continuing deterioration of public schools, have been seen as part of neither the problem nor the solution. California demonstrates just how detached the different levels of the educational system have become from one another. California generally ranks among the top five states in its support for higher education, yet somewhere south of forty-fifth in its support for elementary and secondary schools. As one might expect, the quality of the state's K–12 schools reflects that allotment of public support.

Equally telling is what has *not* happened. A friend and former university president heard us say that in most state campaigns to promote adult literacy, universities play only tangential roles. Not happy with that aspersion, he bristled back, "Believe me, if the governor and the chairs of House Ways and Means and Senate Finance committees told me that adult literacy was a priority, I would have found a way to make it . . . my priority." And that's the point. The governor and legislators never asked, probably never thought to, having decided in their own minds that simply supporting higher education was what they did to help the citizens of the state—as individuals who also happened to be voters.

Watch instead what politicians actually do, and the same lesson is driven home with even greater force. The big higher education news from Washington on the cusp of the 2004 presidential election centered on the efforts of Congressman Buck McKeon, Republican from California, to punish institutions whose price increases exceed federally established maximums. McKeon's initiative was a chilling reminder of just how much public policy had come to focus on prices—and on what many had come to see as the failure of the market to ensure fair and effective competition. Leave aside for the moment that McKeon proposed a system of federally mandated price controls and that his proposal read better as a press release than as a piece of serious legislation. Motivating the congressman's proposal is a principle that everybody now inherently knows: a higher education is primarily a consumer good. The underlying questions are hardly ever asked: just how do colleges and universities spend their tuition income, or might money to support public purposes be spent more effectively than it is now?

This slope has proved to be increasingly slippery. As more people have viewed universities as providing principally personal advantages, institutions have been able to charge even higher prices to provide those advantages. As a result, public universities are less dependent on public appropriation, to the point where many of the nation's best-known public institutions have become like private ones. At the same time the presidents of the nation's major private universities, many of them blessed with billion-dollar endowments, have simply given up defining their institutions in terms of their social and economic contributions to the community, state, or nation. What has come to matter most is the pursuit of quality and excellence—as largely expressed in terms of the competitive advantage enjoyed by its faculty and students.

At this point, some may well ask, "What's wrong with what we have? Modern universities are working fine, teaching students, pushing out the frontiers of knowledge, serving their communities principally as engines of economic development. Why long for an earlier time that was not nearly as romantic or progressive as today's critics of higher education would have us believe?"

The answer lies in what is lost when universities are shaped almost exclusively by the wants of students seeking educational credentials and businesses and governmental agencies seeking research outcomes. When universities are wholly dominated by market interests, there is a notable abridgement of their roles as public agencies—and a diminution of their capacity to provide public venues for testing ideas and creeds as well as agendas of public action. In no arena is this reduction more apparent than in the universities' near absence as active players in the struggle to make public primary and secondary education work in the United States. Finally, what is being lost is the idea that knowledge has other than instrumental purposes, that ideas are important whether or not they confer personal advantage.

What can be done? The first answer to that question is a catalog of what won't happen and in that sense can't work. There will be no return to a simpler era when a much smaller proportion of the population sought a college education. Nor is there any likelihood that either market forces will play a less dominant role or that universities will become less costly or less complex enterprises. No matter how practiced the disaffected become at denouncing the "commodification" of higher education, the conversion of their institutions into market enterprises will proceed apace, if for no other reason than that market income continues to substitute for public appropriation.

Mission-Centered, Market-Smart

Given that reality, we came to understand that the key to making the modern university more publicly relevant ironically lies in making it more market sensitive—or, to use the term we have come to favor, making the university more market-smart. When faced with the kind of revenue shortfalls that now confront higher education, most presidents and their institutions simply hunker down by making the preservation of current jobs and operations their top priority. Confronting the inevitable, those institutions hew to a largely conservative strategy of across-the-board cuts and postponed investments. The result, despite everyone's best intentions, is an institution even more dependent on its current markets and less able to invest in its own future, let alone pursue policies and programs of public as opposed to personal interest.

There are important exceptions; consider the University of Michigan. In the 1980s the university identified ways to encourage its schools and institutes, as well as individual faculty members, to develop new markets to offset the declining value of state appropriations. As Michigan gained mastery of the market, those at the university came to talk openly about "The University of Michigan, Inc." What that mastery provided was both institutional confidence and added funds. In the 1970s Michigan and UC–Berkeley received roughly the same levels of core revenue. Three decades later, however, Michigan's core revenues exceeded those of Berkeley by more than $400 million per year.

Michigan succeeded largely by making itself less dependent on funding from the State of Michigan and substantially more dependent on market-generated student tuition and fee revenue, thus more than offsetting a big drop in the relative value of state funding. By the late 1990s, the State of Michigan was actually supplying less than 20 percent of the university's total revenues (including the operation of its hospital and auxiliary enterprises). The University of Michigan had become the face of privatization.

The experience of UC–Berkeley suggests what happens when, in the face of flat or declining public support, the institution does not "go to market" in the sense that Michigan has. For most of its history, the University of California system had declined to charge students tuition; it believed instead that, as a public good, a college education ought to be provided by the state. In this respect, the University of California resembled European and publicly funded Japanese universities. Faced with the need to increase revenues to remain competitive, the University of California modestly increased student fees; later, when confronted with a substantial reduction in funding from the state of California, it began to charge students a rapidly escalating tariff. If, however, the goal was to remain competitive with Michigan in terms of revenue, then the price increases came almost a decade too late. By 1991, when the new California policies were put into effect, Michigan was already drawing 31 percent of its *core revenues* from student tuition and fee income. By the end of the 1990s, UC–Berkeley drew only 23.4 percent from the same source, even though its other sources of revenue largely mirrored those of the University of Michigan.

In embracing the market, Michigan chose a future that allowed it to surpass the University of California, certainly in terms of financial infusion and, in the eyes of many, in terms of scholarly clout. Not so coincidentally, we believe, the University of Michigan also played the leading role in the decade's most important litigation concerning higher education. In defending its use of race-conscious admissions policies, the University of Michigan and its tough-minded, market-smart administration demonstrated what a mission-centered institution can accomplish in the defense of public principle. Michigan's defense of affirmative action reinvigorated the national debate over social inequity and its causes in modern-day America; at the same time it reminded the citizens of Michigan that their university remained a place of public purpose.

By using funds earned in the market to fund programs that reinforce a university's sense of itself as an institution of public purpose—being market-smart to remain mission-centered—one answers the question of what universities must do to remain places of public pursuit. All the essays in this volume seek to provide detail and context as to what it means to be market-smart and mission-centered. Some reflect on how the university needs to be better organized as well as more entrepreneurial. Some focus on the required culture change if universities are to become effective as well as efficient market enterprises. Others outline the kind of slippery slope on which many universities today find themselves—on the way down to becoming institutions that are much less than they ought to be.

In *Science, the Endless Frontier,* Vannevar Bush defended his choice of the university—as opposed to the industrial lab—as the best place for the federal government to make its investment in research by noting: "Industry is generally inhibited by preconceived goals, by its own clearly defined standards, and by the constant pressure of commercial necessity." It is sad that this description is increasingly apropos of the modern academy as well—a place that has learned well to be market-smart, often at the expense of being mission-centered.

The question we still ask, twenty years after we first began our explorations, is: "Can universities, at this late date, still choose to be places of public purpose?" Though the answer ought to be a resounding yes, we are still not sure. This volume argues that to thrive, universities must be different, more creative, less rhetorical in their pursuit of excellence. They require leaders who want their institutions—as institutions—to become market enterprises that are ready, willing, and able to play public roles. Higher education institutions also require public officials who treat them as more than shopping malls in service of their constituents. Governors, budget directors, and legislative leaders have to ask more of their universities—again as institutions—

even if that means increasing their public appropriations. Most of all, administrators and politicians must publicly reaffirm the principle that the American university, an educational asset, can powerfully serve both public and private purposes.

Perspectives on a Changing Enterprise

We come then to the focus of the present volume. Our goal is to convey a better understanding of how the interplay of markets, strategies, and purposes are remaking American colleges and universities.

Given that our subject is markets, however, there is no single insight, no "aha moment" that clarifies everything or resolves all apparent contractions. There is neither plot nor narrative, neither heroes nor villains. Markets beget purposes and strategies, some of which actually work in the sense that they achieve the desired ends. Very often, however, the larger result is that individual strategies and purposes work against one another, in large part because the champions of particular causes do not fully understand how perfectly good ideas in a market world can lead to genuinely perverse outcomes in terms of public purpose. We seek a better understanding of that perversity, if you will, and how good choices and carefully crafted policies—institutional and personal as well as governmental—can and sometimes cannot achieve desired ends.

Thus, we offer a series of essays; we call them perspectives. In general, we have sought to track historical developments as a way of understanding the context in which choices are currently being made and will likely be made well into the future. The markets that reshaped American higher education did not emerge suddenly as a result of some Machiavellian scheme to make colleges and universities less than they ought to be. Rather, the shaping forces of the market were introduced piecemeal, occasionally as the result of some stated action, like the decision to use a market mechanism to distribute federal financial aid, though more often as the result of seemingly disconnected events and initiatives whose cumulative impact was mostly unexpected.

Because people and the worlds they inhabit changed, colleges and universities changed, along with the people they appointed and employed. What held sway in the quarter-century following the Second World War no longer compels. While the larger purposes of the university—the passing of knowledge from one generation to the next and the production of new knowledge—may still be understood as the constants of the enterprise, they are also purposes whose scale has changed dramatically. During the last fifty years a college education has come to be perceived as an economic necessity pursued by the many, rather than a privilege reserved for the few. The changes in the scholarship of the academy are even more astounding. The pace of discovery, the dissemination of findings, and the commercialization of products and results now proceed at lightning speed. Students talk regularly about being hit by "fire hoses" spewing out facts, proofs, and opinions that they are expected to absorb and master. Those who train physicians talk about the need to create in their students the skills and intuitions of a medical librarian, simply because it is no longer possible to master the knowledge base of most medical specialties. It is the age of just-in-time learning and even just-in-time discovery.

The commingling of these circumstances, along with a growing belief that governments too often did things badly, created and shaped the markets for learning and research that are the subjects at hand. Our volume falls roughly into thirds, focusing first on concepts, then on consequences, and finally, though in a more limited way, on prescriptions.

Concepts

Chapters 2 through 4 explore the markets in which colleges and universities compete along three dimensions. The first reprises the concept of the academic ratchet and the administrative lattice to examine how markets have impacted the behaviors and hence the organization of academic enterprises. The academic ratchet has freed faculty in general, and entrepreneurial faculty in particular, largely to pursue interests of their own choosing and definition. As the faculty have taken less responsibility for operating the institutions they inhabit, the administrative lattice has turned administrators and bureaucrats into internal entrepreneurs and professionals in areas as diverse as student services and financial management.

We turn next to the shape of the markets for educational services, with a specific focus on the market for undergraduate education in the United States. It is, as Michael McPherson has observed, a market ruled by an admissions arms race gone mad. In this chapter we ask why the market for undergraduate education has neither controlled prices nor promoted the kind of quality most educational reformers believe essential. Why instead have the rankings supplied by *U.S. News and World Report* come to play such a dominant role in expressing student preferences and family choices? The answer, not surprisingly, requires an understanding of just what students and their families know and what they seek from a market in which price, like the rankings themselves, becomes a surrogate for excellence.

The third concept we explore is the relationship between missions and markets embedded in our title. In terms that we hope fit with the intuitions most people bring to a marketplace, we explore the similarities, but more importantly, the differences between for-profit and nonprofit enterprises. Here we sketch a kind of calculus of choice that helps make more rational and transparent the kinds of tradeoffs colleges and universities need to make as they seek to remain mission-centered.

Consequences

The middle section of this volume deals with what we have labeled the consequences of market competition. Knowing how particular aspects of higher education have been impacted by market forces brings with it a more general understanding of how markets are reshaping most aspects of an academic enterprise. Chapter 5 focuses on intercollegiate athletics, particularly at institutions that practice selective admissions. We argue that the crisis brewing over what proportion of a medallion institution's spaces in its freshman class needs to be reserved for recruited athletes is an object lesson of what happens when market competition—or just plain competition—is pursued by communities that no longer talk about values.

Our sixth chapter, "To Publish and Perish," transforms that historical lament of assistant professors on the need to publish or pay the consequences into an exploration of what happened when just a handful of commercial publishers came to enjoy near-monopolistic power over the publication of research findings. Almost no one in the academy worried very much when the commercial houses suddenly appeared bearing gifts, promising to bail out the universities and learned societies that could no longer afford to subsidize the scholarly journals responsible for disseminating research findings in the natural, engineering, and biomedical sciences. How the academy came to lose its ability to use the knowledge generated by this research it had paid for is an unhappy, though instructive, tale.

Chapter 9 is a morality tale of a different sort. In the late 1990s American higher education seemed on the verge of being transformed by the technological and commercial forces that had given birth to *e-*

learning. Promises were made, money was spent, and what emerged was decidedly less than expected. Proponents of e-learning promised a revolution in teaching to allow truly customized learning to fit the needs of each individual student. Instead, e-learning has become principally a way of distributing correspondence courses on the Web under the label of distance education. Most big commercial ventures in e-learning have folded, including a number of high-profile enterprises like Columbia University's Fathom and New York University's NYU.Online, each of which cost its institution tens of millions of dollars. Why is e-learning a thwarted innovation—and what does its blunting tell us about how prepared universities are to enter markets dominated by rapidly changing technologies?

The commercial prospects that once swirled around e-learning also contribute to the fourth of the market consequences we trace. Asking "Who owns teaching?" provides an important means of engaging a subject often talked about in the abstract, though seldom explored in sufficient detail to allow an institution to recast what happens in the classroom. One of the more intriguing possibilities just over the horizon is that the academy's embrace of the now-commercialized electronic technologies that its engineers and physicists invented may actually force a discussion of property rights in a different cast: Who has the right to copy or commercialize what faculty do?

Prescriptions

The final section of this volume focuses on prescriptions, though we hasten to add that we have no answer for those who want to put the genie back in the lamp. The educational and research markets now shaping—some would say distorting—higher education are here to stay. Indeed, they will only become more powerful in the years ahead. Hence our prescriptions are about maximizing flexibility and independence; we counsel learning how to be market-smart to remain mission-centered.

Our first prescription, reflected in the title to Chapter 9, is about "Making Quality Job One." In the long run markets do reward those enterprises that help define and then produce what the market comes to see as quality products. Other industries and universities in other parts of the world have mastered the art and craft of quality assurance. What will it take—what will have to happen inside American colleges and universities—for those same lessons and techniques to take hold in the United States?

Next we turn to the question of access. In a world dominated by the admissions arms race, how can colleges and universities in partnership with public agencies, including primary and secondary schools, create sufficient incentives that result in more at-risk youngsters succeeding both educationally and economically? For more than thirty years, public policy's response has been to create a voucher system designed to make a college education within the grasp of every potential student regardless of economic means. Although Pell grants and student loans have expanded access, they have not closed the gap between majority and minority participation in higher education. Our prescription is different: use the market, though not just by providing vouchers and loans to students. Instead use the power of the market and the purchasing power of governmental appropriations to create the kind of joint ventures necessary to promote the climate of opportunity so long pursued.

Chapter 11 is a more general prescription for public policy in an age of markets. We focus on what institutions have and have not learned throughout the last thirty years about the political arena, and we suggest what additional lessons they need to absorb quickly. In part, these lessons entail a public acknowledgment by institutional leaders that their industry, more often than not, enters the policy arena out of self-interest. And paradoxically perhaps, colleges and universities must act out rather than simply reassert their commitments to public purpose. In the end, it means coming full circle by understanding that being mission-centered and market-smart means being politically savvy.

Our twelfth and final chapter begins with the story of the time we asked one thousand eight hundred college and university presidents to meet us in St. Louis, and nearly five hundred actually showed up. It was a moment of change in higher education—a moment, as the *Policy Perspectives* that derived from that conclave proclaimed, when higher education was being asked to dance with change. Throughout the ensuing decade we have sought to catalog what dancing with change would mean in terms of practices, perceptions, and policies. Chapter 12 is our current answer to that question.

2 | The Lattice and the Ratchet

In the mid-1980s then Secretary of Education William Bennett and his sidekick, Checker Finn, were using the bully pulpit their offices afforded to excoriate American colleges and universities for their failure to control costs, for the disinclination of their presidents to hold faculty accountable, and for the fact that student interest as much as faculty consensus appeared to be the driver of curriculum. Shouting was in vogue, along with the kind of institution bashing that reflected a well-honed instinct to make political hay at higher education's expense.

Bennett's and Finn's critiques found plenty of echoes from both within and outside the academy. Such studies as *Integrity in the College Curriculum,* undertaken by Fred Rudolph for the Association of American Colleges, as well as Bob Zemsky's work, *Structure and Coherence: Measuring the Undergraduate Curriculum,* were demonstrating that there was neither integrity nor coherence to what colleges and universities were teaching and hence to what their students were learning—or not learning. Even *A Nation at Risk,* now best remembered for its critique of K–12 education, actually lumped together the nation's educational institutions, noting the "growing impatience with the shoddiness . . . reflected in our schools and colleges." Reflecting on the then-emerging importance of the markets in American higher education, *A Nation at Risk* went on to observe that "in some colleges

maintaining enrollments is of greater day-to-day concern than maintaining rigorous academic standards. And the ideal of academic excellence as the primary goal of schooling seems to be fading across
the board in American education."

Bennett's and Finn's repeated cannonades gained attention because
they hit targets on which colleges and universities—or at least their
presidents and trustees—felt genuinely vulnerable. What the secretary
criticized most vociferously was higher education's profligacy: American higher education was a land of waste and inefficiency. Too many
people were being paid too much to perform tasks for which there was
neither sufficient demand nor well-defined purpose. What the faculty
wanted the faculty got. There were no sunsets in universities; programs
that had outlived their rationale were continued simply because no
one could summon the political will to close them. Every new program or initiative required new funds beyond the existing base—a "that
and more" mentality that inevitably made the whole enterprise more
costly. And always the bill for higher education's lack of discipline
was paid by somebody else—by state governments in the form of increased appropriations, students and their families in the form of higher
tuitions, or the federal government in the form of higher indirect cost
recoveries. Bennett tapped the anger of many critics who believed these
expenditures were chiefly in support of an academic lifestyle that had
little to do with either research or the dissemination of knowledge.

In the late 1980s these charges reached their apotheosis in the hear-
ings of the Dingle Committee, which charged Donald Kennedy, then
president of Stanford University, with siphoning off federal funds paid
as indirect cost recoveries to support, among other things, a yacht and
flowers for the president's table. Kennedy personally sought to answer
Dingle's charges—all to no avail, though in the final accounting
Stanford was held largely blameless of the charge that it had artificially inflated its indirect costs. Stanford in the 1980s was just too inviting a target for those who thought the American university had lost
its way. It was the new, west-coast university, the brash upstart that
was already benefiting from the surge in new technologies that would
make the Silicon Valley a household word. Stanford was also the university that had understood how to take advantage of a rising real es-
tate market, principally by launching a research park and upscale
shopping center. Not coincidentally, Stanford was also the first university to launch a billion-dollar fund-raising drive.

As part of the launching of that campaign and just before Stanford's accounting procedures became the subject of a national inquiry, Kennedy sought to address the principal conundrum plaguing the nation's research universities by asking, "How can we look so rich and yet feel so poor?" The answer he offered was an eloquent explanation of why research universities, in particular, had grown by accretion rather than substitution. He took as his metaphor the constant addition of new elements to the Periodic Table. Universities, he said, had to teach and explore all the elements that preceded each new addition, as well as the new element itself. The nonlinear, not-quite-exponential increase in knowledge across the curriculum was making the nation's universities ever more complex and hence expensive. For Kennedy, as for most university presidents, the dilemma was all about costs and the near impossibility that their institutions would ever have enough money to satisfy their hunger for new knowledge.

Focusing on Money Instead

And then higher education moved on. By the early 1990s Kennedy had given up the Stanford presidency. Dingle had lost interest in the pursuit of purloined indirect costs. Bennett became the Bush administration's drug czar. University presidents became less aggressive in their defense of how their universities spent their money. There even were fewer claims that what higher education needed was a good media campaign to remind the public of the inherently high cost of excellence.

As the fevered pitch of censure and defensive justifications subsided, one might have expected a return to more routine circumstances. However, it became clear that higher education was changing irreversibly. It was a change process that had begun some two decades earlier and ironically had as much to do with the prospect of campus violence as with institutional finances. Thirty-some years after the fact, it is hard to conjure up the sheer terror the events of 1970 evoked among the leaders of American colleges and universities. The college campus had become not just a figurative but a literal battlefield. The knoll from which the National Guard troops fired upon and killed four Kent State students became the symbol of a polity in control of neither itself nor others.

Within a year of those shootings, most American campuses had come to roughly the same conclusion. Most needed was a cooling out that depended on not just lowering voices but changing subjects. Something else had to absorb higher education's energies, something that shifted the focus back to the campus in a way that would not arouse passions or question fundamental values.

Serendipitously, just such a focus was at hand. In the 1970s much of American higher education faced the daunting prospect of running out of students and money simultaneously. The book everyone was reading—Bud Cheit's *The New Depression in Higher Education*—was frightening simply because it was so logical. The great wave of public investments in higher education that had more than doubled the enterprise's capacity, largely through the creation of new campuses, had spent itself. Institutions in the Northeast were beset with a triple whammy: changing demographics, double-digit inflation, and the soaring price of heating oil. Across the region the number of young people was declining; first, elementary schools closed, followed by junior and senior high schools. It took little imagination to see that the Northeast's famed colleges and universities could be next on the endangered species lists. Stagflation—the combination of inflation and the absence of economic growth—was sapping the energy of nearly every American enterprise and institution.

Not immediately and certainly not all at once, campus communities began to focus more particularly on their financial vulnerability; in part, the baby-boomers' graduation in the early 1970s had taken the wind from their enrollment and revenue sails and prompted many institutions to seek new markets in adult and returning students. By the early 1990s some old battles still raged, but, for the most part, money—or rather, its absence—came to absorb each campus. What happened at the University of Pennsylvania in the late 1970s became emblematic of what was about to happen elsewhere. Driven in part by its peculiar financial vulnerabilities, in part by a new president committed to harnessing market forces, and in part by luck and happenstance, Penn began examining to what extent its then eleven schools were really paying their own ways. What lay behind the resulting critique of university finances was a notion that individual units ought to be responsible for both income and expense, an idea that broke a decades-long tradition of allocating resources to the schools and then hoping they lived within their allotments.

Thus was born Responsibility Center Management, a budget system that permanently changed the politics on campus—at Penn, and ultimately at an array of institutions across the country. There was so much more to argue about, starting with the rules for allocating central costs, the distribution of the subvention funds the central administration had reserved for itself, and ultimately the appropriateness of treating academic units as economic enterprises. Underlying much of this new, but actually safer quarrelsomeness, was the revelation of just who was subsidizing whom. The financial winners wanted to retain more if not all of their earned income; the losers, not surprisingly, felt they had been twice wronged—first by being denied sufficient central appropriations to meet current needs, and second by having their dependency made embarrassingly public.

By making deans and schools responsible for generating their own income, the new budget system was initially seen as a way of reigning in wasteful expense. The way to a balanced budget was presumably to eliminate programs that did not pay for themselves, reduce administrative costs, and hold down the growth of the faculty. In fact, Responsibility Center Management taught a fundamental lesson: it was easier to raise additional revenue than to enact painful cuts, particularly if those cuts involved people. It was the system's income incentives that transformed campuses and unleashed a torrent of entrepreneurial energy. There was a burgeoning of new research centers and institutes, new programs to educate professionals in the field, new service bureaus.

The ultimate lesson of the mega battles of the past—whether they concerned the shape of the curriculum, the importance of diversity, or an institution's relations with its immediate neighbors—were less compelling than they might have seemed before. What mattered most was the interdependence of good ideas, energetic people, and the status that being a successful university bought in the marketplace.

The Administrative Lattice

Institutions that mastered this discipline succeeded, but they also changed in ways that higher education's leaders in the 1980s were just beginning to understand. The emergence of such understanding is an important though at times less obvious aspect of the transformation of the American university. To better understand the changing dynamics of higher education institutions, we developed the twin concepts of the administrative lattice and the academic ratchet to map the interplay of traditional administrative functions, the growing importance of entrepreneurial activity, and the resulting recasting of roles and responsibilities across the institution.

We began with the recognition that, then as now, on most campuses there is an inherent tension between academic and administrative units, between faculty and staff. Sometimes that tension is genuinely creative, as each half of the institution strives to strengthen itself while recognizing the inherent value of the other. More often, the tension yields an unproductive competition for resources. Faculty members remind themselves and the community that they are "the business" of the institution, all other activities being nonessential and frequently wasteful. For their part, staff members gleefully recount tales of faculty mismanagement and waste, secure in their sense that the only thing businesslike about the institution is their own ability to discharge increasingly complex management tasks.

We know now that as institutions became market sensitive (though not necessarily market-smart), the number and variety of administrative staff they employed veritably exploded. In March 1990 the *Chronicle of Higher Education*'s Karen Grassmuck used data submitted by the nation's colleges and universities to the U.S. Equal Employment Opportunity Commission to chart that growth. She found that the category of "other professionals"—academic support personnel filling such roles as financial aid counselors, auditors, research specialists, and systems analysts—had increased by more than 60 percent between 1975 and 1985, a period during which the size of the average faculty increased by less than 6 percent. Increases were also substantial for many institutions among the ranks of executive, administrative, and managerial personnel. No less telling than the data was Grassmuck's report of the impression among some higher education officials that, in spite of this growth, "many universities are making do with smaller staffs than they need."

The analysis documented the pervasiveness of the growth of administrative personnel; it was occurring across the board in nearly every type of institution, rich and poor, big and small, public and private. Just as most institutions enjoyed real revenue growth in the 1980s, so did most institutions substantially expand their administrative and academic support staffs. As a result, an extension of the scale and scope of an administrative lattice was growing, much like a crystalline structure, to incorporate ever-more elaborate and intricate linkages within itself.

Increased Regulation and Micromanagement

The growing importance of markets in the 1980s was accompanied by both a general increase in federal regulation—

ironically, perhaps, a side effect of the federal government's own use
of market mechanisms to make policy—and a new eagerness to make
colleges and universities subject to federal regulation. The Dingle
Committee's exposé of what it considered higher education's abuse of
federal rules for determining indirect costs was simply one manifestation of the fact that higher education was now regarded like every
other American industry.

Although they frequently protested too much, university presidents
were at least partially right when they blamed increased regulation
and external micromanagement for their ballooning administrative
functions. OSHA, EEOC, EPA, FISAP, A21, OFCC—the acrostic lexi-
con of regulatory and reporting agencies became all too familiar. Each
new federal program imposed substantial monitoring requirements that
often led to establishing new internal bureaucracies whose principal
function was to create more work for others. Health and safety regulations provided a prime example. Most research universities increased
their staff of health and safety inspectors fivefold; essentially, they hired
more inspectors to find problems that others would in turn be hired
to fix.

Micromanagement, principally by state agencies in the public sector and by energetic and sometimes intrusive boards of trustees, had
much the same result—more paper, more procedures, more staff, without substantial increases in the quality of the product or the productivity of the institutions. Public commissions of higher education, either
as coordinating or governing boards, became increasingly insistent that
they had a right to know, well in advance, what institutions under their
purview intended to do. The filing of ever more detailed plans and
the seeking of approval for each new certificate or degree program generated sufficient reporting requirements to keep small battalions of
administrative staff busy. Boards of trustees were beginning to have
the same effect; they demanded that they be "kept in the loop" on all
major administrative decisions. The result again was more paper, more
reporting, and, not surprisingly, more personnel, some of whom were
charged with explaining to governing boards just why administrative
costs were increasing at such an alarming rate.

Administrative Entrepreneurialism

Less understood was the pressure for growth cre-
ated by the administrative staffs' own energies and the willingness of
the faculty to consign to them what had traditionally been regarded

as academic service functions. Because colleges and universities were expanding administratively and had the reputation for being "good places to work," higher education attracted a new cohort of experts who brought an important sense of professionalism to the industry and who expected their energy and creativity to be rewarded with increased responsibility, enhanced status, and better pay.

One result was much better management. Universities became better at managing their monies, acquiring sophisticated technologies, making their campuses more efficient in the use of utilities, and servicing the needs of their students and staffs. The second, largely unforeseen and seldom acclaimed result was that higher education's newly professionalized experts came to "own" their jobs, much as faculty already "owned" their appointments. This outcome was less a product of implied administrative tenure (though such understandings often accompanied the expansion of administrative services) as of the staffs' ability to define the content of their positions, much as faculty defined the content of their teaching and research. Professional staff, precisely because they knew what was best administratively, were acquiring the capacity to put into place their visions of how a well-run institution should look. They defined their goals, built their staffs, and then used their initial successes to reach out for broader responsibilities and opportunities to do their jobs even better.

The shift of responsibility for advising from faculty members to professional staff is one example of how such expansions fed on themselves. On most campuses where faculty gave up responsibility for undergraduate advising, there was a corresponding shift in the scope and scale of nonfaculty advising that was available to the institution's student customers. Having arrived in the hands of competent professionals whose sole job was to develop and deliver academic advising, the advising function itself came to require more and better computer support, greater flexibility of hours, and a broader range of services, including career placement, tutoring, and counseling. Where advising had once been subsumed within the faculty role, it became instead an enterprise in itself with its own impulse for expansion.

Throughout the 1980s, most administrative activities became similarly complex, a development justified largely in terms of improved services and greater efficiencies at the unit level. The result was a proliferation of increasingly independent agencies, each competing to be the very best at delivering its administrative specialty. The impulse at almost every turn has been to develop the lattice further, rewarding administrative personnel who show initiative with larger staffs and increased responsibilities.

Because most universities had seldom, if ever, mastered the discipline of "growth by substitution"—that is, the ability to substitute one kind of administrative or support function for another—each improvement meant more administrators. Most new problems were tackled separately; new groups were formed, new administrative functions were defined, leading increasingly to a set of ad hoc relationships with on-going administrative functions. The more discretionary revenue an institution generated—that is, the more successful it was in the marketplace—the more likely it was to make further investments in its administrative lattice, often with the implicit acceptance of a faculty who saw substantial improvements in work conditions deriving from the eagerness of the professional administrators to take on tasks the faculty found burdensome—tasks like advising.

Market Management

While increased regulation and staff entrepreneurialism were responsible for much initial growth of the administrative lattice, in the 1990s the need to manage the new markets the enterprise had spawned became the lattice's principal driver. Institutions everywhere suddenly became aware that they had student-customers who expressed needs and expected to be served. On many campuses Student Affairs became Student Services. Dormitories, now often renamed as student residences, had to be better managed. Campus dining supported by mandatory meal contracts became a thing of the past. A host of new auxiliary enterprises—some with separate fees, others included in the price of attendance—became standard features, first at the nation's most expensive and selective institutions and subsequently at most colleges and universities. The list of services came to rival those offered by a first-class resort—high-tech recreational facilities, wired campuses, writing centers, counseling centers, improved and expanded student health centers, as well as centers that offered career counseling, better management of student finances, and a host of extracurricular activities.

Each activity became an enterprise in its own right, complete with managers and staff who saw themselves competing for an increased share of an internal market for student services. Pricing became important whenever the activity was supported by fees or, as in the case of residences and dining, by outright student purchases. And just like managers in a for-profit enterprise, this new breed of student-service professional simply assumed that success would lead to increased responsibilities, which in the world of the administrative lattice meant bigger staffs, more independence, more latitude to launch new ventures.

The growth in enterprises serving student customers was but the first wave of new functions to expand the administrative lattice. The next wave was continuing and executive education—activities for which there was a burgeoning external market that universities and their professional schools were eager to tap. Successful programs were almost always managed by a professional who in turn built a staff of equally eager professionals—"entrepreneurs in waiting" was how one disgruntled faculty member described them. Each new educational program had to be staffed, organized, marketed, and evaluated. The fact that this new leveraged workforce was shifting the balance of the campus workforce, to the extent that faculty were becoming an important minority, was simply glossed over, given the economic returns the programs promised. Most participating faculty were more than satisfied with the arrangement: teaching in these programs was interesting, most continuing and executive education programs enrolled students who really wanted to learn, and, not least, teaching in these programs was personally remunerative.

Almost simultaneously the universities' research units, particularly those that supported themselves by winning competitive research grants, began taking on similar organizational arrangements. While research institutes continued to be directed by a member of the standing faculty—usually senior, tenured scholars of significant national or international standing—they now began requiring the support of professional managers who knew how the research game was played. Increasingly as well, the actual research these institutes were contracted to perform was undertaken by professionals with advanced degrees who were employed as support staff—that is, as part of the institution's expanding administrative lattice.

The rest of the institution quickly followed suit. The development function, now often dubbed "Institutional Advancement," organized itself as a sales force concerned with how the institution was branded among the public in general and the alumni in particular. If more money was needed, then more money could be raised, by hiring more professionals who really understood the business of the business. Public relations was next, often followed by the professionalization of the president's office as well as the offices and staff of the deans, who increasingly defined their own roles as the chief operating officers of the institution's principal subsidiaries. What paid for the expansion of the administrative lattice was the fact that the new organizations were in fact doing what they promised—they were bringing in more money than they spent, providing increased opportunities for entrepreneurial faculty, and making sure that the institution's students were in fact satisfied customers.

The Academic Ratchet

In truth, at most universities faculty members themselves were among the principal beneficiaries of the entrepreneurialism that expanded the administrative lattice. The nearly five-and-a-half decades since the close of the Second World War have witnessed a fundamental transformation of the American professoriate. In 1940 there were approximately 147,000 full-time faculty in about 1,700 colleges and universities. By the mid-1980s, the number of institutions had nearly doubled, while the number of faculty members had quadrupled—an expansion accompanied by a substantial shift in the focus of faculty efforts, particularly at the nation's most expensive, selective, and research-intensive institutions. Because reliable quantitative data are maddeningly absent, our best guess is that by 1990 professors in such settings were spending substantially less time in the classroom than their counterparts before the Second World War. Faculty were spending less time advising, less time teaching, teaching fewer courses outside their specialties, and were in general less committed to a commonly defined curriculum.

Such shifts were the visible evidence of a pervasive change in the definition of the academic task: what it is that a member of the standing faculty is formally paid to do and for whom? At work over the decades was an "academic ratchet" that had steadily disengaged each faculty member's greatest energies and attention from his or her home institution. Each turn of the ratchet further displaced the norm of faculty from institutionally defined goals and toward the more specialized concerns of research, publication, professional service, and personal pursuits.

Part of what made the ratchet work was the uniformity with which faculty members expect to be treated with respect to workloads. It proved all but impossible, for example, to maintain substantial differentiation of teaching loads within a single department. As long as a few faculty members were advantaged, there was strong, irresistible pressure to lower the average load for everybody, thus advancing the ratchet by another click. Rare was the faculty member who wanted to teach more general courses at the expense of his or her specialty; eventually everyone got to teach his or her specialty. The number of general courses declined, the number of specialized offerings increased—and the ratchet turned again.

Wins and Losses

It is a process that produced gains as well as losses—increased research productivity, a more expansive set of courses, more freedom for students, particularly those prepared to join their faculty mentors in specialized study. Such gains were achieved, however, at substantial costs—the need for academic support personnel to leverage faculty time, administrative staff to perform tasks once routinely assigned to the faculty, and a need to increase the size of the faculty. The larger cost, however, lay in the shift of faculty attention and effort away from institutionally defined goals and toward personally and professionally defined pursuits.

A sad paradox had come to describe the changing responsibilities and perceptions of the American professoriate. Many of those who chose an academic career did so as a result of having been taught well as an undergraduate, often at a smaller, teaching-oriented institution. After years of graduate teaching and experience in the academic profession, however, college faculty learned to seek "relief" from the responsibilities of teaching, mentoring, and curriculum development within their departments and institutions. Not many failed to perceive that the real winners were those faculty members who earned more discretionary time to pursue their own definitions of purposeful work. Faculty everywhere understood that professional status depended as much, if not more, on one's standing within a discipline as on one's role as a master instructor within an increasingly complex institution.

The Market Effect

The workings of the academic ratchet were not necessarily tied to the introduction of market forces into the academy. All the attributes we have described (lowered teaching loads, more time for independent research, more recognition of professional accomplishment) could have happened simply because the faculty wanted them to happen. The critical proviso is that they could have happened as long as the institution itself was experiencing real revenue growth.

What made the operation of the academic ratchet possible in the first place was that for most years throughout the past half-century, institutions had found themselves with more money to spend than in the previous year. Much of the growth stemmed from the marketplace. If public appropriations for higher education had expanded in the 1980s and 1990s at the same rate that they had expanded in the 1950s and 1960s, institutions would have gained sufficient new funds to drive the ratchet almost without trying. But public appropriations did not increase; instead, growth came dramatically through market-generated revenues in the form of escalating student tuitions, new entrepreneurial ventures like executive education, and more money for sponsored projects from foundations, corporations, and the federal government. From our vantage point, what really drove the ratchet was the escalating importance of market revenues, particularly among the nation's research universities. The lesson was seldom lost on the academy's most competitive faculty: market income bought greater independence.

Faculty Lessons

Though they often pretend to have forgotten, faculty absorbed two additional lessons. First, increasingly, someone other than themselves could be expected to make the institution work. In their own institutes and departments faculty readily added administrative personnel to handle student demands, operate labs, and assist in winning additional funding to support their research. When today's faculty complain about the growth of administrative costs, they usually mean the cost of the "central administration" or the "dean's office" or the ever-increasing number of student services personnel—not the growth of those essential personnel who provide direct support that relieves faculty of the tasks they find onerous or in which they are less than fully productive. The resulting division of labor leveraged the faculty members' time while simultaneously diminishing their engagement with the university as a whole.

Second, even the task of teaching, once considered the most basic of faculty responsibilities, could be assigned to someone else. Starting in the 1980s and escalating through the 1990s, the number of part-time and adjunct faculty exploded. These faculty most often taught the introductory and general courses most standing faculty now eschewed. That the growth of this contingent workforce inside the academy paralleled the growing reliance on temporary and transitory workers in the economy at large was just one more sign that universities were themselves becoming more like enterprises, more able if not exactly ready to apply the lessons of the larger economy to their own operations. The net result was that faculty, particularly at the nation's research universities, were becoming a smaller minority in the institutions they once dominated.

Advice from the Belly of the Whale

Faculty members were also becoming increasingly detached from the life of their universities. Some of that detachment was attributable to the increasing complexity of family life in America. In earlier decades, most faculty members had been men who were supported at home by a wife whose principal responsibility was to run the household and care for children. Faculty often lived near or adjacent to campus as part of an extended community enveloping the university. By the mid-1990s, women had won a permanent and expanding place in the academy. Increasingly, academic spouses had jobs and careers of their own and expected their partners to share in the running of the household and the raising of children. Faculty began to live more distant from campus and to spend less time as active leaders in their campus communities. Increasingly, the university was becoming simply a place of work.

At the same time the workings of academic ratchet were having an even more profound impact on faculty lives. The kind of academic success the ratchet promoted and the market rewarded was turning an institution's most highly regarded and marketable faculty into independent contractors who were coming to conceive of their institutions principally as platforms for personal achievement—good places to work and thrive, but ultimately, with the right opportunity, good places from which to move on. Even while "at" the university, these faculty were less likely to be "in" or "of" their institution—less likely to take an active role in governance or to consider their own future as necessarily conjoined with that of their institution.

There are many ways to describe this gradual process of separation, but Henry Rosovsky, as he stepped down for the second time as dean of the faculty of arts and sciences at Harvard in 1991, offered our favorite. Rosovsky minced no words; as a dean, he found that too many of his Harvard colleagues were no longer part of the university simply because they spent so little time on campus.

Rosovsky's observations reflect a lifetime in academia—first at William and Mary as an undergraduate, later at Harvard as a graduate student, at Berkeley as a blooming economist, and finally back at Harvard as that institution's principal academic leader. In his eleventh and last "Annual Report of the Dean of Arts and Sciences," Rosovsky voiced his concerns about the evident decline in Harvard teaching loads, a growing unavailability of faculty for student consultation and mentorship, and a more general absence of the professoriate from the institutional setting—too few faculty in their offices, too many rushing back on the "red-eye" to teach their morning classes.

> There is a very close relationship between absences from Cambridge and the spread of outside activities. It is difficult to discuss because we have so little hard information, but I do have the clear impression that, for a significant minority of our faculty, the sum of their efforts outside Harvard is greater than their efforts inside Harvard. We are dealing here with a mixture of activities: business ventures, professional activities, lectures, consulting (worldwide) for governments, etc. These activities have varying degrees of legitimacy and may be valuable for the individual and the University. But at the moment they are almost entirely controlled by individual professors. There is no knowledge, and no real control or management from the administration.
>
> This brings me to the crux of the matter. FAS has become a society largely without rules, or to put it slightly differently, the tenured members of the faculty—frequently as individuals—make their own rules. Of course, there are a great many rules in any bureaucratic organization, but these largely concern less essential matters. When it concerns our more important obligations—faculty citizenship—neither rule nor custom is any longer compelling.

A *Cautionary Note*

It is not impossible to imagine a scenario that could reverse the academic ratchet. A depression would certainly do it—so might a consumer revolt over higher education's escalating prices. A third and ironic possibility would be the rise of a for-profit sector that has absorbed up to 15 percent of higher education's current enrollments. What distinguishes the University of Phoenix is the notion that faculty are paid solely to teach. There is no academic ratchet; rather, a management system assigns nearly sole responsibility for the development and marketing of new programs to the corporation's professional managers.

What is not likely to yield a fundamental change in faculty priorities is new government regulation at either the state or the federal level. Even reduced appropriations will not do much more than temporarily slow the process, given the likelihood that most public agencies continue to allow institutions to substitute market revenue for public funds—a practice, as we have seen, that feeds the lattice and speeds up the ratchet.

Two final observations before we turn the other ways in which markets are remaking the American university. As the effects of the lattice and the ratchet become clearer, there will be a tendency on the part of some to say, "I told you so!" There is a class of faculty politicos who are particularly prone to use studies of administrative growth to wage again that ancient battle between academic and administrative functions. These academics seldom note that they have been primary beneficiaries of administrative growth—that the administrative lattice is the natural complement to the academic ratchet. In effect they seek a return to a past that never quite existed, wishing for a scenario in which public agencies provide the necessary funds as a form of entitlement to support learning for learning's sake and faculty for faculty's sake. While decrying the present, these critics never really identify where the money that supports faculty efforts is to come from if not from the market.

We worry just as much about those within the business community who are likely to say, "It's about time!" Yet to urge colleges and universities to be more "businesslike" will hardly be persuasive after a decade in which businesses too often engaged in a frenzy of mergers, acquisitions, leveraged buy-outs, spectacular bankruptcies, and out-and-out fraud. It would not be churlish for higher education to note that, in terms of cost, the problem of student loan defaults nowhere approached that of the federal bailout of the savings and loan industry or the bills sent to the state of California for electrical energy by an industry that redefined the meaning of industrial gouging.

The final lesson that the lattice and the ratchet teaches is that the challenges facing American higher education are remarkably similar to those facing most American enterprises. Colleges and universities need to evolve management systems that work, that yield leaner, more agile, certainly more focused, organizations. In a word, universities need to learn how to shape their administrative lattices as well as control their rates of growth. At the same time, colleges and universities must remember why they are in business in the first place. They need to learn better how to use the proceeds from being market-smart to invest in such ways that they remain mission-centered. Unable to reverse the academic ratchet, colleges and universities must improve the process of making sure that both individual and institution share fully in the resources that success in the marketplace brings.

3

The Admissions Arms Race

Michael McPherson—the president of Macalester College, now head of the Spencer Foundation, and long-time professor of economics at Williams College—first taught us to see the competition for top undergraduates as a kind of self-perpetuating arms race. Each institution seeks an edge it can never hold, but each joins in the race, fearing it will otherwise be left behind. There is, as it turns out, practically no limit to what the nation's most selective institutions are prepared to do, spend, or offer to attract the high school seniors everybody wants.

It is an admissions arms race no one ever wins—certainly not the students who are the objects of these institutions' intense attention. In the late 1980s Bob Zemsky and Greg Wegner conducted a roundtable on behalf of the Consortium on Financing Higher Education (COFHE)—then a friendly cartel comprising the nation's thirty most selective and expensive undergraduate institutions. The purpose of the roundtable was to imagine an alternate admissions process that might prove less disruptive to students seeking admission to a highly selective institution, a process that would help prospective students make the choices that are best for them rather than one designed mainly to benefit the college. In the paper Bob and Greg wrote following the roundtable, Bob told the story of how his daughter, Tobi, had come to understand the college selection process. That story is worth repeating here just as Bob told it on the eve of Tobi's enrollment in Carleton College.

Tobi's Lament

She is small and quiet, my daughter, but once her passions are engaged she looms larger than life. On a drive home from the airport last spring, I mused that now that she had finally chosen Carleton, she might tell me how she had actually gone about making the decision. I realized immediately that the question was a mistake, my interest in her and my research notwithstanding. With an innocence of the etymology of the phrase she used with such abandon, she turned to me and hissed, "Dad, you just don't understand. College choice sucks!"

In the nearly hour-long soliloquy that followed, Tobi detailed what eighteen months of worry about choosing a college had done to her and her friends—how it had affected the terms of their friendship, their sense of priorities in the last year of high school, and, finally, their confidence in their ability to make mature, responsible decisions. Despite each of their successes, neither Tobi nor her friends really felt they understood how or why they made their choices, or what they were expected to learn from such a process except, perhaps, that life was a crapshoot (my term, obviously, not theirs).

The part of the process that most troubled Tobi was her application and acceptance to one of the nation's most selective institutions. Her guidance counselor had suggested this school as a good "stretch"— meaning she probably wouldn't be admitted, but it was worth an application, just to see if she was competitive. She went to visit this particular campus only after being admitted; in fact, she had pretty well decided on Carleton by then. The trouble came when she told her friends she had been accepted by her "stretch" school but had decided to go elsewhere.

What she uncovered was a barely disguised vein of resentment among three friends who had been denied admission to that institution. Each made the same charge: "If you weren't interested, why did you apply? Don't you understand that they only admit a limited number from our high school?" While the college in question would no doubt deny that Tobi and her classmates were in direct competition with each other, these youngsters were remarkably perceptive about how selective institutions build their classes on the principle of broad diversity. That translates into not admitting too many applicants from the same high school, regardless of their quality. Tobi understood that her friends had a point; by applying to an institution in which she had only mild interest, she effectively lowered her classmates' chances of acceptance, including those who may have had greater interest in the institution from the beginning. She simply had neither an answer for them nor any real explanation for why the college selection process should have proven such an ordeal.

Mutually Assured Destruction

By the time Tobi graduated from Carleton in the early 1990s, the admissions arms race was in full swing. Institutions of every stripe were spending more money not just on brochures but on state-of-the-art publications that included videos and then DVDs extolling virtues, both real and imagined. Marketing was in vogue everywhere. The College Board and later ACT had begun selling names and addresses of prospective applicants. Consultants proliferated, admissions budgets grew, admission officers became marketing professionals, deans of admission became vice-presidents for enrollment management. The annual ranking devised by *U.S. News and World Report* established itself as *the* market publication—higher education's equivalent of *Jane's Fighting Ships.* And through it all the pressure on young people increased—to make the right choice, to present themselves in the most favorable light, to tailor their interests to the task of winning not just admission but also the financial aid they would need to enroll in a selective college.

The silver lining in these high-stakes games was supposed to be the prospect that the market would exact the same kind of accountability from the nation's colleges and universities as it did from American manufacturers. In some respects, institutions of higher learning were already coming to resemble car companies, pricing their products like automobiles complete with sticker prices, discount rates, and accompanying credit packages. Why not expect the public to follow suit by viewing colleges as commodities that could be compared and ranked for quality, if not actually tested as *Consumer Reports* tests automobiles? Hadn't *U.S. News and World Report* done just that each year with its increasingly complex methodology since the mid-1980s?

What we expected of the market was progress on two key fronts. Better-informed consumers would make better decisions; they would send messages to colleges and universities that ever-escalating prices would not be tolerated and that educational processes that ignored customer wants and needs would no longer suffice. Like the engineers and workers in the American automobile industry, faculty would get the message that the way forward lay in a fundamental investment in educational quality. The American Association of Higher Education, and subsequently the Carnegie Foundation for the Advancement of Teaching, had already placed teaching and learning at the center of a national reform agenda that sought a fundamental reordering of higher education's priorities. In short, what the government and the media had failed to accomplish by jawboning, the market—in conjunction with a growing reform movement within higher education—would achieve through the forces of competition.

It just didn't happen. The prices colleges and universities charged continued to rise substantially faster than the underlying rate of inflation. While discussions of quality and accountability have gained some renewed intensity within governmental circles, there is scant evidence that much is happening at the institutional level.

Why didn't the market have the expected impact? Why didn't market forces impose the kind of accountability on colleges and universities that was being imposed on hospitals and health-care providers, as well as on the manufacturers of consumer products? A variety of answers could be given; none is necessarily conclusive, but taken together they attest to how the market has unexpectedly changed higher education. Just as the lattice and the ratchet recast relationships within most institutions, the admissions arms race fundamentally changed the relationship between higher education's most sought-after customers and the institutions that were doing the seeking.

Why the Market Didn't Impose Price Accountability

A first insight into the college admissions dynamic is that the relationship between price, product, and demand is different for different purchasers in different parts of the higher education market. The segment of this market that commands most attention comprises those young people—and their parents—interested in full-time undergraduate enrollment, most often at a private or public institution practicing selective admissions. For these consumers, what is being purchased at great expense is a degree, the value of which depends on the reputation of the institution no less than on the purchaser's natural abilities or the effort expended in earning that degree. Think dance lessons—the quality of the certificate doesn't amount to much if the studio is not highly regarded, if the student has no rhythm, and if the genre is outmoded. The combination of reputation and achievement makes this kind of transaction very different from buying an automobile. Automobiles are consumables in the sense that they are not expected to last forever. Most drivers own several in the course of a lifetime. But purchasing a college education from a selective college or university is a singular event for most Americans.

For this select group of higher education's consumers, deciding where to enroll is also a shared experience in a double sense. The choice of institution is something to be negotiated with one's parents or other adult helping to pay for the purchase. As such, it is an event in which family forces and tensions can be expected to play a role as great as, if not a greater than, market forces. Questions of price can get lost amidst the family drama.

At the same time, the choice of a college is also a transaction in which the selling institution has a direct role in the purchaser's choice and hence willingness to pay a premium price. In fact, the selected college or university may choose not to sell its product to the would-be purchaser; in the most sought-after institutions, the decision not to sell is made much more often than the decision to sell. The duality of the decision is made more complex because the normal rules of supply and demand have been suspended. While the prices the top institutions charge are high, they are not as high as they could be. That is, most medallion institutions at the top of the pecking order could fill their freshmen classes at substantially higher prices, but they choose instead to enhance their prestige from the surplus of applications. To make matters even more convoluted, the price an individual consumer is charged in this part of the market reflects his or her ability to pay: when a selective institution admits and enrolls a so-called full-pay, it makes money on that transaction. If, however, the purchaser is found to have "financial need," then the selling institution may spend considerable amounts of its own funds to educate that customer.

For a second group of young Americans the choice of a college follows a less arduous path. Many of these students are not sure they want to go to college, but their friends are going, the job market isn't very promising, and, what the heck, they just might like it. These young people develop largely local options; for the most part they choose among reasonably priced privates and even lower-priced public institutions. In contrast to those youngsters who compete for a place in a medallion institution, these students exhibit a price sensitivity from the fact that they are not sure what they really want, not even sure they intend to graduate within four or five years. While increasingly most college-going youth work, for those in this part of the market work is often as important as college itself.

The third and fastest-growing group of purchasers in the higher education market see colleges and universities principally as providers of spot courses and skills. They buy their college education one course at a time, often attending a variety of institutions over a wide span of years. These are higher education's most price-sensitive shoppers, though ironically they often end up paying higher prices than a student who attended full time and was eligible for financial aid.

Finally, in considering price and market accountability, it is important to note again that state governments, their rhetoric notwithstanding, have consistently used market forces to solve their own short-term budgetary shortfalls by driving up the prices publicly owned colleges and universities charge. This phenomenon occurs every time the business cycle reduces state revenues and forces state governments to choose between reductions in services or increased taxes. What the governor and legislature rediscover at that moment is that prisoners don't pay rent, Medicaid recipients can't pay much for health care, and public schools can't charge tuition—but thankfully, publicly funded colleges and universities can. Each time the college-attending public pays the increase; they grumble, to be sure, but not enough to reduce enrollments or spur a revolt next election day. As a result, state governments use the robustness of the market, not to control prices or hold public institutions accountable, but to raise the revenue they cannot or will not raise through increased taxation.

The larger result is the smoke of confusion that encourages most institutions to charge what they think they need to in order to balance their books. So pervasive, in fact, are the pressures to increase, rather than reduce or control prices, that genuine price cutting—the tried and true way to increase volume in a saturated market—is a rarity in higher education. Those few institutions that have announced price cuts are, for the most part, small, struggling privates that provide financial aid discounts to practically all their students, which makes the announcement of a price cut more of an advertising gesture than a real reduction in the amount of money their customers are expected to spend in pursuit of their baccalaureate educations.

Given this set of circumstances, it is hard to imagine a scenario in which traditional market forces can be expected to yield a moderation of the price increases colleges and universities, public as well as private, impose. Indeed, the continued willingness of states to allow their public universities and colleges to supplant reduced appropriation with higher tuition suggests that the prices colleges and universities charge will continue to rise faster than the underlying rate of inflation.

Markets, Quality, and Accountability

Given the willingness of public agencies to make the student consumers pay more to attend public institutions, and the continuing demand for prestige or medallion degrees at very high prices, it is unlikely that market forces will limit the prices colleges and universities charge. But shouldn't those same forces at least hold American colleges and universities accountable for the quality of their educational products? Isn't that what markets are supposed to do? Couldn't the educational equivalent of a *Consumer Reports* lead the purchasers of undergraduate degrees and courses to more discerning choices of those institutions delivering the best demonstrated quality?

By the fall of 2001, at least three major enterprises promised just that kind of consumer information. The biggest, most successful, and most closely followed consumer guide remained the *U.S. News* rankings, which last year provided detailed data on more than 1,500 colleges and universities. For the price of the magazine itself, students and their parents could identify the top fifty universities and the top fifty liberal arts colleges—the so-called "nifty fifty" national institutions in each category—as well as the relative ranking of regional institutions grouped into competitive tiers. All these data were in the public domain—and in those instances when *U.S. News* magazine itself did not present the detailed data, they were available for a nominal fee on the magazine's Web site.

U.S. News's principal competitors were two research projects: one was supported by the federal government; the other was initiated by The Pew Charitable Trusts. The CRS or Collegiate Results Survey is now a licensed product of *Petersons,* the publisher of college guides; initially more than forty thousand college graduates from eighty institutions, six years after receiving their baccalaureate degree, responded, to the survey. The NSSE or National Survey of Student Engagement has been administered over the last four years to a sample of seniors at 730 baccalaureate institutions. That instrument focuses on the extent to which the respondents' college experiences reflected agreed-upon best practices leading to a quality undergraduate education. As its name applies, the NSSE seeks to measure the level of engagement on the part of both the student and the faculty in the learning process.

Both the CRS and NSSE promised to do precisely what *U.S. News* had eschewed—to focus on the educational process itself (NSSE) and to ask whether it mattered if one attended one institution instead of another (CRS). Their best efforts not withstanding, however, neither the CRS nor the NSSE was able to convince a private medallion university to participate. None of the Ivies joined; neither Duke nor Stanford nor the University of Chicago, nor any other universities belonging to the Consortium on Financing Higher Education (COFHE) participated. A handful of public medallions—the University of Michigan, the University of Illinois, and the University of North Carolina at Chapel Hill—used either the CRS or NSSE, but in general public medallions also declined to participate. Among the eight campuses of the University of California offering undergraduate programs, for example, only UC Santa Cruz has participated in the NSSE, and none participated in the CRS.

This absence of medallion participation was in itself an important market sign that should have surprised no one. Already enjoying superior market position, these institutions had nothing to gain and potentially a great deal to lose if their outcomes or levels of engagement were no better than those of institutions charging substantially lower prices. Even institutions that did participate insisted, as part of their formal agreement to administer either the CRS or the NSSE, that they alone could make public their results. It was as if the producers of products or services tested by *Consumer Reports* could decide after finding how well they had scored in the test whether to make the results public.

No one should be surprised that the nation's best-known and most selective colleges and universities dug in their heels; they showed little or no inclination to provide the kind of quality-based data that would let the public decide which products or services were best. Just how entrenched this attitude had become was reflected in an e-mail sent to a designer of the CRS. The sender, a principal consultant of a major firm offering enrollment management expertise to colleges and universities, wanted to know if the CRS, now that it was under license to *Petersons*, was available under any other terms. "I'd like to learn more about the Collegiate Results Survey for a client. Client doesn't want to give information to Petersons (fear of ranking), but loves the CRS."

It is not a fear that hampers *U.S. News*. Begun in 1983 as an almost casual experiment, the rankings started out as a kind of beauty contest in which college and university presidents were asked to identify the best undergraduate institutions in the country. Once the public's appetite for these rankings became palpably obvious, a steady stream of presidents and association spokesmen visited the editors responsible for the survey and told them that such an important measure of quality should not depend on the vagaries of institutional gossip. *U.S. News* responded by assembling an extraordinary array of data, much of it supplied directly by the institutions themselves. The more precise and detailed the data requirements became, the clearer it became to institutions how they could improve their rankings—by increasing their six-year graduation rates, increasing their yield rates, giving more weight to an applicant's SAT/ACT scores, and increasing the newsworthiness of the institution.

It is hard to overestimate just how important the rankings game and *U.S. News* annual reciting of America's Best Colleges has become. No matter how the results are pooh-poohed, everyone pays attention. Everyone's strategic goal is to move up in the rankings: from tier two to tier one, or from there into the top 100 and ultimately the "nifty-fifty." But what does it mean? What exactly does *U.S. News* measure? What are the terms of the admissions arms race?

What U.S. News *Measures*

U.S. News does not measure the quality of the educational experience. The data *U.S. News* so arduously collects tell nothing about what actually happens on campus or in the classroom. Some have argued that the rankings reflect institutional prestige—and they do, though that concept is sufficiently amorphous as to lose most of its meaning when one tries to describe the difference between two institutions with similar profiles but ranked twenty places apart.

Throughout the last decade we—with the assistance of our colleagues Susan Shaman, Dan Shapiro, and Andrea Wilger—have periodically returned to this question of determining precisely what *U.S. News* measures. In 1997 our initial exploration resulted in defining a market structure for higher education that ranged from a relatively small, extraordinarily high priced "medallion" market segment at one end of the spectrum to a slightly larger, more moderately priced "convenience/user friendly" segment at the other end. The single largest segment, comprised of "good buy–good opportunity" institutions, occupied the middle of the distribution. The analysis that produced this structural description of the market used admit- and yield-rates as surrogates for demand to predict price. Quite unexpectedly, however, the key variable turned out to be an institution's six-year graduation rate. Given that *U.S. News* used the same measures in its ranking scheme, not surprisingly our market structure and *U.S. News* rankings overlay one another. We concluded then that what *U.S. News* measured was market position: the higher the ranking, the better the market position, and the higher the price the institution could charge. Put another way, if you knew an institution's *U.S. News* ranking, you would know its market segment and roughly the price it charged. Even more astonishing, all one really needed to know was the six-year graduation rate for any set of institutions to order them and in that sense define the market. Private medallion institutions graduated 75 percent or more of each freshman class within six years of matriculation; private name-brand institutions, comprising the next market segment, graduated 65 percent of their freshmen within six years, and so on down the line. The same logic applied to public institutions at slightly lower graduation rates.

For the top of the market, we could replicate the *U.S. News* rankings by using only graduation rates, and once we added the reputation variable from the *U.S. News* survey, we could almost replicate the exact order of institutions in the "nifty fifty." For a full one-third of the twenty-five top liberal arts colleges, we were able to predict the precise *U.S. News* ranking. For the next one-third we were off by no more than two places. The analysis was not as clear cut for the universities, largely because this set of institutions included both public and private campuses. Nevertheless, using graduation rate and reputation, we could place two-thirds of the top twenty-seven universities (because of ties) within three or less places of their actual positions in the *U.S. News* rank ordering.

What then is being measured? The answer is remarkably simple: both the *U.S. News* rankings and our market analysis measure competitive advantage. The higher the ranking—or conversely, the better the market position—the better the institution is able to attract students, faculty, and revenue. That's half the answer. The other half derives from an understanding about why graduation rate is the best proxy for a *U.S. News* ranking and the market segment designation for any given institution.

Zoomers and Amblers

U.S. News itself believes that an institution's graduation rate is an output measure—an index of how well that institution serves its customers as well as the public. Graduation rates in general have come to be seen as a critical measure of accountability; for example, when leading politicians and media pundits list higher education's failures, they principally cite just two: the inability of colleges and universities to control their costs and hence limit their price increases, and the fact that many more students enroll than graduate. Why, they have taken to asking in increasingly harsh terms, must students, their parents, and the tax-paying public pay so much for a system that fails to deliver what it promises?

Such attacks betray a fundamental misunderstanding of how the higher education market has evolved, how it sorts students and sets prices. Twenty years of intensifying competition have produced a market in which the higher the probability the student has of graduating in four or six years, the higher the price that student is prepared to pay for his or her college education. The market then sorts those students in terms of their probability of graduation, which not so coincidentally is correlated with their SAT/ACT scores, their rank in class, their parents' level of education and income, and, certainly not least, their academic and professional ambitions. Those with the highest probability of graduation can be aptly described as "zoomers." For them, secondary school is a preparatory experience in much the same way that an Olympic training village prepares athletes for Olympic competition. Primarily in secondary school these zoomers get ready, not just for college, but also for the rigors of the selection process through which top-ranked institutions pick the students to whom they will sell their high-priced products and services.

For the nation's medallion institutions it is a win-win situation. They preserve their position in the marketplace principally by enrolling students who are seeking the competitive advantage a medallion degree confers. The top-ranked institutions win precisely because they can choose those students most likely to succeed and most willing to pay an extraordinarily high price for an undergraduate degree. Why? Because zoomers know that the baccalaureate degree is the next gateway in their run to the professional and academic credentials they have spent their young lives preparing to acquire. The better the undergraduate medallion, the better the law, medical, business, or graduate school to which they will win admittance. It is more than worth the price—because the prize is great and because they and their parents know that there is very little chance they will not graduate in four, let alone six years.

Twenty years into the admissions arms race, however, most college-bound high school students are not zoomers, but rather amblers; they are less certain about what the future holds, and about their graduation from the institution in which they initially enroll, and less willing to cut their social ties to their home communities. Because most college students are in fact amblers, most colleges and universities face the challenge of turning their amblers into bloomers—the young, and sometimes the not-so-young people, who discover relatively late the rewards, even the joys, of learning. When an institution succeeds in transforming amblers into bloomers, the first telling sign is an increase in the freshman-to-sophomore retention rate, followed by a slow but measurable increase in the institution's six-year graduation rate.

U.S. News has recognized both the importance and the difficulty of increasing the graduation rate by awarding extra points to institutions whose actual six-year graduation rate is higher than its predicted rate based on the average SAT/ACT score plus average rank in class for an enrolling freshman class. In our terms, this bonus calculation becomes a kind of bloomer index. In terms of the actual rankings, however, this adjustment appears to make little difference and suggests perhaps that even greater weight ought to be given to this corrector.

At the same time, however, there is simply no evidence that the students who consider these institutions pay much attention to their graduation rates or their success in nurturing bloomers. The population for whom graduation rate matters are those students and parents interested in medallion and name-brand institutions. The rest of the market seemingly understands that timely graduation is largely up to the students themselves. To be sure, most of these "good buy–good opportunity" institutions can do a better job converting amblers into bloomers; success can be fostered by smaller classes in the freshman year, more individualized attention, more willingness to serve vocational interests during the years traditionally devoted to general education. Private institutions in these segments have generally done a better job, not because of market demand, but because they have worked to preserve enrollment and reduce marketing costs. These institutions have learned that a student retained is a student paying tuition. Public institutions, despite the use of enrollment-based funding formulas, do not seem to have the same incentive to increase retention and thereby maintain stable enrollment.

Through the last twenty years both public and private institutions have learned that the market accords no advantage to institutions that go to extraordinary lengths to provide quality educations. Indeed, plenty of institutions with exemplary teaching programs—Alverno comes first to mind—have in fact struggled for enrollments. What foundations or the media may find attractive, the market largely discounts. What matters in this environment is not quality, as defined by Lee Shulman and his Carnegie Foundation for the Advancement of Teaching, but rather competitive advantage. *U.S. News* has learned the lesson well and ensures its dominance as the collegiate consumer magazine of choice.

Making Educational Quality Matter

Could it be otherwise? Could market forces in concert with public initiatives and institutional practices somehow be linked or combined to make colleges and universities more accountable in terms of the prices they charge and the kinds of educational experiences they offer? Could, to use Joseph Burke's Accountability Triangle, market forces be somehow linked to state policies and academic concerns to create what some have called managed markets capable of restraining price increases while simultaneously rewarding institutions of demonstrable educational quality?

Our answer is simple: the only way in which educational quality will come to matter is when there is a demonstrable, market-based demand for it. Educational quality will have to become a real and tangible attribute that contributes directly to an institution's competitive advantage in the marketplace. Higher education's consumers will have to be taught first to recognize, then to understand, and ultimately to value quality. Metrics will have to be developed. Consumer information that touts quality instead of competitive advantage will have to become widely available and actually used by the consuming public.

Measuring Up, the state-by-state report card first compiled by the National Center for Public Policy and Higher Education in the year 2000, represented an important step in the launching of just such a campaign of public awareness. At the same time the document exemplifies the difficulties inherent in using the tools of public policy to shape the market for higher education. Among the attributes *Measur-*

ing Up sought to gauge was the extent to which each state had succeeded in fostering successful learning as a central principle in the organizational and reward structures of its higher education institutions.

Measuring Up's goal of making student learning a spur to institutional accountability encountered the same problem others have confronted when trying to build a consumer movement that takes quality seriously; there are no readily available public data reflecting the quality of either individual institutions or state systems of higher education. No one really knows what students are learning or how well they feel prepared to apply lessons learned in college to a world in which jobs, families, and careers assume center stage. As a result, *Measuring Up* gave every state an "Incomplete" in the learning category.

In the 2002 edition of the National Center's *Measuring Up*, Peter Ewell described the path ahead. "What is needed for the future," he wrote, "is to extend the administration of the NSSE and CCSSE [NSSE's community college companion] to all states, and administer the CRS (or similar surveys) to national samples of college graduates." Having previously noted efforts funded by the Pew Charitable Trusts to test the usefulness of these and other instruments, Ewell observed:

> Creating new instruments to reliably assess college-level learning will require considerable time and effort. . . . But individual states can improve their ability to monitor their educational capital by taking two steps right now: (1) states that have not participated in existing national surveys such as the NAAL [National Assessment of Adult Literacy] could elect to do so, and (2) states could work proactively to induce testing and licensing authorities to open their databases to researchers seeking to improve the state's store of policy-relevant information. With more data in hand, state leaders could begin to realistically assess the mix of key abilities among their citizens in relation to state economic and workforce development plans. They could use these data to help persuade firms in key industries to locate in their states, direct state investments to remedy identified gaps in workforce skills, and adjust their plans to respond to changing economic conditions on an ongoing basis. These immediate actions will admittedly not give us the measures we will ultimately need to monitor and improve the nation's store of educational capital. But we have to start somewhere.

Ewell's proposal would constitute only a first step because he focuses almost exclusively on the makers of public policy primarily at the state level. Yet to be addressed are the institutions that provide the educational services along with the consumers whose demand for those products shape the market for postsecondary education in the United States.

In addition to those Ewell has proposed, state governments in partnership with the relevant federal agencies would have to take at least two additional steps to stir demand for consumer information required by a market in which quality mattered. The first would be a commitment to pay for the collection, analysis, and distribution of the learning-outcomes data consumers require if they are to make quality choices. It is unlikely that sufficient consumer demand for that kind of information in the foreseeable future will attract the entrepreneurial capital to make the effort self-financing. At the same time governmental agencies would have to find a way to encourage, if not actually require all institutions to collect and make public data on the learning outcomes of their students and graduates.

No less essential would be the willingness of organized higher education, and the industry's medallion and name-brand institutions in particular, to join in developing consumer information that focused on learning outcomes as a significant measure of educational quality. These colleges and universities would have to accept publicly the challenge of demonstrating that quality matters. The faculty of these institutions, already largely responsible for the standards defining the quality of research outcomes, would have to be persuaded that it is in their own as well as the public's interest to have similar standards defining the quality of learning outcomes.

The Pessimists among Us

The prospects for now, however, are that the admissions arms race will continue unabated and that the market for baccalaureate education in the United States will become increasingly more competitive and further stratified. The college admission process will continue to be a dysfunctional mélange that drives highly motivated students to seek prestige at any price while saddling students at less prestigious public institutions with higher tuitions to fill the vacuum caused by reductions in state funding.

Here it is interesting to note what happened to the 1986 discussion paper that presented the story of Tobi's Lament with which we began this chapter. The proposal for ameliorating the admissions arms race, which that roundtable eventually investigated, was to adopt the same kind of process that matches newly graduated medical students with hospitals seeking interns and residencies. In that process, which is also used to match would-be pledges to sororities on most American campuses, the senior medical students list, in order of preference, the hospitals at which they would like to continue their medical training. The hospitals, at the same time, rank the medical seniors they find most attractive. The challenge facing the medical students is to have sufficient range in their rankings that they appear high enough on the list of at least one of the hospitals to which they have applied to ensure a successful placement. Just like Tobi, the medical applicants need to develop a list that includes at least one "stretch," one "safety," and a limited number of "probables."

Our discussion paper invited those institutions practicing selective admissions to consider adopting a similar matching process. We imagined that such a system would include both public and private institutions and would appeal to the high schools already being recast by a competitive process that had little educational purpose. Our proposal, however, went nowhere—zip. No interest, no discussion, end of story. The COFHE presidents, to whom the discussion paper was addressed, buried it.

Since that initial discussion, we have periodically presented the same idea; most recently, a 2002 meeting of the assembled deans of admissions and their staffs of the Ivy League offered much the same response. When we asked why this idea has so little traction, a variety of answers were suggested. Such a system would be too complex. Combining public and private institutions would lessen the possibility of genuine price competition. The matching would actually lessen student choice because they would no longer be able to visit and reevaluate the institutions that had actually offered them admission. Eventually, our proposal was dismissed as being impossible; the matching process we had envisioned would constitute an illegal restraint of trade.

We come at last to the rest of the story. In 1980s the federal government, prodded by a series of articles in the *Wall Street Journal*, opened an investigation into the pricing and financial aid policies of the Ivy League and the handful of equally selective liberal arts colleges that annually compared the financial awards they were prepared to make to applicants who had applied to two or more institutions participating in this overlap group. The stated rationale behind this comparing of prospective awards was to prevent members of the over-lap group from "buying" students by offering them more aid than the standard need formula allowed. If, for example, it was determined that a particular student was entitled to a larger financial award based on Harvard's than on Penn's calculations, then Penn could match Harvard's award—or conversely, Harvard could accept Penn's calculation instead of its own. The outcome, achieved in an actual meeting of the directors of financial aid, was a set of common awards to any successful applicant to two or more institutions participating in the overlap process.

To the feds and the *Wall Street Journal*, the practice smacked of price fixing by a powerful cartel of elite institutions. The *Journal* had also pointed out that these same institutions, along with the other members of COFHE, were similarly sharing information about how much they were planning to raise tuitions prior to making final decisions on next year's sticker prices. What the feds wanted—and after considerable threat and bluster got—was an agreement to end the overlap process and to stop sharing information about prospective price increases.

Alone among the institutions charged with restraint of trade, the Massachusetts Institute of Technology chose to fight the case, arguing in a trial before Judge Bechtel that, as a charitable institution, MIT was not subject to the same antitrust laws as are businesses. Indeed, MIT claimed that, as a charitable institution, it was required to do all it could to keep its costs down, even if that meant entering into cooperative agreements with other institutions to set standard financial aid awards.

Bechtel would have none of it. Labeling as "pure sophistry" MIT's contention that the distribution of financial aid was not a commercial endeavor, he noted:

> MIT provides educational services to its students, for which they pay significant sums of money. The exchange of money for services is "commerce" in the most common usage of the word (*Goldfarb*, 421 U.S. at 787–88, 95 S. Ct. at 2013). By agreeing upon the expected contribution of aid by applicants' families, the Ivy Overlap Group was setting the price that students would pay for educational services. The court could conceive of few aspects of higher education that are more commercial than the price charged to students.

The importance of the federal investigation into the admission and financial aid practices of the Ivy Group was twofold. First, the investigation itself, along with the MIT trial, dramatically reinforced the idea that higher education was essentially a commercial activity. Second, the investigation made clear that colleges and universities, as commercial entities, were subject to the same regulatory constraints as every other business. Not only did universities price their products like General Motors, but as far as the regulators were concerned, universities were indistinguishable from GM.

Two important postscripts are worth noting. The linking of market forces and federal regulation has not diminished. In early 2004, a major challenge was mounted to question the matching process used by hospitals to select their interns and residencies. Critics charge that the hospitals, with the collusion of the medical schools, are engaging in a practice that keeps the salaries the hospitals pay their interns and residencies artificially low.

It is also important to remember that market forces have been part of higher education from the very beginning. Stanley Chodorow, medieval historian and former University of Pennsylvania provost, is fond of pointing out that the modern university has two roots. The first is the monastic school, a place of contemplation as well as labor, separate from worldly affairs. The second, even stronger root was the medieval university, which grew as students flocked to Paris to attend the lectures of Peter Abelard and others. Chodorow, addressing an All-University of California Conference on the Relationship between Universities and Industry in 1997, observed:

> Where there were flocks of students, there was money to be made in teaching. Teaching masters soon came to Paris to take advantage of the opportunity that Peter Abelard and a few others had created. By the middle of the twelfth century, there were dozens of teachers and thousands of students, and, by the 1180s, it appears, the teaching masters there had formed the guild—the *universitas*—that would be the seed of the modern university.
>
> The university was a craft guild, with the form and functions of all other craft guilds, [that] . . . organized and regulated the business of the teaching masters in the city. The guild was a collective entity, the very definition of a corporation. The teaching masters who belonged to the university made

and sold knowledge. They made knowledge by applying logical analysis to the classic texts in grammar, philosophy, theology, medicine, and law. They sold this knowledge to students who came to take lectures and to get tutorial assistance.

For Chodorow, as for Bechtel, institutions that maximize revenues, for whatever reason, are commercial enterprises. Eight hundred years later, the admissions arms race is a logical, though not necessarily inevitable, result.

4 On Being Mission-Centered and Market-Smart

Our argument that colleges and universities ought to be mission-centered and market-smart will surprise no one who has followed our work throughout the past two decades. We can also report that few presidents or provosts are troubled by the juxtaposition of mission and market, no doubt because they spend so much of their time striving to balance the traditions of the academy against the demands of the market.

Those who are discomforted—and in some cases offended—by linking academic and commercial pursuits are principally faculty, particularly those whose scholarly pursuits are centered in the humanities. They are the ones most likely to see in their institutions' pursuit of market opportunities a future that can only undermine the traditional values of the academy.

To be sure, not all faculty are similarly discontented. Academic entrepreneurs across most campuses readily embrace the market, often with little regard to how market initiatives square with the dictates of either mission or tradition. They are often the first targets of the traditionalists' scorn that, from the perspective of the entrepreneur, too easily translates into opposition against every proposal to launch a new venture.

What both sides can usually agree upon, except when the humanists have really dug in their heels, is that markets are becoming evermore important—so important, in fact, that today they compete with mission for institutional attention. The question likely to be posed by all but the most energetic entrepreneurs is not whether the escalating importance of markets is detrimental to the academy, but whether anything can be done about it.

Actually, markets have been part of the academic scene since the beginning. Clark Kerr, president of the University of California during its growth years and later head of the Carnegie Commission on Higher Education, once described the tension between the acropolis, with its focus on values and mission, and the agora, the Greek word for marketplace. Arguing that universities always have served the market, Kerr went on to observe:

> The cherished academic view that higher education started out on the acropolis and was desecrated by descent into the agora led by ungodly commercial interests and scheming public officials and venal academic leaders is just not true. If anything, higher education started in the agora, the market, at the bottom of the hill and ascended to the acropolis at the top of the hill. . . . Mostly it has lived in tension, at one and the same time at the bottom of the hill, at the top of the hill, and on the many pathways in between.

If the central role given to the markets for higher education's products today is not exactly an anomaly, what accounts for the cynicism and bitterness that now swirls about so many discussions of the academy and the market? Why are so many within the academy not just anxious but truly angry?

Part of the answer, we suspect, can be traced back to the period of extraordinary prosperity that graced American higher education from the end of the Second World War through at least the 1960s. New campuses were being built everywhere. Faculty salaries were on the rise. There was an abundance of students to teach, graduate students to train, and, in the nation's leading universities, a wellspring of funds to support basic, as well as applied, research. Markets were something one studied in economics departments and business schools—not something anyone in higher education really needed to be concerned about.

Then in the 1970s higher education rediscovered both hard times and the market. Like the rest of the nation, colleges and universities were coming to live with double-digit inflation and the impact of an economy that somehow had stopped growing. The market was proving a tough taskmaster as the demand for college educations also stopped growing—the product of a baby-bust having followed the baby-boom that had fueled much of higher education's growth in the 1960s. No longer were new campuses opening. Well-trained graduate students were not finding jobs. With the near-universal tightening of belts, college and university faculty could be forgiven for asking, "Who rained on our parade?" When the answer came back, "the market," the expected reaction set in, particularly among those faculty whose prospects were most limited by the new realities.

But the 1970s slide into stagflation provides only part of the answer. The rest of the story reflects how ill-prepared then, just as now, higher education was to navigate a set of educational markets increasingly in flux. Too many old shibboleths, too many rules of thumb, no longer made sense. For a generation, higher education leaders had told their students, as well as themselves, their trustees, and their faculty that their institutions only charged what was necessary to "cover our costs." In fact, nearly every institution was practicing cost-plus pricing, using their surpluses to offset unexpected losses and the subsidies with which they covered the costs of programs without sufficient markets. While research and teaching were still described as joint products, the reality was that the former was underwriting the cost of the latter. On the administrative side of the house, most colleges and universities were still being shaped by entrenched bureaucracies that saw their principal task as the enforcement of regulations designed to keep students in check, faculty in their offices, and entrepreneurs out of sight.

Almost no one talked about the impact of markets or the new rules colleges and universities were being asked to live by. Even radical experiments, like Responsibility Centered Management, were cloaked in the language of the traditional academy: despite the new rules, it was still business as usual. Absent much discussion about or even interest in how a struggling economy and a saturated educational market were reshaping American higher education, few thought much about the dysfunctional practices embedded in the lattice and the ratchet or the unbridled competition introduced by an admissions arms race gone mad.

All the while colleges and universities were trekking up and down the mountain, sometimes inhabiting the lofty heights of the acropolis, though more often wandering through the bazaars of the agora. What they were discovering—though again not talking much about—was that there were actually myriad pathways up and down Kerr's metaphorical mountain—choices that, as often as not, were a reflection of each institution's standing in the market itself. What was lacking—and what we hope this present volume helps provide—was an articulated understanding of how this emerging system of pathways actually worked.

Different Pathways

Nowhere are the differences in pathways colleges and universities traverse more apparent than across the spectrum of American liberal arts colleges. At one end are the medallions—think Williams, Amherst, Wellesley, or Pomona—institutions that attract the market's zoomers, along with strong faculties, a commitment to need-blind admission, an excess of applicants, and large endowments. These institutions enjoy an abundance of revenue that allows their faculty to pursue teaching and scholarship without worrying about securing the dollars needed for their programs. They are also colleges that seldom if ever invest in big science and other especially expensive undertakings; and while more funding is always welcome, these colleges need not put academic values at risk in order to obtain it. One hallmark of a medallion liberal arts college is its fealty to an arts and sciences curriculum that all but eschews the practical and vocational. Their faculty take pride in their ability to educate gifted students. They practice a brand of pure scholarship, leading them generally to resist efforts by administrators to pursue market opportunities that are not fully aligned with the college's mission.

At the other end of the spectrum lie the many struggling nonselective liberal arts colleges, most of which have only small endowments. Most have now introduced business majors, opened weekend colleges and programs of continuing education, launched vocationally targeted masters programs, and have been willing to consider almost any market-oriented offering that promises to bring more students, if only for a little while. The higher teaching loads and a paucity of support facilities in these institutions often prevent faculty from pursuing serious scholarship. Academic purists may decry such changes, but most within the institutions themselves say the substitutions and introductions were as appropriate as they were necessary for survival.

In time, many institutions in this circumstance reach a point where the shift toward serving nontraditional students ceases to be viewed as a distortion of a historic full-time liberal arts mission. Then the result is a productive embrace of the new mission in its own right. Still, the stories told by these struggling institutions reflect what happens when the market comes to define the mission—sometimes to the point of changing the very nature of the institution itself.

Expanding Perimeters, Melting Cores

Research universities present a mixed set of examples. The arts and sciences core of medallion universities almost always holds mission-driven values—not in as pure a way, perhaps, as the elite liberal arts colleges, but it reflects the same commitment to the acropolis and resistance to the agora. In the research universities the core sees itself as the keeper of the academy's traditions and its commitment to unfettered scholarship. The core is the home of the liberal arts, of most programs of undergraduate as opposed to graduate or professional education, of the hallmarks of student life—fraternities, sororities, student government, and intercollegiate athletics. The element that best epitomizes the nature and allure of the academy's core, however, is the central library: usually large and imposing, often physically dominating the center of campus, symbol of the academy's ancient traditions. The central library, like the core of the campus, is a place of congregation, a resource that belongs both to no one and to everyone. It is a place, as any good professor of English will remind you, that is hard to imagine having markets or even customers, just as it is difficult to calculate the library's productivity or measure its worth in anything except its own terms.

Among those who inhabit the core of these institutions the sense of being diminished is also the most pronounced, as if somehow what is most important to them is being melted away while entrepreneurs who inhabit the institution's perimeter enjoy expanding horizons. In this world of melting cores and expanding perimeters the evidence for the growth of the latter lies in the very nature of the entrepreneurial enterprises being spawned—research institutes and centers that for the most part operate independently from the rest of the university, though frequently in partnership with similarly chartered enterprises on other campuses.

Joining the research entrepreneurs along the perimeter are those graduate and professional programs with strong market positions; law, medicine, and business are the prime examples. Taken together, the perimeter's research and professional programs have grown relative to or even at the expense of the core arts and sciences, and often at the expense of undergraduate education. These entrepreneurial out-posts along the perimeter of their institutions, on the academic side of the house, fed the administrative lattice.

The perimeter also allowed the freedom and flexibility to pursue big science and the funding streams that made it possible. The nation's mega-universities achieved that status and grew dramatically in the process; they organized themselves to compete in the market for spon-sored research that evolved in the years following the Second World War. Important scientific discoveries required ever-greater amounts of funding—more money than even the best-endowed institutions could provide from their own resources. The necessary funds came instead from the Department of Defense, the National Science Foundation, and the National Institutes of Health, and more recently from private cor-porations. The resulting marketplace for research was both very large and very competitive. In this market, research universities had to suc-ceed if they were to enhance their reputations and hence their rankings.

Many elements of the research market actually aligned well with the academy's traditional mission—principally the emphasis on schol-arship and discovery and the empowerment of faculty. Other aspects of the research market were distorting. While the entrepreneurial pe-rimeter was feeding the administrative lattice, the competitive forces that dominated the market helped drive the academic ratchet. The re-sult was a seemingly inexorable shift of faculty attention from teach-ing to research.

In public institutions, growth along the perimeter accelerated the process of privatization, particularly among the nation's more entre-preneurial public universities. Recall the varied experiences of the University of Michigan and the University of California–Berkeley we recounted in our first chapter. From the 1980s onward these two great flagships pursued quite different pathways: Michigan was the more entrepreneurial, and Berkeley was more protective of traditional aca-demic programs and values. Today, Michigan has nearly $400 million more to spend per year than Berkeley. The difference stemmed not from more generous public funding but rather from revenues earned mainly in the marketplace. Michigan's success with out-of-state en-rollments, nontraditional research sponsors, and fundraising enabled it to invest in academic programs that otherwise would have been unaffordable, while at the same time reducing its dependence on state funds. By relying on market power rather than public appropriations it gained more control over its own destiny, while simultaneously making itself more vulnerable to the vicissitudes of the market.

Not only research universities have expanding perimeters. New programs along the perimeters have changed the cast of community colleges and most public and private comprehensive institutions, often at the expense of their traditional missions. Community colleges were among the first to offer customized training courses for the workers of firms prepared to pay market rates for such training. Joint ventures—sometimes with local school districts, sometimes with public agencies, occasionally with corporations—have proliferated along the frontiers of almost all of these two- and four-year institutions. When struggling liberal arts colleges went to expand their markets through the offering of weekend masters, evening classes, and courses leading to vocational certificates, for the most part they located these new programs along the perimeters of their institutions.

A *Mission-Market Model*

For nearly two decades now the mantra that has held sway in most state capitals has been "Read my lips—no new taxes." For public higher education, the most obvious result of this political disposition was the enhanced role market revenues came to play in determining institutional strategy and mission. Though it is largely the consequence, rather than the conscious intention of policy, this process of privatization is not without justification.

One rationale holds that users should pay a greater proportion of the cost of their education. The idea that higher education confers private as well as public benefits fuels this view, leading, among other things, to policies that focus on student loans and need-based student financial aid as the principal means of guaranteeing access to higher education. A second, complementary rationale holds that ultimately the market can monitor the cost and performance of colleges and universities better than government bureaucrats. The market represents the summation of individual decisions about what to demand by way of education, research, and other university outputs, and from whom. Because in principle such decisions reflect the self-interest of consumers rather than of institutions, the public benefit becomes not just lowered taxes or a smaller government, but a range of higher education options and providers that meet real needs through the provision of cost-effective outcomes.

The question too often unexamined is, "But what happens when markets dominate mission?" The struggling liberal arts college that stays in business by changing its mission to better fit the market offers one answer. A no doubt more glitzy example is the case of big-time athletics. A century ago intercollegiate athletics was an inexpensive activity undertaken by undergraduates for pleasure and exercise. Like other cocurricular activities, athletic competition was expected to develop qualities of good citizenship and self-discipline. Today that same enterprise is a complex, highly commercialized business, managed by professionals, often separated from the institution that hosts it, and tangential to the lives of most students except in their role as spectators. Intercollegiate athletics, as practiced by nearly every NCAA Division I institution, has emerged as a market-driven juggernaut whose principal mission is to entertain. For the nation's big-time athletic powers, the market is the athletic mission.

Institutions that go to market—whether liberal arts colleges that need to attract more students or athletic powerhouses in search of national championships—find it all but impossible to reverse course. Only a very few institutions have ever put the genie back in the lamp. They become trapped, as it were, in Kerr's agora. But then again, whether a college or university should be "at bottom of the hill, at the top of the hill, [or on one of] the many pathways in between" is not necessarily an answerable question. To stay safely within the acropolis means sacrificing funds and opportunities the market brings. However, dwelling too much in the market exposes the institution to forces outside its control—forces that may or may not align well with either the institution's mission or its values. Then again, institutions sometimes have no choice: public policy or their own lack of resources may force them into the market. But does embracing the marketplace mean subordinating mission to market?

Not necessarily, particularly if an institution uses the proceeds derived from being market-smart to invest in remaining mission-centered. Our argument, to repeat, is that being mission-centered and market-smart is an effective, we would even say necessary, strategy for taking account of the changing realities of the market. Bill Massy would add that being mission centered and market smart is also shorthand for explaining university behavior from a rigorous model that is firmly rooted in economic theory.

Beginning economics courses teach that businesses try to maximize profit. Other factors may enter the equation, but, when all is said and done, firms that cannot provide adequate returns on investment will eventually be forced to merge or go out of business. Absent the Midas touch, even the most successful firms are limited in the amount of profit they can make. A firm cannot sell more than its customers want to buy, given the prices they are willing to pay for the level of quality they deem essential. The firm's costs are largely determined as well, in this case by the prices it must pay for its own inputs and its ability to use them productively. More formally, microeconomic theory holds that "business firms maximize profits subject to limitations imposed by the marketplace and their own productivity." In technical terms, the theory tells us that firms will "maximize profits subject to demand and production functions."

Although no one claims that universities maximize profits, the for-profit model does inform an analogous not-for-profit model that applies directly to universities. What do universities try to maximize? The answer, of course, is that they try to maximize mission attainment. They want to produce as much high-quality education, research, and public service as possible given their circumstances. But like for-profit enterprises, universities are limited by the marketplace and productivity. Tuition revenue cannot exceed what students are willing and able to pay, and research revenue is limited by the university's success rate on proposals. Productivity is limited: faculty and staff can only accomplish so much, and computers only run so fast. So far, then, the not-for-profit model looks like the for-profit model, but mission attainment is substituted for profit.

What about the relation between revenue and cost? While universities are not in business to make money, neither can they operate without it. Any model seeking to describe the behavior of a university must take money into account by adding a financial constraint to the maximization of mission: "Over the long run, universities cannot spend more money than they take in without merging or going out of existence." The for-profit model does not need this side condition because the difference between revenue and cost, better known as profit, is the quantity to be maximized. Just as business firms maximize profits subject to limitations imposed by the marketplace and productivity, non-profit entities, like universities, are said "to maximize mission attainment subject to limitations imposed by the marketplace, productivity, and finance." Maximizing mission attainment thus becomes what we mean by our phrase, "being mission-centered."

Market-smart institutions exploit opportunities to gain revenue, money relaxes the financial limit and thus permits greater mission attainment. But the opportunities must be reasonably well aligned with the university's mission itself. If not, the activities required to get the revenue will hurt mission attainment more than the extra money helps it. Institutions that are truly market-smart avoid getting caught in this trap, no matter how enticing the extra revenue may appear. They view marketplace success as a means to an end rather than an end in itself, just as envisioned by the nonprofit model.

Market Power

Market power means control over price and the quality and quantity of the goods or services provided. The nation's medallion or elite colleges and universities meet this test. They charge high tuitions, determine the benchmarks for education quality, and enjoy excess demand for student places. Their market power confers a high degree of discretion, in not only pricing but also in setting the admissions criteria that shape the student body. For-profit entities with this degree of market power are said to be earning monopoly profits. They might also dictate product specifications, as in Henry Ford's famous dictum, "They can have any color they want, as long as it's black." Medallion institutions go even further. They define what it means to provide a good education and then use their market power to make their pronouncements a self-fulfilling prophecy.

Institutions with less market power must respond quickly to competitive price cuts and shifts in consumer preferences. For example, struggling nonselective colleges and universities have little pricing discretion. They operate under the pricing umbrella of the elite institutions but compete strenuously with other nonelite institutions for every dollar of net tuition. They also must offer programs with direct and demonstrable appeal to the market segments they target—for example, programs with a demonstrated history of advantageous job placements. Accreditation sets a floor on what is required for a college education, but, beyond that, consumer demand trumps academic values—including institutional desires to emulate the elite schools' academic standards.

Research universities operate in a highly competitive market for sponsored projects. Here the medallion institutions still exercise a degree of market power based on the qualifications of their faculty, though some of that advantage may be slipping as a tight academic labor market has dispersed scholars trained at the nation's top graduate schools across a wide spectrum of institutions. Price competition has also intensified as federal agencies have come to insist that universities provide substantial cost sharing on direct project expenditures and top-class facilities while strictly capping the rate at which an institution can recover the space and administrative overheads attributed to a sponsored or otherwise externally funded activity. Major research universities, however, have no choice but to compete in the sponsored-project marketplace, even if it costs them substantial sums to do so.

Virtually all institutions experience the tension between what Gordon Winston calls "university as church" and "university as car dealer." Winston's classification is another expression of the "mission-market" and "Acropolis-agora" dichotomy—in a way that points more specifically to the price component. From the "churchy" perspective, universities care deeply about access and establish need-based financial aid policies to ensure that qualified students can attend regardless of ability to pay. From the car dealer perspective, universities wheel and deal in the marketplace to bid for students with both merit-based and need-based scholarships. Newly admitted students have learned to negotiate their aid packages before they agree to matriculate: a behavior known in the trade as "dialing for dollars." But whatever the motivation, the result is a high degree of price discrimination. This, too, is consistent with the behavior of for-profit enterprises. Such enterprises often prefer to adjust price on a case-by-case basis rather than make global adjustments through the sticker price. Firms with market power may become what economists call "perfectly discriminating monopolists," by setting a high sticker price and then discounting selectively they extract the maximum each customer or group of customers is willing and able to pay. The analogy to selective colleges and universities is obvious.

The evidence is unclear as to whether or not medallion colleges and universities use their selectivity-based market power to earn monopoly profits in undergraduate education. To the extent they do, the money helps support faculty research and scholarship, including, for research universities, the cost-sharing required to compete for sponsored projects. Here the analytic uncertainty arises because universities do not, and insist they cannot, separate the cost of teaching from costs they associate under the heading "departmental research," by which institutions ordinarily mean research that is not separately paid for by grant or contract.

Faculty members also share the fruits of their institutions' market power in the form of higher salaries and better amenities than are available at less elite institutions. Student amenities, too, are first class at the medallion institutions, although they represent benefits received for tuition payments rather than gain-sharing.

As nonprofit entities, universities are not allowed to distribute profits to owners as for-profit enterprises do. They can improve mission attainment, however, by reinvesting the margins or profits earned in one activity to enhance other worthy activities. Bowen's Law, first specified by the economist and former University of Iowa President Howard Bowen, holds that "universities will raise all the money they can and spend all the money they raise." The question is whether all the money should get plowed back into the programs that generated it. Most universities receive subsidies overall, either from current donors or the government, and some receive additional subsidies from endowment. The result, however, is not an economy in which each and every activity is subsidized, as some apologists for higher educations would have you believe. It is more than possible, for instance, that full-pay undergraduates pay more than the real cost of their education, especially at institutions that find themselves under intense pressure to compete for sponsored-research projects.

Cross-subsidies R Us

Such cross-subsidies are a way of life in nearly every nonprofit college and university and indeed in any nonprofit enterprise that operates in multiple markets. To see why, imagine for the moment that you are looking over the shoulder of a provost as she ponders next year's faculty allocations for her college's business and philosophy departments. She knows philosophy lies at the core of the college's value system but that the department scrambles for enrollments and loses money. Business is not as central to the college's traditional values, but it turns away good students and produces surpluses. Many professors in the philosophy department think business's success threatens the college's identity and hence its mission, despite— or perhaps because of—its profitability. They want new faculty slots to better cover the full range of specialties that comprise the modern discipline of philosophy. Not so incidentally, they see adding slots in philosophy as an important counterbalance to recent growth in the number of business faculty.

Some provosts, and perhaps most chief financial officers, would expand business to make it even more profitable and perhaps contract the philosophy department to make it better fit its real revenue base. This strategy is one of "following the money," in effect letting department size be determined by the market rather than by mission. Other provosts might reallocate a few faculty slots from business to the philosophy department—a strategy that would cater to mission but ignore the potential market consequences of larger classes or increased teaching loads in business.

The provost you are observing, however, is an economist, and she knows that the nonprofit model requires a more complex calculus. Her thinking runs something like this:

> Every program produces two "goods"—*mission attainment* and *revenue from the marketplace*. One might say these represent "love" and "money." I'll expand a program if the extra love plus the extra money exceeds the variable cost of expansion, and visa-versa; and I'll continue expanding or contracting until the sum of love and money just balances the cost of expansion. By doing this I'll produce more value overall than if I considered either love or money alone.

Using this logic leads the provost to expand both business and philosophy.

Her decision rule speaks volumes. To maximize a college's or university's mission attainment, the provost is saying that she needs to take money as well as love into account. For her, money is no more a dirty word than love is a dreamer's escape. When called to explain why she is allowing business to expand, thus further distorting the college's historic mission, the provost responds:

> No, I've not debased the college's values by "putting money above love." I'm using the "profits" obtained by expanding business to boost mission attainment elsewhere, which will leave the college better off overall. Without the extra profits from business, for example, I might have to contract the philosophy department.

Contrast this way of thinking with that of a CEO of a for-profit enterprise, educational or otherwise. His mission is to maximize shareholder value, which in the present context is synonymous with maximizing profits. His decision rule is to "expand a program if the extra revenue from the marketplace exceeds the variable cost of expansion, and conversely reduce or close those units that fail this test. Continue expanding or contracting until the extra revenue just equals the variable cost." More formally, this dictum becomes the *marginal revenue = marginal cost* rule that is taught in beginning economics courses, with marginal meaning incremental in this context. Only money enters the equation. Love comes in as a side condition if it is considered at all. Such considerations differ significantly from the nonprofit decision rule that holds that *marginal mission attainment per dollar spent + marginal revenue = marginal cost*, where both love and money enter the equation.

We constructed the college example so the profits from the business department compensate for losses generated by the philosophy department. We have also assumed that it is not difficult to measure cross subsidies at the level of departments or schools—an assumption largely borne out in practice. We have been using the term "profit" loosely to describe what the accountants would calculate as "contribution margin" or "margin" for short. Margin is simply the difference between the revenue a unit generates and the direct cost it incurs. Educational revenue can be calculated by multiplying student credit hours taught times the tuition rate, with or without an adjustment for student financial aid. Cost equals faculty and staff salaries and fringe benefits plus applicable nonsalary costs. It is not necessary to allocate overhead as part of the margin calculation, although some institutions do include use charges for facilities in the definition of direct cost. Positive contribution margins provide sources of funds for cross-subsidies and negative ones represent the cross-subsidies themselves.

Calculating margins need not be a precursor to decentralizing the budget process. In fact, information about margins is as important in centralized as in decentralized budget systems. To see why, suppose the provost you are observing has in fact maximized mission attainment as she and her colleagues see it. Suppose also that the accountants calculate contribution margins of +$35,000 per faculty member for the business department and −$70,000 for the philosophy department. One can describe this result as favoring either business or philosophy. Business professors make money on average while philosophy professors lose it, so the former are more valuable in market terms. However, there must be some reason why the college does not expand business to produce even more contribution margin: because the department turns away good students, the reason must be that expanding business would detract from mission attainment as viewed by the institution as a whole. Similarly, the college must value philosophy professors highly in terms of mission attainment: if it did not, the provost would save money by employing fewer of them.

Nonprofit theory shows that when an institution is perfectly balanced, its programs' incremental contributions to mission attainment are inversely proportional to their contribution margins. One must carefully define "incremental with respect to what," however, and the resulting calculations can be complex. For present purposes, it is enough to say that contribution margins provide key information for decision making even in a centralized environment. If the provost is comfortable with the contribution margins, well and good; if not, she will begin searching for adjustments—for example, fewer students or more faculty or visa versa—that will increase her degree of comfort. The data on contribution margins allow her roughly to quantify the influence of mission and market on her decisions and to do something about whatever imbalances she perceives.

Also important in this example is the provost's acquisition of the necessary data and willingness to share them with the leaders of both business and philosophy. To make the mission-centered–market-smart strategy succeed, the institution must commit itself to transparency—and such transparency must mean more than revealing the president's salary or the athletic department's deficit. Transparency means, as a minimum, an agreed-upon set of rules and the necessary data to calculate contribution margins—even if, in the process of making those calculations, it becomes obvious that some departments, for example, have lower teaching loads or higher average salaries.

When Nonprofits Struggle

The president of a midlevel private university once described what happened when the University of Phoenix opened a campus down the street from her institution. "In a few years," she said, "the new competition had squeezed all the profit from my MBA program." She didn't have to describe how losing the MBA cash cow had curtailed her ability to provide cross-subsidies for other programs or the loss of mission attainment this entailed.

Universities have just two sources from which to subsidize unprofitable programs: contribution margins from profitable programs and so-called "fixed revenue" from endowments, current donors, and governmental appropriations. Fixed revenue means income not earned by any particular program, but rather by the institution as a whole. Such revenue can be used to defray the university's fixed costs and subsidize unprofitable programs. All programs can receive a subsidy when fixed revenue exceeds fixed cost. There need be no cross-subsidies in this case, but some programs probably generate positive margins anyway; thus, they contribute to the pool of funds available for cross-subsidies. When fixed revenue is less than fixed cost, the university must rely on margins from profitable programs to cover the difference and to provide cross-subsidies for unprofitable programs.

But what happens when a university is barely making it financially? The nonprofit model gives a clear answer: it must behave just like a business. No money is available for subsidies because every dollar of contribution margin and fixed revenue must go to cover fixed cost. Without the ability to subsidize programs, the institution has no way to assert its mission. The "marginal mission attainment per dollar spent" term vanishes from the nonprofit decision rule, which becomes simply "marginal revenue = marginal cost." The institution must remain market-smart to survive, but it can no longer be mission-centered.

The payment of cross-subsidies distinguishes the for-profit from the nonprofit enterprise. For-profit enterprises do not subsidize programs or product lines over the long run because they use their discretionary funds to provide pay-outs to shareholders. Nonprofit enterprises use their discretionary funds—assuming they have discretionary funds—to subsidize activities they believe will enhance mission attainment. The noble purpose of the nonprofit—that is, its mission—can be achieved only if it has discretionary funds.

Why Markets Matter

The potential for destructive competition might suggest that markets are a necessary evil or perhaps something to be avoided altogether. Stanford, for example, charged no tuition during its early years. All funding came from endowment and so was, in the present context, discretionary. But Stanford soon realized that it could do more, much more, if it tapped the tuition its students would pay for the instruction the university wanted to provide. Stanford made the same kind of decision a half-century later when it chose to expand faculty research by pursuing the newly lucrative sponsored-research market. Both revenue streams enabled substantial gains in mission attainment.

The lesson from these top-line growth examples is that markets confer great benefits when the needs and wants of the marketplace and its inhabitants are well aligned with the university and its value system. Markets also confer a benefit in making institutions more responsive to user needs and wants. While academic traditions are important, so are the needs of today's world. Few would wish to restore the classical education in Latin and Greek, for example. Although missions can change as the result of conversations within the institution, there is nothing like an external stimulus with an economic edge to drive the conversations forward. One announced principle governments proclaim when embracing market mechanisms to distribute public funds is that their efforts will make public institutions more responsive to market forces. While we remain skeptical as to the motivation for this argument in an era enamored of ever-lower taxes, over the long run markets ought to impact both price and quality, provided that consumers come armed with the right kind of information.

Markets also provide incentives for productivity improvement. The nonprofit model shows that a dollar saved in production cost is a dollar freed up for cross-subsidies, other things being equal. In principle, the nonprofit calculus is no different from that underlying the incentive in the for-profit sector to boost shareholder value. Colleges and universities, however, have no shareholders to insist on market rates of profitability or corporate raiders waiting to step in if such profitability is not forthcoming. What can and should impact institutions is the squeeze of competition on contribution margins, as well as the effects of changes in the price and the availability of lower priced or more malleable inputs. Such pressures can trigger productivity improvements that would not have been feasible without an external stimulus.

Market forces drive institutions to evaluate what they do as well as how they do it. Universities trim subsidies to their least-valued programs in times of financial stringency. Sometimes such evaluations unearth more low-priority programs than are needed to balance the budget, in which case schools may shift subsidies toward higher priority programs. We call this "growth by substitution," which is also a productivity improvement. Such substitutions might have occurred anyhow, but stimulus from the marketplace often provides the impetus. A similar process occurs when corporations, in response to competition from others, mount cost-cutting drives to rescue their profits. Less-than-necessary functions that grew up during good times get excised when times are tough. Shedding unproductive lines of business is an example of the same phenomenon, one that we have suggested might apply to colleges and universities as well as to businesses.

The anonymous and decentralized market forces tend to override arguments against change from inside the institution, no matter how powerful the proponents. While institutions may not really want to make all such changes, change is a necessary condition for efficiency in a dynamic environment. Market forces disrupt the status quo as in the old classroom experiment where iron filings are placed on a paper that sits atop a magnet. Nothing happens until one taps the paper, at which point the "disruption" overpowers friction and allows the filings to align themselves with the magnetic field. The same thing happens with markets. By overpowering organizational friction, even random shifts in supply and demand can produce worthwhile adaptations.

The bottom line, then, is that markets can help institutions do better in attaining their missions. Sometimes markets effect changes in the mission, but most often they are enablers and stimulators. The challenge for the academy is to guard against allowing market success to become a reason for being in and of itself. Being market-smart is the means, not the end. The goal ought to be remaining mission-centered by spending wisely and productively the margins generated by being market-smart.

5 | To Publish and Perish

One of the more endearing as well as dangerous aspects of the academy is its penchant for self-deception. University presidents often talk about the market for undergraduate education as a kind of metaphor that helps make real the unpleasant fact that their institutions cannot stay in business if they do not enroll sufficient numbers of students. In fact, the undergraduate education market is not a metaphor. It is a system of transactions that, among other things, determines the prices institutions can charge and the value attached to their educational products.

One consequence of this rhetorical sleight-of-hand is the notion that only some parts of the university are subject to market forces—such as the undergraduate admissions office, where "marketing" has become acceptable as well as necessary. In the rest of the university, the search for knowledge ostensibly remains the principal if not the exclusive force that determines how the institution invests in people and ideas. What matters are neither prices nor products, but rather research and scholarship. From this perspective, the university remains a sanctuary apart from the hurly-burly of the marketplace.

This perspective also bears less and less resemblance to the reality of most universities. What troubled Henry Rosovsky at Harvard, for example, was the fact that his faculty had become market players, flitting off to consulting assignments and speaking engagements, building their careers and networks outside the university that gave them stature as well as tenure. They had become or were in the process of becoming independent contractors, free agents in a market fundamentally at odds with the ideal of the university.

The academy has now begun to talk more openly of an academic marketplace in which a few internationally prominent professors and their research have become the focus of recruitment wars that are often little more than auctions in disguise. At the same time, among the universities that compete for these luminaries there is often talk about the market for sponsored research and foundation support—though most academic commentators hasten to point out that in this competition it is not price, but peer review that is important.

The conclusion too quickly drawn is that the "research market" is a metaphor describing the competition among and between academics rather than a term defining the transactions that distribute research opportunities. In truth, the research market, like all markets, determines how much, to whom, from whom, and at what price.

In the mid-1990s Bill Massy, in partnership with Charles Goldman, demonstrated the importance of understanding how such markets work. Their research initially focused on a central conundrum in graduate education in the sciences in the United States: the continued overproduction of new Ph.D.s. Despite the sustained absence of job opportunities, particularly at universities, the recruitment and training of new graduate students in the sciences went on unabated. While the story of legions of physics Ph.D.s being reduced to driving cabs was apocryphal, too many do not work in their chosen specialty once they have completed their initial training and a postdoctoral fellowship. At the same time, the salaries of those limited number of scientists with academic appointments have not been reduced, as one might have expected from an oversupply of trained professionals in a limited market.

Bill and Charles discovered that signals from the demand side of the market are overwhelmed by those from the supply side. Most departments continue to overproduce Ph.D.s even when they know most of their graduates lack opportunities for good appointments in their specialties. What matters most, finally, is the role of graduate assistants in producing research and undergraduate education. Although there may be various rationalizations of the demand-side market imbalance, the fundamental fact is that departments are hooked on the cheap and expert labor provided by their doctoral students.

On reflection, the Massy-Goldman results raise deeper questions about the market for scientific publications and the link between publication and the production of new scientists. Why? The most productive role advanced Ph.D. students and postdoctoral fellows play initially is as members of a research team engaged in multiple projects resulting in multiple publications; these publications in turn play significant roles in determining the distribution of research funds in the sciences. The more publications, the more funds. The bigger the team, the more publications. Despite the seeming oversupply of trained personnel, this research market is both efficient and rational precisely because its ultimate demand is not for new scientists but rather for new knowledge packaged in scientific publications.

The lesson is clear: higher education often misrepresents to itself and others what it actually produces and which markets it ultimately serves. As the admissions arms race has made clear, critics of higher education, and to some extent higher education itself, have misunderstood the core business of these institutions. While most believe the task of universities and colleges is to supply quality educations at reasonable prices, their real business is to sell competitive advantage at necessarily high prices. The research market that Bill and Charles analyzed was not about jobs or degrees but rather about the efficient production and publication of scientific findings. Had the market been thus understood, scientists when they recruited their students might have been able to offer a more honest explanation of why so many Ph.D.s experience often short-term roles in the processes of research and discovery. Instead, the explanations of the oversupply of trained personnel became ever more tortuous.

A Problem in Search of a Solution

The market for the training of scientific personnel involves less than two hundred major research universities that principally supply graduate education in the sciences, medicine, and technology. The market for scholarly publications, however, involves the entire industry—or at least every institution with a library and faculty members who expect access to the research literature in their fields. Colleges and universities are both the prime producers and prime consumers of these products—they constitute the market. As with the market for the training of scientific personnel, this market has developed largely unnoticed with a host of unintended consequences that have provided painful lessons in the new economics reshaping the academy.

From the 1970s onward the leaders of America's universities and colleges have sought relief from the growing costs of providing access to an ever-expanding volume of scholarly output. The challenge they defined for themselves principally concerned maintaining access to significant research and scholarship at a time when both the volume and price of information have continued to increase at rates that consistently exceed the general increase in the cost of operating an institution of higher education. As time passed and money disappeared, institutions have discovered that, however straightforward the problem may have at first appeared, the path to resolution increasingly comes to resemble a perambulating rumba: two steps forward, three steps back, one to the side, twirl, and repeat.

On most campuses the descriptive handle most often attached to the issue has been "the library problem"—a seemingly permanent imbalance between the funds accorded to academic libraries and the volume of scholarly output these libraries are expected to purchase and manage. Libraries that once sought to support an array of specialties within and among academic disciplines were finding it necessary to ration their purchases of monographs and subscriptions to journals. While university libraries could once field powerful collections to support their faculty's research and teaching, most had come to settle for inadequate assemblages that existed at the intersection of what scholars deemed critical and librarians judged they could afford.

And then the problem got worse. By the 1980s universities and colleges were finding themselves trapped between the expectations of their faculty, who often consider the work of research and scholarship as essentially a free good, and the market strategies of the commercial publishers, who recognized sooner than the institutions themselves how valuable these commodities were to the workings of the academy.

Actually the focus on the library as the problem was in its own way misleading, a confusion between symptom and disease, or between market cause and effect. The underlying issue has always been the disjunction between the sociology and the economics of academic publication itself—those processes through which the research community disseminates knowledge and judges the quality of work produced by its members.

Role, Purpose, and Profit

Academic publication accomplishes four objectives of critical importance to universities and colleges: the certification, dissemination, indexing, and archiving of research and scholarship. Publication both advances the state of knowledge within a domain and provides the mechanism to assess the quality of contributions that individuals make to a discipline. Publication is understood to be the primary channel through which individual faculty demonstrate their worthiness for tenure, promotion, grants, and fellowships. The peer review mechanisms that underlie the decision of any publisher to accept an article or full-length manuscript help to certify the value of the contribution as well as its contributor to the field.

What gives this market its peculiar cast is the fact that the producers of knowledge are also its principal consumers. In most fields the market for scholarly publication is driven largely by the internal mechanics of a culture, in which further specialization increases greatly the volume of published work at the same time that individuals come to read more narrowly within their fields. For the faculty of a university or college, the act of publication constitutes a "gift exchange" among a community of devotees bound by a common interest; the giving of such gifts is intended to win the regard of other members of the community. Any personal gains from the publication of research are the result of the positive esteem an article or book receives in its field of inquiry. Superior achievement is gauged not by the volume of sales but by the number of research citations, the approbation of peer review, and the prestige of the journal in which an article appears. The personal rewards of significant accomplishment accrue indirectly in the form of tenure and promotion within one's home institution, the awarding of grants and fellowships, or the appearance of attractive offers from other institutions.

However logical and proper the operations of this gift exchange society seem, in market terms an environment flourishes in which individual producers of knowledge experience no direct consequences of the market. Those contributors to a knowledge base who are faculty of universities or colleges simply assume that their institutions will provide the current information that makes possible their own engagement in a field.

The premise that a university and its library should provide access to all or most materials that support its faculty's research derives from a time when the volume of published material was smaller, the cost of acquiring such material was lower, and the resources available to institutions to accomplish their objectives were proportionately greater. Donald Kennedy elaborated on these ideas at an informal session with alums at UCLA: If the resource base of research universities grew in real terms since that time, the demands on those resources grew at a substantially faster rate. It is a prime example of Kennedy's sense of looking rich and feeling poor as knowledge increases geometrically while resources expand linearly. His observation also persuades few faculty members who insist that "the institution should provide," regardless of cost, regardless of changes in the circumstances of academic publishing.

In the 1960s it was possible for most major institutions to provide "full coverage" in a given field of study. Their ability to do so reflected the economics of an era in which enrollments were growing, the Cold War prevailed, federal money flowed in abundance, and the number of higher education institutions aspiring to research status increased. Vannevar Bush's vision that universities would become *the* engines of scientific discovery was being fulfilled daily. Ultimately, however, the quantity of research simply overwhelmed the capacity of a publishing apparatus consisting for the most part of journals operated by scholarly societies housed on university campuses.

At this point, the academic enterprise turned to the market in what became in everything but name higher education's largest experiment with academic outsourcing. What the academic publishing apparatus so clearly lacked—sufficient time, capital, and expertise—commercial publishers had in abundance. With little thought or understanding of the dynamics of the publishing market, the academy turned over—in effect gave away—to just a handful of commercial publishers the right to produce and control the dissemination of research findings in most scientific, medical, and technical disciplines. With the broad support of the faculty who served as editors, reviewers, and members of the editorial boards of the journals, higher education had seemingly purchased what it needed most: an immediate increase in capacity. Existing journals expanded, and new journals were formed to accommodate the growing quantity of research in a host of increasingly specialized domains.

For a while, the bargain seemed to make eminent good sense. Individual scholars gained an increased number of outlets for the dissemination of their work; universities and scholarly organizations were relieved of a set of production activities they were not well-disposed to perform; and commercial publishers gained a new client base to augment their businesses.

If You Own It, You Can Sell It

In time it became apparent that the true winners in this arrangement were in fact the commercial publishers. Universities found themselves taking two steps back, reeling in the grip of rising prices from an industry that shared few of their fundamental values. While members of university and college faculties regarded publication as an exchange of free goods, the publishers who were coming to control access to and utilization of intellectual property saw opportunity for enlarged profits. What the publishers understood and the universities and scholarly societies simply missed was the fact that scientific research represented a form of intellectual property that—when skillfully managed, cleverly packaged, and properly controlled—had real and sustained value in the marketplace. The crucial issue was, as the universities and their libraries were about to find out, simply a matter of making clear who owned what.

The principle of requiring authors to assign copyright to a publisher had been standard even before commercial publishers had come to control so much of the industry. Because they did not conceive of the publication as providing direct financial benefit to themselves or their institutions, most scholars willingly and regularly agreed to what, on the surface, appeared an inconsequential stipulation. They assigned the publishing rights of their articles to the entity willing to bear the cost of publishing it.

Somehow the academy had glossed over the fact that commercial publishers were in the business of making money. Having quite literally given away the property rights associated with research they had largely underwritten, research universities now found themselves paying the substantially higher subscription costs commercial publishers charged to recover their direct costs and earn their often substantial profit margins.

The lesson hindsight affords is that the ripest moment for creating a fair and cost-effective system of scholarly discourse in printed form occurred some thirty years ago. At that time universities might have exercised a stronger hand in shaping the publication system and the disposition of rights to intellectual property created on their own campuses. In considering what might have been achieved in the case of copyright, it is interesting to note what it took to succeed in the case of patents. In the latter, universities followed a dual strategy: they provided the technical help their faculty needed to acquire and market their discoveries, and they insisted that they maintained a financial stake in the returns on research conducted in university facilities by fully employed university personnel. A clear understanding of the role that institutions played in supporting the research of their faculty yielded a logic of mutual benefits.

No such logic prevailed in the case of copyrights. In the heady days of rapid expansion of both institutions and funded research opportunities, neither institutions nor their faculties fully understood what was at stake when establishing—or rather declining to establish—rules concerning the publication of research and scholarship that faculty produce using university facilities and university personnel. Missed was not the value of the blockbuster textbook or best-selling monograph, but institutions overlooked the value of the scholarly articles that were becoming the staple of the research enterprise itself. While the faculty rightfully protected the former, both faculty and institutions gave away the latter; they had accepted publishers' tacit assurances that, in exchange for the consignment of publishing rights, they would undertake the broadest possible dissemination of scholarly research.

In time a second painful lesson was learned as well. A commercial publisher, unlike those operated by universities and scholarly societies, expects to be paid every time its intellectual property is used. There are, in a word, no free samples—not for one's students or colleagues or local libraries. Faculty in the sciences often realize that their research findings do in fact belong to someone else—someone both willing and able to charge market rates for the privilege of accessing what was earlier regarded as essentially the academy's public domain. As it turns out, the constraints to the flow of scholarly information result not just from prohibitive pricing but from the restrictions that commercial publishers impose on the kind of use an individual faculty member can make of his or her own published work.

Differing Circumstances

A third lesson from this experiment is that the outsourcing of research dissemination contributes to a growing disparity between the sciences and the rest of the scholarly world. Commercial publishers are not very interested in the market for scholarly publications in the humanities and social sciences. Journals in these fields continue to be owned and operated predominantly by nonprofit organizations—major disciplinary societies, smaller scholarly societies focusing on a specialized field, offshoots of university presses, and state-supported organizations established to promulgate scholarship in a particular field.

Each of these publications, like their commercial counterparts, is compelled to cover the costs of its own operations, even as the sources that once helped to subsidize those costs are reduced or eliminated. With fewer subsidies and rising publication costs, scholarly journals in these fields face a continuing cycle of increased subscription prices followed by a decline in subscriptions, which in turn necessitates further price increases. To those responsible for library acquisition budgets, the nonprofit publishers of scholarly materials in the humanities and social sciences seem no less avaricious than the commercial publishers that have become the dominant suppliers of scholarly materials in medicine, science, and technology.

At the same time, scholars in the humanities and social sciences have decried a shift of funds and emphasis away from their kind of scholarship. However hard institutions and their libraries work to distribute evenly the pain of limited means, scholars in these disciplines have come to believe, rightfully we suspect, that acquisition funds are migrating away from publications in their own fields to meet the escalating cost of electronic and print journals in the fields of medicine, science, and technology.

In more than one respect, the academy's humanists and social scientists have found themselves disadvantaged by a market that runs counter to their own values. Take, for example, the question of digital publication as a mode of scholarly discourse that could potentially expand both the accessibility of scholarship and the potential readership of works in these fields. This means of dissemination does not meet the needs of humanists and social sciences in anything like the same degree it does the medical, scientific, and technical fields. Scientific endeavor is deliberately cumulative and immediate in its impact. Investigators in the scientific fields depend directly on one another's data and findings, even as they compete to advance the state of knowledge. The need for rapid dissemination of findings has made the scientific article the staple unit of expression in these fields, while helping to secure digital publication as an increasingly preferred mode of dissemination. To be sure, these are also the characteristics of substantial parts of the social sciences with research methodologies closely aligned with those of the natural sciences: for example, most aspects of economics, psychology, and those areas of political science rooted in the mathematics of game theory.

Within most of the humanities, however, the concept of academic inquiry requires consideration of a greater range of evidence than in scientific investigation. For this reason, the unit of expression tends to be longer than the scientific article, and the scholarly monograph has proven to be remarkably well-suited as a vehicle for scholarly dissemination.

At the same time, the enhancements to infrastructure and equipment that have made electronic publication feasible in the scientific fields derive from heavily subsidized investments by the federal government and others; the humanities, in contrast, have received far less external support for the development of new modes of scholarly expression. The only major exception has been a set of initiatives by the Mellon Foundation in support of electronically archiving materials for the social sciences and humanities.

Squeezed from below by the rising costs of publication, and from above by the declining ability of academic libraries to purchase their scholarly wares, a few iconoclasts in the humanities and social sciences have begun to argue that the answer lies in cultivating a broader readership by producing works of more general appeal. What the nonsciences need to do, they suggest, is go to market; more readers willing to buy more products can result in lower unit costs, thus making publishing in these disciplines a viable economic activity. A number of university presses, faced with declining support from their home institutions, have become leading exponents of this strategy in searching out "crossover" books that appeal beyond a circle of specialists to a more general readership.

Most scholars of the humanities, however, are simply not interested in either broadening the circle of their disciplines or in experimenting with electronic or digital publication as a means of expanding their audience. Electronic publication from this standpoint makes scholarly communication less singular, less permanent, and, above all, less tactile. Nor has the search for a wider audience seemed to offer anything more than an awkward embrace of a market that is essentially antischolarly. What the humanists and social scientists want most is the same kind of public recognition and subsidy they have seen flow-ing to the sciences. What they have gotten instead are lectures on how to appeal to a market that has little appreciation for or interest in their scholarship.

The workings and nonworkings of the scholarly publication market have always been entwined with one of the most basic functions of the academic workplace—the awarding of tenure—leading to our final lesson deriving from the academy's failure to understand how the market for scholarly communications would evolve. What have all these market machinations meant for junior faculty in the humanities and social sciences, particularly as they bid for tenure and promotion? The answer has been almost perverse in its antimarket message. At a time when being market-smart means expanding the base of support for work in these fields, the scholarship that is most highly rewarded at the junior level is that which speaks predominantly to the interests of specialists. In addition to their need to produce what Ernest Boyer called the "scholarship of new discovery," every young scholar quickly learns that the scholarship that "counts" needs to be published in the form of printed articles or a scholarly monograph.

The scholarship of young faculty may very well draw extensively on images and other material obtained through the Internet, and an electronic medium may often prove the most suitable venue for communicating one's thoughts about these subjects. Given the choice between this medium and a traditional print journal, however, young scholars know that their portfolio is weakened if they abandon the high road of print. In addition, untenured faculty members know that efforts expended on such projects as Web sites, textbooks, and other scholarly activities addressed to a more general audience are inferior currency in the pursuit of tenure and promotion.

The larger lesson, applicable in the sciences as well the humanities and social sciences, is the tenure process's intrinsic link to the market for scholarly publication. Colleges and universities everywhere use the process of review and publication to evaluate the scholarship of current and would-be faculty members. Every time a journal, whether commercially published or not, sends a paper out for review, it is doing the work of the academy. Accordingly, a key part of the subscription price to any journal is the indirect purchasing of the results of the journal's evaluation process. What the publishers supply is both vetted information and vetted scholars—two products the modern university requires to operate.

Regaining the Initiative

The emergence of a commercially dominated market for scholarly publication provides an important framework for exploring the academy's options in a world that is increasingly shaped and then reshaped by market forces. At this point one question remains central: Can a market-smart strategy, even at this late date, give the academy greater control over its intellectual products and allow it to pay more reasonable prices for the vetted research findings it needs to acquire? Answering that question becomes an interesting exercise in market analysis, one of imagining what might work—and why.

From the market for scholarly publications the academy needs two essential elements. First, colleges and universities need an efficient means of disseminating scholarly findings to achieve the greatest possible volume and distribution at the most reasonable cost; and second, the institutions need *a system for providing qualitative evaluations* to judge the scholarly work undertaken on behalf of the academy.

As with all markets, achieving these goals is a matter of discipline plus strategy—and just a modicum of luck. Having largely created the current market for scholarly publications by first giving away the intellectual property its own faculty creates and then buying it back at increasingly higher prices, the academy should be able to change the market's calculus by using the lessons of the last two decades to help reduce the escalating cost of obtaining what its faculty in fact produces.

First, peers must disentangle the quality from the quantity of scholarly research produced in evaluating the achievement of faculty credentials. The habit of mind that equates the number of articles published with academic quality in a tenure portfolio is one that stretches the essence of a candidate's contribution so thin as to make its real value scarcely discernible. This custom also encourages greater specialization of publication, which thereby reinforces the power of commercial publishing. One suggestion might seem jarring: because demand for research findings always rises to match supply—"Whatever you publish in my field, I will expect my library to acquire"— one way to lower demand, hence price, is to produce less supply.

Second, university and college libraries must become much smarter shoppers, turning away from that mindset that accords status and prestige by "the tonnage model." In the kind of market we are imagining, the best libraries will be agile—those in which the principles of selectivity have been applied to build a collection of distinctive value that can support well-defined lines of inquiry. Selective excellence is itself a market strategy that forces buyers to make and stand by decisions to forego some opportunities in order to exploit others.

Smart shoppers also recognize other shoppers not as competitors but as potential partners. Universities and colleges must come to see themselves as something other than independent consumers of scholarly research. The consolidation of printed-volume purchases and the volume discounts that result from group subscriptions to electronic information resources have yielded a notable increase in buying power for the libraries that have worked together as regional collectives. The leverage from such linkages can only increase as the range of cooperation among libraries expands.

Third, the academy reshapes the market for scholarly publications by requiring the academy to get a handle on property rights. Most faculty members understand that the economic value of a research result lies not so much in the fact of publication as in the stature and hence market position that a consistent history of publication brings to an individual. To the extent that further research depends on reasonable access to previously published work, individually and collectively faculty must understand that "the library problem" is their problem, one they helped create by giving away what have turned out to be truly remunerative property rights. Indeed, to the extent that members of a faculty—and not simply the librarian or senior administrators—come to decry the drain on institutional resources posed by the escalating costs of scholarly acquisitions, the likelihood of embracing alternatives to the current system of academic publication increases.

Required here is a broad commitment to educate faculty about the impact of intellectual property rights on institutions. It means understanding that getting tough in a market world ultimately means being willing and able to take your business elsewhere. Two rules of thumb for faculty seeking to publish the results of their research: understand your options, and never give anything away absolutely. Don't give away the publishing right without getting something concrete in return; for example, the right to distribute your published work for purposes of teaching or for sharing with colleagues in your own institution. One might conceivably press further and demand the right to distribute published material freely to colleagues within the field at other institutions. Particularly in the case of university presses and other nonprofit publishers, however, it is important to recognize that a wholesale sharing of published work in this manner can substantially diminish a publisher's likelihood of recouping its own costs in reviewing, editing, producing, distributing, and marketing a publication. A successful education campaign might result in faculty themselves coming to affirm that the funds that their institution must devote to the acquisition of increasingly expensive published materials are really a diminishment of funds available to support their own research and teaching.

Fourth and, in many ways, the most difficult, departments must decouple publication and faculty evaluation for the purposes of promotion and tenure. To repeat an observation made above—in most markets prices reflect the relationship between supply and demand, with the latter driving the former. In the market for scholarly publications, however, supply generates demand with disastrous results: more product to purchase at ever higher prices.

What is driving up the supply of publishable research? In part, of course, it is the explosion of knowledge compounded by the fracturing of fields and specialties. As fields divide and then divide again, each new section establishes its own journal. But something else is at work here, something much more directly attributable to the academy itself.

Indeed, much actual growth in published scholarly research has been occasioned by university and college personnel processes that make publication in peer-reviewed journals the *sine qua non* for promotion and tenure. The more specialized the journal, the smaller its circulation, the more likely its function is that of an outlet to accommodate the work of a relatively closed network of individuals who, in the pages of their journal, speak principally to one another and to the personnel committees that judge them suitable for promotion and tenure. The commingling of publication with peer review for purposes of promotion and tenure produces information at a rate that far exceeds the capacity for consumption within the enterprise. In a world ruled by "publish or perish," what perishes first, it turns out, are trees and library budgets. Breaking this logjam requires disentangling or "decoupling" the processes of faculty evaluation and print publication.

In this case, being market-smart means lessening, not the importance of research, but the importance of publication in print journals as a means of certifying an individual's worthiness for promotion and tenure. Because the push to make a profession out of what had once been seen as a calling helped create the market for scholarly publication at almost any price, decoupling promotion and publication is one way to turn off the bubble machine. Were universities and colleges to assume a more direct role in certifying the value of research results—a function once collectively performed by the academy itself, though now almost exclusively performed by scholarly journals—the result would be less publication and lower prices. If the net savings to the library budget were substantial enough, then some funds would be available to help pay the costs of operating a more localized faculty evaluation system that relied heavily on external evaluators.

Fifth and finally, the academy must invest broadly and collectively in electronic forms of scholarly communication. The Internet is bringing about a steady and fundamental change to the process of scholarly communication—a change occasioned less in the interests of cost than of time and convenience. A growing practice of faculty in many fields is to post preliminary accounts of their work on private Web sites for review and comment by a circle of colleagues in the field. Within a handful of traditional disciplines, most notably physics, postings to public Web sites are also becoming a standard form of collective communication.

This push for electronic forms of scholarly communication reflects both the growing power of the Internet and a search for more timely and convenient means of announcing and certifying new research results. Such findings typically take far too long to review, edit, and produce in printed form. The Internet dramatically increases both the speed and the audience for this kind of initial circulation. Post a working paper or a draft on the Internet, either before or during the time it is being reviewed for publication, and its potential impact is instantaneous. Particularly in the sciences, it is only a slight exaggeration to say that by the time a piece of work reaches the printed page its greatest research impact has already occurred, and its remaining value is primarily archival.

The obvious problem with postings to the Internet is the unruly nature of a communications channel in which the attributes of tangibility, permanence, quality, and authority are all notably absent. For most researchers, the printed page connotes an accomplishment of lasting value, more so than any image on a computer screen or data consigned to a disk. However pure and incorruptible the digital environment may seem in theory, its dependency on equipment that can break down or grow obsolete gives rise to skepticism about its suitability for the permanent archiving of scientific or scholarly achievement. Experience has also taught that however appealing electronic publication may appear as a means of reducing cost, the margin of difference between electronic and print publication is much smaller than it might seem. The cost of editing, producing, distributing, and marketing is essentially the same, regardless of the final mode of distribution.

Beyond the factors of tangibility and permanence, an environment of purely open, undifferentiated electronic communication does nothing to certify the value of individual contributions to a field of inquiry. Part of the reluctance to embrace the digital medium is the seeming absence of any certification or branding convention. In the unfettered democracy of the Internet, anyone can be a publisher, and the profusion of information makes it hard to delineate the quality of individual works. It is clearly within the realm of possibility, however, to develop a branding system in the digital environment that works just as effectively as the conventions currently recognized through print journals. No venture into a different system of communication can gain the support of the academic community unless it provides a mechanism for denoting what peer review determines to have greater or lesser importance to a field. A key role of the scholarly publication process in its current form is distinguishing work that is correct and helpful from that which significantly advances the state of understanding.

In recent years important steps have been taken to increase the acceptance of digital publication and explore different models of meeting the cost of disseminating scholarly work. The "open access" movement has gained particular attention as a means of accomplishing these purposes, especially in scientific, medical, and technical fields. In place of subscription fees, this approach assesses a fee to the authors of works accepted for publication.

Doing Something

The outcome we have imagined is a set of specific arrangements—a complex bargain, really, linking institutions, their faculty, and their scholarly organizations—that protects the rights of faculty and secures for their appointing institutions a more assured ability to provide access to research and scholarly information.

For the presidents, provosts, and library directors of the nation's research universities confronting the phenomenon of expanding publication volume and runaway acquisition costs, there will be an exasperating familiarity to the issues raised and the solutions proposed in our scenario. It is not for want of discussion that the problem continues to intensify.

Why is there so little focused action to solve a problem so well understood? The answer lies in part with the fragmented nature of the academic enterprise, in part with the tenacity of the commercial entities that now exert disproportionate influence on the price of acquiring scholarly information, and in part because, despite their understanding of the "problem," most academic communities still do not understand the market. It is not surprising that there are, across the academy, those who have proposed that the only practical solution to the "problem" is to take no action at all; they hope that the commercial exploitation of scholarly publications will prove just another bubble, another dot-com whose demise in the long run is foreordained.

Our guess is that the risks of doing nothing substantially outweigh the difficulty of doing something—and doing it now. A moment of opportunity is at hand, occasioned by the potential for peer-reviewed electronic publishing and a sense of desperation spawned by runaway acquisition costs. Missing this opportunity means more rapidly accelerating costs, greater commercial control, and, in the end, less access to scholarly communications. The result will be all market and no mission—an outcome no one would consider very smart.

6 A Value Proposition

For much of higher education the market has proved a tough master—difficult to decipher, seemingly impervious to academic values and virtues, relentless in its demand for economically efficient behaviors. As the academy's dependence on market-generated revenues has grown, so has the faculty's unhappiness with the idea that students are customers, with the glib speeches by presidents and trustees about marketing and the importance of brand, and with the institution's pursuit of for-profit ventures of dubious value.

The growing list of complaints and wrongs is best filed under the general heading: "The Three Cs." The first C is competition and its consequences. Winning has become singularly important, even though it proves increasingly transitory as well as expensive to accomplish, as the admissions arms race demonstrates. In the academy there is competition for students, for faculty, for A-rated athletes, for research grants and facilities. Increasingly, the arbiters of this competition are the "dreaded rankings," which prove to be fully acceptable as long as "my institution comes out at or near the top." In this competition a few institutions emerge as winners, and everyone else becomes an "also ran."

The second C is commodification—an epithet best delivered with curled lip and resonant sneer. By making education a commodity—something to be bought and consumed rather than cherished and preserved—the market is making the university less about ideas and more about things (degrees, credentials, connections) leading to other things (jobs, positions, careers). Less important—some would say all but vanquished—are the ideas that education is about either learning for learning's sake or the application of knowledge to the pursuit of public purpose.

The Third C

The third C is commercialism—the impulse that leads universities to invest in for-profit ventures, to push their faculties to pursue ideas for which there will likely be an economic return, to see themselves as branded enterprises protective of their standing in the market and hence their ability to charge ever-higher prices. In the 1980s such commercialism became federal policy with the passage of the Baye-Dole Act, which both gave universities ownership of the products of their research labs and mandated that they aggressively bring them to market. Princeton University's experience is typical. Initially slow to capitalize on the avenues Baye-Dole was opening for other universities, Princeton, in the 1990s, revamped its strategy, empowering its Office of Technology Licensing to take full advantage of the university's "technological strength" and move Princeton to the forefront among research universities. The results were spectacular. In less than a decade, the number of patents annually issued to Princeton quadrupled, while in the rankings published in *Technology Review* Princeton jumped from forty-seventh to sixth. Princeton was not at all subtle in its trumpeting of this achievement, in no small part because the rankings' publisher was none other than the Massachusetts Institute of Technology.

More than just bragging rights are at stake here. At America's major universities commercially sponsored research has become big business, involving billions of dollars and often resulting in favored sponsor agreements giving individual businesses the right of first refusal for products being developed by some of the nation's most prestigious laboratories. Critics worry that the science being pursued will itself become warped—that the definition of good science will become that which has commercial potential. By linking commercialism with competition, not only warped but also fragmented science results as cooperation among scientists and their labs falls victim to the search for market advantage.

A Defining Issue

For many Americans, this talk of commercialized science seems more than a little arcane, though it reflects a deeper perception that is in fact held by many: the academy has become greedy and all but detached from the public purposes that historically defined its missions. Press for an example of greed, and nine times out of ten the answer is "intercollegiate athletics." Why, people ask, should coaches get paid more than presidents or professors? How come so few name athletes actually graduate? How come so many of them misbehave—a few truly atrociously? Why should universities be in the entertainment business? How did a set of amateur competitions that students undertook in their spare time become commercial commodities in which, in the name of competition, winning is the only acceptable outcome?

For those who like neither markets nor athletics, the unnatural combination of the two is simply proof positive that universities have become commercial enterprises run amok: big money, big risks, truly outlandish—at times even criminal—behavior. Although this indictment is as much caricature as fact, the larger truth remains: intercollegiate athletics provides a lens that brings into remarkable focus the often troubling connections among and between the three Cs (competition, commodification, and commercialization), the academy's pursuit of learning, and the public purposes associated with an informed citizenry.

More than most issues, competitive athletics and the controversies that so often swirl about them have the effect of casting complex and ambiguous disputes into sharp relief. Historically, participation in collegiate sports has been the hallmark of the well-rounded student— serious, disciplined, competitive, yet equally exemplifying the virtues of good sportsmanship, team camaraderie, and institutional loyalty. In the pantheon of collegiate aspirations, athletic achievement has always held a special place—for both individuals and institutions.

But as sports have become more intense in every level of society, higher education institutions of all kinds have confronted the question of how well practice in fact follows precept. Within the last three years, the perennial debate about the role of athletics has become more acute, particularly in those highly selective institutions that often define the collegiate market. For these institutions, it is not so much a question of commercialization—though they too have on occasion sought the luster that comes with a nationally prominent team—as a matter of the academic purpose. To what extent, academically elite colleges and universities have begun asking, are our recruited athletes truly representative students? Do they have the same academic qualifications? Do they perform as well in the classroom? Do they gravitate toward a certain limited set of majors, effectively distorting demand on the curriculum and potentially diverting resources from the departments athletes shun? Is participation in a team sport still an extracurricular activity?

Just how important is winning and to whom? What is the price athletics exacts—in terms of expenditures, priorities, and institutional self-identify? Have the recruitment and admissions practices of the nation's most selective and best-endowed colleges and universities conferred too strong a market advantage on students who are recruited to participate in team sports?

In 2001 the publication of *The Game of Life: College Sports and Educational Values,* by James Shulman and William Bowen, gave new bite and saliency to the asking of these questions. The distorting competitiveness and commercialization of big-time athletics was not something about which only the football factories needed to worry. Here was the former president of Princeton and his Yale-educated colleague arguing that competitive intercollegiate athletics, because they had reshaped the admission practices of the nation's elite colleges and universities, was in the process of changing academic communities. That most of these institutions neither awarded athletic scholarships nor expected their athletic programs to turn a profit had not shielded them from the corrosive effects of big-time athletics. Indeed, the questions that had come to swirl around intercollegiate athletics at the kinds of institutions Bowen and Shulman knew best, were, if anything, harder to resolve precisely because they involved institutional priorities and purposes. Along with the increasing ferocity of the admissions arms race, these institutions had discovered that remaining competitive on the playing field meant reserving an increasing proportion of places in the freshman class for recruited athletes.

Defining the Context

We understand that some observers will say of our interest in the impact of intercollegiate athletics on elite institutions, "There you go again—focusing on the few rather than the many." Our answer is simple enough—in this case the few do matter as both market leaders and academic icons. They set the standards. That they are not immune to athletic and competitive controversy is in itself an important insight into how time and circumstance are changing American higher education.

Any discussion of intercollegiate athletics at colleges and universities that practice selective admissions while also fielding robust athletic programs needs to begin by taking stock of some basic facts. Few students who participate in athletics in selective colleges and universities ever expect to become professional athletes, and in that sense athletic participation on these campuses remains preparation for life rather than preparation for work. The athletic departments at these institutions are supervised by their institution's designated academic leadership: there are few boosters gone amok; few cases of brutish behavior on the part of athletes; little, if any, TV money.

That said, these elite institutions do have something in common with big-time intercollegiate athletics: both fundamentally confront the allocation of scarce resources. For colleges and universities of every kind, athletic programs require a substantial investment of funds—a point driven home each time a new budget is effected. For those institutions that practice selective admissions but do not offer athletic scholarships, the mounting of broad-based, competitive athletic programs requires an equally explicit investment of a second scarce resource: places in the freshman class. Because athletes comprise a larger proportion of the student body than is true at larger, less selective schools, these institutions must establish the degree to which athletic ability should be a factor in admissions decisions; they must consider that the coaches of each sport need the ability to recruit athletes with specific skills in order to field competitively respectable teams.

Ironically, at universities that offer athletic scholarships, athletic ability is not an admissions issue in the same degree as in smaller, highly selective institutions. The very size of the freshman class in those larger settings makes the proportion of athletes comparatively small, and it is unlikely that recruited athletes will displace prospective students who excel in other pursuits. Those who would be athletes at larger institutions compete against other, similarly motivated high school seniors for a specified number of athletic scholarships; it is simply assumed that the best athlete wins, position by position, provided he or she meets necessary academic qualifications.

Among the smaller, selective institutions that supply our focus here, however, the student-athlete competes against every other applicant for a limited number of spaces in a freshman class. In these institutions, intercollegiate athletics places much greater pressure on the admissions process itself. As the competition intensifies for admission to these leading institutions, so too does the contention over how much athletic ability should figure in the mix of factors that determine which students gain admission from a pool of highly capable and promising applicants. The press for gender equity in athletic programs mandated by Title IX of the Education Amendments of 1972 only puts more pressure on institutions seeking to balance academic and athletic competitiveness.

Specialization and Early Excellence

A joint effect of intensified admissions and athletic competition has been to increase the drive toward specialization in students, whether they seek athletic scholarships or admission to an elite institution that does not offer athletic scholarships. The athletic and academic zoomers, particularly those in high-aspiration communities, come to understand the need to excel in a specific area—to develop a distinctive talent that distinguishes them in the competition for admission to the most selective colleges and universities. The composition of a freshman class at selective institutions is the result of an increasingly intense national competition for the most competitive and promising students—nearly all of whom, it is assumed, demonstrate exceptional ability in at least one particular domain, such as science, mathematics, history, music, theater, public service, or, in particular, sports.

This heightened competition for admission underscores another basic fact that any discussion of intercollegiate athletics at selective institutions must address: athletic competition has itself undergone fundamental change through the past fifty years and particularly within the last two decades. No one understands this alteration better than the college president who must contend with angry alumni and trustees who are convinced that the college is abandoning its athletic traditions. Most of these advocates are successful men and women who have fond memories of playing, sometimes even acquiring, a new sport during their time at college. They likely recall team membership as an integral part of their own undergraduate experience, and they are distressed by what they perceive as attacks on the ability of current students to discover and benefit from athletic competition in college.

These alumni and trustees seldom realize, however, the degree to which athletics, like almost everything else in the modern world of markets, has become a highly specialized endeavor. Playing a sport is not something discovered in one's college years. It is something begun early in childhood, first by choosing a sport and position and then by honing the necessary skills while developing the fortitude and discipline to become truly competitive. Nearly gone are the athletes who excel in several sports at a variety of positions. Gone too is the idea of a sport having a particular season. Maintaining a competitive edge is a year-round endeavor, something an athlete expects to practice every day. More than ever before, in college one perfects one's skills and draws strength from the camaraderie of being part of a team of similarly motivated students—in sports, as in any other field of pursuit.

These developments make clear that students who played football for Amherst, Bucknell, Princeton, or any of the fifty or so institutions that practiced selective admissions in the 1950s were not the same as those who make up the teams today. Although members of those earlier squads also played in high school, doing so was less likely to have been a deciding factor in their admission to college. Getting into any of these schools was also simpler back then; a smaller cohort of students and parents was prepared to seek or pay for that kind of education. The student body of these institutions was far more homogeneous than today in terms of socioeconomic status, race, and religion: many of these selective colleges and universities were single-sex institutions through most of the twentieth century. There were certainly fewer guidebooks, special admissions professionals, media stories, and national rankings comparing colleges and universities that have made the scramble for admission to a selective institution the hurly-burly it is today.

Difficult Debates

What has also changed is the increasing frequency and ferocity of discussions that have made athletics a focal point for a deeper set of uncertainties within the academy—uncertainties that are increasingly being expressed in terms of market forces vs. academic and public purposes. At the heart of these concerns, though seldom expressed so boldly, is the preeminent question of what values these institutions seek to foster in their students and their learning communities. Like affirmative action, athletics draws attention both inside and outside the academy because of the admissions "tip"—the power to tilt the balance of forces that are otherwise nearly equal and to shape the incoming class to meet particular objectives of the institution. The questions are being asked by not only prospective students and their parents but also institutions themselves: By what criteria do we select an incoming class? Who determines those principles of selection, and how are the decisions made? Do they result from broad campus deliberations of purpose and value in shaping an incoming class? Finally, is the selection process fair to all qualified students, including those with exceptional skills in other areas?

A telling instance of the pressure intercollegiate athletics exerts on admissions occurred in Swarthmore College's decision to eliminate varsity football in December 2000. The decision was made, not to reduce the proportion of freshman admissions earmarked for athletes, but to allow the college to allocate those places among players in other team sports. In fact, the football team had made real headway in reversing a pattern of losing steadily through the seasons; what became clear over time, however, was the price exacted for such progress in terms of admission slots. In the most general terms, the college realized that maintaining competitiveness in other sports would require a greater number of athletic tips for those sports as well. Simply increasing the total number of spaces earmarked for athletic admits would constrain the college's ability to meet other goals in shaping its freshman class.

Not long afterward, Williams College—by anyone's accounting a national leader in Division III athletics—raised questions about the role of athletics on its own campus. An internal study and report found that athletes had a decisive advantage in the admissions process and that a strong culture of athletics on campus at times detracted from the college's academic environment. Then briefly the presidents of the Ivy League added to the existing rules that limit practice activity by stipulating that student-athletes should have a minimum of seven off-season weeks each year with no supervised practice. The ruling was designed to allow these students to meet regular academic obligations and also to explore other kinds of learning experiences and resources on their campuses. The uproar was as effective as it was spontaneous. Faced with the angry demands of their student-athletes to be left free to choose how to spend their time, the Ivy presidents backed down; they successfully but inadvertently demonstrated once more just how contentious the question of athletics could be within their campus communities.

Each of these events—at Swarthmore, at Williams, and across the Ivy League—exemplifies the increasingly complicated and difficult debates about the future of collegiate sports at elite colleges and universities. At these institutions, which receive eight or nine applications on average for every spot in their freshman classes, there is an escalating competition for goods of fixed scarcity: budget dollars; hours spent in pursuit of cocurricular activities; and, what is proving the most contentious resource of all, spaces in the freshman class.

The increased scrutiny of athletics has affected people in all kinds of roles in these institutions. Student-athletes often feel a sense of betrayal: heroes on game day as exemplars of the ideal of a college education that stresses achievement and performance, but otherwise undefended against those who would question whether athletes are smart enough to belong in their institutions. Not surprisingly, many of these students feel victimized, denigrated, placed under the microscope. There is a sense of needing to prove themselves academically, of being held to even stricter standards than their classmates from the perception that they were admitted under different and less demanding criteria.

Coaches and athletic directors also feel themselves put on the spot—on an almost daily basis called upon to justify their presence in a learning community. The perception that coaches and athletics exert a disproportionate influence on the admissions process generates charges of misplaced institutional priorities, particularly among faculty who feel their own academic programs are deprived of institutional admissions or financial support. Those faculty members who question the role and importance of athletics in their institutions often feel marginalized simply for having brought up the issue.

In some respects the pressure on coaches in these settings is greater than it is for coaches in institutions that provide athletic scholarships. In any kind of institution, coaches understand that building a winning team depends to a considerable degree on their ability to recruit a critical mass of proven athletes. Because these selective institutions do not offer scholarships to students admitted as athletes, coaches have no assurance that team members will play for more than a single season— or, indeed, whether a given student will play at all once admitted.

Winning, Markets, and Values

The questions surrounding athletics—often colored by the particular, some would say peculiar, insularity of highly selective as well as highly expensive institutions—arise today amidst the growing national debate over the excesses of big-time college athletics. Throughout all of higher education there is an uneasy disparity—a lack of resolution between the drive to academic distinction, on the one hand, and to athletic prowess on the other. This circumstance results in institutions trying to look like an ivy institution six days a week and a football powerhouse on the seventh.

In fact, even those selective colleges and universities that are leaders in the academic domain find themselves drawn to an intensified competition—for the best students, for research dollars, for donors, and for prestige. Different as they are from larger public institutions that play big-time athletics, many small selective institutions find themselves being drawn into the same athletic waters as those bigger fish. The performance of athletic teams, in football and basketball as well as in a range of other men's and women's sports, sends a strong market signal about an institution's sense of itself and its ambitions. The concept of loyalty to the college team regardless of its standing may last for awhile, but ultimately no one wants to affiliate with something generally perceived as a losing enterprise. There is nothing like a winning season to rally team supporters. An institution that seeks to distinguish itself in the market for students and donors may well perceive that athletic performance becomes analogous to academic strength. In these and myriad other ways, athletics at selective institutions has become central to an intensified process of market competition among institutions generally.

Some may wonder why such rancor surrounds the issue today. Hasn't athletics always been an issue, lurking somewhere in the midst of things, ready to ignite and then subside once the moment for demagogy has passed? Perhaps so, but the larger, more interesting question might be: Why, over the past few years in particular, has athletics been the catalyst for a much deeper set of conflicts within the academy? The answer is both simple and complex. The simple answer is that athletics is more easily understood than most aspects of campus life; the questions of budget, winning vs. losing seasons, and slots in the freshman class—all take on a sharpness often lacking in other areas of campus contention. The more complex and important answer is that too often these same colleges and universities have left undefined the core values that, in a world of markets, might be expected to resolve the apparently simple questions of resource allocation to different parts of the institution, including athletics.

Presidential Leadership

One of the most emphatic points made in the Knight Commission's 1991 report on intercollegiate athletics—and reaffirmed in the 2001 report of the second Knight Commission—was that athletics is the president's business. Presidents who seek to avoid the issue—either by having their athletic programs report "elsewhere" or, amidst the inevitable contretemps that bad behavior engenders, by suggesting "boys will be boys"—are putting their institutions at risk just as certainly as if they had tolerated scientific fraud or financial misconduct. In each of these cases the president's role—both as CEO and community leader—is necessarily the same: he or she makes certain that values as well as policies keep the institution on track and moving forward.

That's the theory. In practice the option that many, perhaps even most, presidents choose is to do nothing; they hope that the peculiar problems surrounding competitive athletics in selective institutions will go away as they have so often in the past. They argue, with more than a little justification, that other problems—more pressing as well as more resolvable—need their attention. The friction, whether increasing or not, generated by the competition for places in the freshman class is simply noise in the system, yet another of the inevitable consequences of higher education's surrender to market forces.

A second option is to have presidents "bite the bullet," as many of their most vocal faculty would have them do. By arguing that the time for clarity and resolve is at hand, they could propose a substantial reduction in the number of intercollegiate teams their institutions field. Fewer teams translate directly into less money spent and fewer places for recruited athletes. The resulting policy thus becomes one of "selective excellence." Fewer teams but more winners.

There is, however, a third option, one that perhaps ironically uses the "clarity" of the debate over athletics to facilitate a larger, more important discussion of the institution's core values and how they help frame the institution's response to the pressures of market competition. The challenge facing the presidents of the nation's most selective colleges and universities is not so much to "fix athletics" as to lead their communities toward an articulation of core values of sufficient vibrancy that the disputes centering on athletics become resolvable.

On the surface the first of these options might seem the least controversial and therefore most attractive to many presidents. But adherence to the status quo simply allows the current muddle of issues and emotions to persist. Doing nothing actually encourages a continuation of the disputes centering on athletics and its relation to the institution's academic and educational mission. Choosing more of the same most likely results in a continued escalation of emotions, greater confusion in the competition for admission, more public scrutiny and criticism about questions of privilege in the admissions process, and continuing questions about the allocation of its financial resources.

The second option attempts simply to dispel the controversy about athletics through executive decision. While a presidential decision to reduce the scale of athletics would certainly have an impact on how and where the institution invests its resources, the residual effects of such a decision would only increase the fractures that already exist within a campus community.

Not surprisingly, we suspect, our favorite is the third option, which argues for a full and frank discussion of core values capable of shaping the institution's market strategies and of resolving the questions of purpose and advantage that now swirl about intercollegiate athletics at elite institutions. At this juncture higher education needs discussions centered on the core values that unite the college or university as a learning community.

Any conversation about core values is as difficult to describe as it is to convene. From our vantage point, the core values that a roundtable that began by focusing on athletics would want to define include the importance of community, of scholarship for its own sake, and of diversity as an element for determining the shape of the freshman class. There is a sense, for example, that even at selective institutions, athletes become a separate, inward-looking subcommunity too often detached from the rest of the institution. If one key virtue in having athletes on campus is the diversity they bring to the institution, then how can we better promote intracampus communities that include a few athletes and a whole lot of other people as well? Where are the other, nonathletic cliques or self-selecting and exclusionary communities on campus? Is it possible to make them less important or less of an element of fragmentation?

Or take the core value of scholarship. Does athletic competition and the need to field competitive teams make intellectual discovery less important? Are athletes less interesting than others on campus? And again, are there other groups of which the same could be said? The roundtable might similarly ask, do we want all of our students to look like our faculty—same interests, same devotion to scholarship?

Here there is a double challenge: first, an institution must successfully conclude a discussion of core values; then it must ensure
that the values thus identified are actively employed in the institution's
decision-making process. In reaching a common understanding and
affirmation of core values, an institution establishes a foundation for
every decision it makes: which goals it pursues, what activities it un-
dertakes, what human and financial resources it expends. The crucial
missing element on many college and university campuses has not been
a discussion of athletics per se. Missing is rather the articulation of
institutional and educational values to provide a context for considering the role that athletics should play and the resources it should
command. Discussions are needed to lead to a strong—even if not
unanimous—consensus about the institution itself, the values it seeks
to foster, and the goals it seeks to achieve.

Convening discussions of this kind inherently carries risk; in many
ways it is tantamount to holding a constitutional convention, providing a forum that could draw an array of latent issues into the open.
Such discussions might make an institution's admission and selection
process transparent in a way that it may not have been before. As a
consequence of such openness, a president might conceivably fear
controversy further intensifying among many constituencies competing for resources in an institution. The sad truth of the matter, however, is that lack of candor on both the issue of values and their
relationship to athletics and to the more general questions of market
competition has already created more damage—in terms of institutional
coherence and market success—than any effort to be forthcoming is
likely to produce. Higher education needs to get this story straight,
and it needs to tell it out loud—for its own sake, as well as for those
it serves.

No one except the president can provide the leadership needed
to begin these explorations. At the same time, no president can expect a productive result without the help of others. First, the president must engage, as essential coconveners of these dialogues, the
leadership of two critical stakeholders: faculty and trustees. It is important that an institution's academic leadership, formal and informal,
be involved as active participants in this process. The chief academic
officer, faculty senate leadership, deans, and department chairs all have
roles in helping to ensure the thoughtful engagement of an institution's
faculty.

Trustee leadership is also essential to the productivity of these dialogues and the success of their outcomes. No conversation of institutional values can occur without the presence and engagement of key trustees reflecting a range of insights at the table. The fact that the values affirmed from these discussions will help guide decisions about athletics' role makes trustee involvement especially important.

The faculty, president, and trustees have ultimate responsibility for the values and direction of a higher education institution. As owners of the curriculum, faculty have primary authority in defining the content of the undergraduate educational experience. Trustees have fiduciary responsibility for an institution, exercising their ultimate authority over the allocation of resources that make possible the fulfillment of an educational mission. Finally, the president bridges these two domains, and the president must ensure that the table is not predisposed to a particular casting of institutional values, whether to favor or oppose athletics, to surrender or defy the market. Among faculty and trustees alike, there must be a range of thoughtful insight about the core values informing the educational mission and the roles that various curricular and cocurricular programs have in the education of undergraduates.

At the outset it will be necessary for a president—and the institution as a whole—to commit themselves to the time a discussion of this kind requires. These conversations must take place over a time period that allows key members of the community to participate. Making progress on these questions entails not just a decision to engage, but a commitment to a kind of engagement: a sustained, reflective dialogue that entertains a range of perspectives. It requires of participants a capacity to listen as well as talk, to move beyond speechmaking and constituency politics, and to focus on the convergence of shared values. Managing a conversation of this sort may require that a president distinguish between a broad consensus and the convictions of a vocal minority that presumes to speak for the whole.

One of the greatest challenges in convening such conversations is to convince its participants that the subject is real. Members of academic communities know all too well that conversations of this kind often fail to produce any substantive result. Presidents must signal to their campus communities that the values defined in this process will provide the basis for real decisions the institution makes in establishing its priorities and committing its resources. Beyond the conversation itself, a college or university must have the political will to act decisively if the discussions should recommend changing the status quo.

In sum then, to succeed these dialogues must follow several guidelines. They must: be convened and managed by the institution's president; include all sectors of the campus community; focus on the purpose of defining core values that unite a campus; be endowed with the political will to act on the values the institution defines; reflect the context of a campus' own particular culture.

Some may find it odd that we have argued for a discussion of values and athletics as a means of beginning the ultimately more important conversation about markets and market values. But that is precisely what we intend—and we intend that such conversations take place on every campus, not just at those institutions that practice selective admissions or run big-time sports programs. Most campuses are far better prepared at this moment for a focused discussion of athletics than of one considering their roles as market enterprises—though, in fact, they are the same discussion centering on the question of how to remain mission centered while becoming market smart. The conversations we have in mind must have the individual college or university as their primary focus. Each campus must define its fundamental values in the framework of its own culture and traditions. What a president might seek from these discussions is not just a decision about athletics per se; rather the goal ought to be as broad an agreement as possible on the central institutional values that in turn guide far-reaching decisions about the role of athletics as well as the place of other programs and pursuits. While the discussion of institutional core values cannot in itself generate an action agenda, it becomes nonetheless the basis for the specific policy decisions an institution makes concerning its programs for undergraduate education.

What a delicious irony it would be if the current contentiousness of intercollegiate athletics would at last engender the kind of value discussions colleges and universities need to undertake, as opposed to being mastered by the commercial pressures of market competition.

7 | Thwarted Innovation

There is nothing so cold as yesterday's invincible revolution. Five years ago e-learning was everybody's buzz—the promise of a trillion dollar market wrapped around the prospects of anytime-anywhere learning. All that is now gone, replaced by a pervading sense of disappointment, all the more dispiriting because e-learning seemingly combined two of the most important educational innovations of the last quarter-century.

The first was pedagogical, resulting from the linking of a set of rapidly maturing information technologies to new insights into how, when, and why people learn. Best described as electronically mediated learning—but dubbed e-learning because of the innovation's close association with e-commerce and the dot-com boom—the new learning and teaching modalities offered a truly student-centered approach to education, one that was both design rich and interactive, that could be delivered anywhere-anytime, and that could be customized to take full advantage of each individual's personal style of learning.

The second major educational innovation of these last two decades was geographical. Although too often dismissed as a kind of political slogan, globalization in fact describes a real process in which economies become linked, market forces triumph, and, as a result, both individual workers and national cultures feel threatened. The educational result is that everyone is on the move, both literally and figuratively. To be competitive more actual and potential workforce members seek to acquire new learning, and quickly. More students are being dispersed across national boundaries, and most scholars now adhere to disciplinary definitions that reflect international standards. Those ranked at the top of their disciplines have increasingly defined their futures in terms of an international labor market remarkably akin to the kind of free-agent system now characteristic of professional sports.

E-learning, with its promise of anywhere-anytime educational offerings, was to be globalization's handmaiden, creating educational communities that literally spanned the globe, thus allowing the rapid—and at times instantaneous—transmission of ideas as well as feelings across a cyberspace in which everyone could have equal voice. E-learning, precisely because it combined the promise of technology and the new realities imposed by globalization, was the educational innovation that garnered the most venture capital, the most press, and, not surprisingly, the most grandiose promises.

Among the claims made for e-learning, three are worth specific notice. First and probably foremost, the marriage of the new, electronic-based technologies and newly accepted theories of learning promised a revolution in pedagogy itself: customized, self-paced, and problem-based learning. Designers and facilitators would replace course instructors; "the sage on the stage" would literally become "the guide on the side." Students would be able to model outcomes, conduct experiments based on well-documented laboratory simulations, rapidly exchange ideas with both fellow students and their instructors, and, where appropriate, join international learning communities, not unlike the international contract bridge networks that were springing up on the Internet.

E-learning's second promise derived from its ability to be delivered anytime anywhere there was a computer and a connection to the Internet. Analysts were independently projecting a boom in adult education as more people sought both to start and finish baccalaureate and post-baccalaureate programs and to acquire the new kinds of skills on which a learning economy depended. For many, e-learning would spur a boom in distance education as both governmental agencies and private providers brought new programs to market. Life-long learning would become an electronic reality.

E-learning's third, and in many ways its most radical promise, was that the market would provide the financial wherewithal to fund the necessary innovations. Initially that funding would come in the form of substantial venture capital with which to launch the panoply of products a learning revolution would require. Thereafter tuition and other forms of product revenues would fund the expansion of the e-learning market. Predictions of e-learning's likely bounty literally knew no limits.

The most quoted projections were those by Michael Moe for Merrill Lynch's 2000 white paper, *The Knowledge Web,* which predicted growth in the online market opportunity for knowledge enterprises from $9.4 billion in 1999 to $53.3 billion in 2003, a 54 percent compound annual growth rate. By 2002, Moe and his colleagues said, students would be spending $3.9 billion online, while overall the market for online higher educational alone would be $7 billion by 2003.

With that level of market anticipation at hand, a uniquely American stampede began. Columbia University launched Fathom; New York University nearly matched those efforts with NYU.online. Cardean University became the model of a for-profit/not-for-profit collaboration in which some of the best-known U.S. and European universities partnered with UNext to launch a high-cost, high-prestige model of international business education. Individual states, making similar investments, chose to focus instead on providing low-cost, but ready, access to the educational assets already available on publicly funded university campuses. California's brief fling with its own electronic university and the more familiar Western Governors University were probably the two best-known examples, though efforts in Massachusetts, Maryland, and Missouri in the end demonstrated more staying power.

The reality never matched the promise—not by a long shot. There was no pedagogical revolution. By 2004 Fathom and NYU.online were gone. Cardean U and UNext were in the process of their third or fourth makeovers. There was but a modest boom in distance education—the limited number of successes owed more to their past market triumphs—as in the case of both University of Maryland's University College and the University of Phoenix—than to the effectiveness of the new technologies.

E-learning's altered fortunes occasioned considerable comment. More often, now, it is the butt of bad jokes—as in, "Can you imagine telling your children to go to their rooms and study college for four years?" In general the cynics had a field day, pointing out that e-learning was just one more fad, more hype than substance whose demise proved little more than an echo of the bursting of the dot-com bubble.

Asking the Right Questions

Not surprisingly, the cynics are no more correct than the evangelists were prescient in their predictions that e-learning would prove an irresistible revolution. The truth is that e-learning has more than survived. Money has been spent. Smart classrooms now abound on college campuses, while an increasing number of faculty count themselves among those who use technology to enhance their classroom presentations. That said, it is also the case that e-learning is not all it was promised to be—or all that it can or should be. What happened to e-learning is another object lesson attesting to how higher education's inexperience with markets and the forces they unleash produce unexpected results.

The story of e-learning is fundamentally about what students of the subject call "radical technological innovation." An innovation is judged to be radical when the invading technology has the potential to deliver dramatically better performance or lower costs in what previously had been a stable industry. The operative word is *potential*. When the new technology first emerges, it often appears clumsy and inferior to its established predecessor. In the beginning, it is the new technology's promise rather than its performance that attracts initial adherents. A large part of that promise is the vision of an altered future—one that is not only different, but also dramatically better.

In the case of e-learning, the convergence of personal computers and ubiquitous connectivity sparked a utopian vision in which teachers taught and students learned in fundamentally different ways. Just over the horizon was a world of active learners with teachers who guided and facilitated rather than proclaimed and judged. Learning would be both continuous and exciting, while the products of such learning would tangibly reward both learner and teacher. When e-learning was first introduced, now more than thirty years ago as Computer-Assisted Instruction (CAI), it was readily acknowledged that exploration of the new technology's future capacities had only just begun. While to the faithful the potential was clear and present, few pretended to know exactly how "going digital" would actually alter the day-to-day practices of professors.

Utterback and the Emergence of a Dominant Design

In actuality, much more is known about the dynamics of innovation, particularly about what happens when a new technology enters the marketplace. For one thing, the introduction of a radi-cal new technology creates fluidity in both markets and product de-signs. New entrants to the field bring novel design concepts and target new market segments. Established firms field additional innovations as they struggle to defend their territory. MIT's James Utterback, a lead-ing authority on technology-based innovation, points out that, in the early days of a radical innovation, "market and . . . industry are in a fluid stage of development. Everyone—producers and customers—is learning as they move along." But the fluidity is not sustained. Ulti-mately, as Utterback notes, in the case of a successful innovation, "Within this rich mixture of experimentation and competition some center of gravity eventually forms in the shape of a *dominant prod-uct design.* Once the dominant design emerges, the basis of competi-tion changes radically, and firms are put to tests that very few will pass." From this competitive process an innovation emerges in a newly standardized format that readily attracts new users.

The early days of automobiles were characterized by just such a cycle. The number of automobile manufacturers peaked at seventy-five in 1923, but then dropped to thirty-five in the late 1920s and to fourteen in 1960, meanwhile the market expanded. Creation of the dominant designs we know today required a period of trial and error in engineering laboratories and in the marketplace. What gelled after 1923 was a standardized conception of an effective automobile: for example, one fueled by gasoline, not steam; a self-starter, with four-to six-passenger seating; and a vehicle with the all-steel enclosed body introduced by Dodge in that year. The pace of innovation, and the num-ber of innovating firms, slackened once this dominant design emerged. Subsequent competition turned to product refinement, cost reduction, styling, and brand positioning. The slower pace of innovation boosted the premium on capital and market dominance, which in turn pro-duced a further shakeout in the industry.

The triumph of the automobile as the world's primary form of trans-portation teaches a second lesson as well. The dominant design may take a long while to emerge, and it may involve changes not directly related to the precipitating technology. For example, the automobile's dominant design did not consolidate until a paved road system came into being and gasoline became widely available.

When cast in these terms, the parallel between automobiles as the key element in an innovative transportation system and computers as potentially the key element in an equally transformed postsecondary learning system is both instructive and prophetic. On and off college campuses, e-learning could not take off until wide-bandwidth Internet access was readily available, until smart classrooms were constructed, and until all faculty and students had access to computers—investments that students and universities have been making and are continuing to make. Still missing, however, are many key elements of a dominant design. The avenues are in place; still lacking is a standardized design for the vehicles that system will employ.

Put another way, a radical innovation for a complex process such as e-learning requires more profound changes than simply creating an infrastructure: one's very conception of the supplying or consuming entity may have to change. When the innovation relieves one constraint, other constraints may well lurk close by. As these limits are overcome, as the innovation marches toward its dominant design, attracting the intellectual and financial capital necessary to establish a supportive infrastructure, the innovation itself becomes transformed—pushed in fewer directions, under the direct influence of fewer innovators, but all the while becoming more practical and hence attractive to a growing number of new users.

The Path of Innovation

The processes of adoption and adaptation that shape most innovations usually start slowly because of the need for experimentation. They accelerate only once the dominant design emerges and then eventually reach saturation.

The actors at the various stages of adoption differ markedly. First, *innovators* seek out and experiment with new ideas, often driven by an intrinsic interest. These pioneers endure many trials and tribulations. Their role is to determine how to use the new product or service and demonstrate its potential value. Collectively, the innovators comprise just 2 to 3 percent of the ultimate market.

The next 15 percent of potential users, the innovation's *early adopters*, embrace the innovation once there is a proven value in the concept. They usually are tightly connected to others in the field and often are viewed as opinion leaders. Early adopters seldom consider themselves pioneers; rather, they are hard-headed decision-makers who pursue the innovation for extrinsic rather than intrinsic reasons. But because they participate in the fluid stage of adoption, before the dominant design has become established, they shoulder a substantial risk. One principal contribution of early adopters to the emergence of a nplex situation that is more difficult to analyze and predict, even gh the underlying dynamics follow the traditional pattern. Today's ications of technology to on- and off-campus teaching and learn-present this kind of complexity, in large part because four classes pes of innovation are now in various stages of adoption by higher ation.

The first wave of innovation—*enhancements to traditional course/ gram configurations*—injected new materials into teaching and ning processes without changing the basic mode of instruction. mples include e-mail, student access to information on the Internet, the use of multimedia and simple simulations. Here the typical lication uses off-the-shelf software, such as PowerPoint, to enhance ssroom presentations and homework assignments.

Next came the *course management systems,* which enabled pro-sors and students to interact more effectively. They provided bet-communication with and among students, quick access to course terials, and support for administering and grading examinations. special subset of these activities came bundled together to enable creation of online courses and learning networks.

Still in their very early stages of experimentation and adoption imported learning objects, learning modules really, which enable ofessors to embed a richer variety of materials into their courses than possible with traditional "do-it-yourself" learning devices. Examples nge from compressed video presentations to complex interactive mulations. Online entities are springing up to collect, refine, distrib-te, and support electronic learning objects, and a few institutions are xperimenting with enterprise-level Learning Content Management ystems.

Finally, and still very much more hope than reality, are the *new ourse/program configurations,* which will result when faculty and heir institutions re-engineer teaching and learning activities to take ill and optimal advantage of the new technology. The new configu-ations focus on active learning and combine face-to-face, virtual, syn-hronous, and asynchronous interaction in novel ways. They also equire professors and students to accept new roles—with each other nd with the technology and support staff.

These four classes of e-learning innovation are currently in dif-ferent stages of their adoption cycles. *Enhancements to traditional course/program configurations* have moved rapidly through the early majority stage. *Course management tools* are just now moving into the

dominant design is their success at finding al
the innovation and test their alterations under i

The innovation's *early majority,* roughly th
lation of eventual users, enters once the domina
The early majority displays less leadership tl
but these people are open to new ideas, tend t
their peers, and committed to staying ahead of
they drive the first big wave of market expansic

Members of the *late majority,* the next thir
eventual users, are people who adopt after half
ready done so. They are followers because eith
interfered or their attention was focused elsewh
adoption stages. Late-majority users drive the ne
pansion, which is characterized by intense com
vation matures.

Finally there are the *diehards,* the last 15 p
sist adopting the innovation despite its now-obv
the risk of becoming isolated. In the end, the di
retire from the field.

Innovation stages are usually described in te
consumers, but the ideas apply to the supply side
firms and the individuals who launch those firms
realize them in practice. Early adopters may be inc
likely they represent parts of the firms that bring
scale and test design alternatives in the marketpla
out to be critical for radical innovations, such as e-
firms expand the market and move it toward maturity
hold on by their teeth in declining markets. The sam
cursors or descendents, may play all five roles at dif

Market saturation occurs when the ranks of poten
been depleted. Further growth may be limited to inci
population, or the stage may be set for a new breakth
adoption cycle. The breakthrough may introduce the ir
market segments, or it may represent new application
ments. Either way, it superimposes a new adoption c
lier cycle.

E-learning's Adoption Cycles

On occasion, new and nearly simul
of related innovations occur. The overlapping of adoption c

early majority stage—not so much in terms of individual faculty using them, but rather in terms of the proportion of students who are enrolled in courses and programs that deploy course management software. These first two adoption cycles have largely built on and reinforced one another.

Their momentum, however, has not transferred to either the *importation of learning objects* or to the *development of new course/program configurations*. Both remain at the innovation stage, still in search of the kind of acceptance that attracts early adopters.

The adoption cycles of off-campus and distance education have followed the same basic track: good use of the presentation enhancement tools represented by PowerPoint; heavy reliance on the kind of course infrastructure that a good course management system provides; computerized assessments; and threaded discussions.

Two Steps Forward, Two Steps Back

The different pace and successes of the first two adoption cycles, as compared with the latter two, suggest how the broader development and adoption of e-learning is being shaped and, in some cases, curtailed, by interactions, both real and potential, between and among these four adoption cycles. It now appears, for example, that the widespread and rapid introduction of teaching enhancements and course management software actually constrained the development of course objects and new course/program configurations. The very real need to catalog some early successes led to e-learning becoming nearly synonymous with online and distance education, which, in turn, reinforced the reluctance of more traditional on-campus programs to move much beyond the deployment of course management systems and the use of presentation tools like PowerPoint. While those innovations developed strong dominant designs—nothing is more dominant than PowerPoint—the absence of similar dominant designs structuring the development of learning objects and new course/program configurations goes a long way toward explaining e-learning's thwarted innovation.

Equally missing was the kind of faculty push for instructional reform that many of e-learning's early proponents believed would be the natural result of linking electronic technologies with a desire to change how students were taught. Alas, only bureaucratic processes have proven more immutable to fundamental change than the basic production function of higher education. Most faculty today still teach largely as they were taught; that is, they stand in the front of a classroom providing lectures intended to supply the basic knowledge students need.

Those who envisioned a changed, more responsive learning environment argued that the most effective instructor is not the master who pronounces but rather the teacher who guides. Learning works best when it is participatory. Students can become effective problem-solvers only when they have mastered the art of critical thinking and acquired the discipline necessary to be self-paced learners. Constant assessment and feedback are critical; thus, both student and instructor can determine, before it is too late, whether the student is mastering the necessary material.

E-learning seemed more than ready to satisfy each of these goals. The most successful e-learning experiment was Studio Physics developed by Jack Wilson, then at the Rensselaer Polytechnic Institute (RPI). Studio Physics was taught wholly on the computer in specially designed "studios" where students worked in two-person teams on upward of 25 computers. Faculty circulated throughout the studio, providing help and instruction as needed, as each student pair worked through a complex set of problems and computer simulations designed to teach the basics of introductory physics.

The program worked at RPI—and at more than a dozen other institutions—because the curriculum itself was problem-based, because simple graphics could be used to simulate physical properties and rates of change, and because the students themselves saw Studio Physics as an example of the kind of system they had come to this engineering school to learn to develop. Yet, this set of characteristics is hard to match for other curricula. It is also important to point out that Studio Physics remained a group activity. The students came to class, and they worked directly with their partners and the faculty assigned to the Studio. No one was isolated—no one was off in a room by himself or herself with just a computer and a set of e-learning exercises.

As Studio Physics at RPI demonstrated, within fully integrated e-learning courses faculty do become guides—and designers and mentors and conveners. They are not presenters, unless they happen to have filmed themselves performing an experiment or conducting a simulation and then made those images available on their students' computers. The student pairs represented exactly the kind of interactive learning groups that educational reformers envisioned. The feedback was immediate and continuous. Students knew if they had the right answer or were at least proceeding in the right direction as soon as they submitted answers to the problem sets on which they were working. The designers of Studio Physics also learned that there could be no hidden assumptions—no relying on one's intuition or past experience to know when and how to introduce new topics. For the first time, many of the faculty involved in Studio Physics were forced to spell out their teaching strategy as well as think through what kinds of learning strategies their students were likely to bring into the Studio.

Studio Physics proved the exception, not the rule. For the most part, faculty who made e-learning a part of their teaching did so by having the electronics simplify tasks, not by fundamentally changing how they taught the subject. Lecture notes were readily translated into PowerPoint presentations. Course management tools like Blackboard and WebCT were used to distribute course materials, grades, and assignments, but the course materials, for the most part, were simply scanned bulk packs, and the assignments neither looked nor felt different. Even when the text book came with an interactive CD-ROM or when the publisher made the same material available on a proprietary Website, most faculty did not assign those materials. Only modest breakthroughs occurred, faculty used e-mail to communicate rapidly and directly with students and adopted computerized testing materials, many of which provided a more robust, but still static, means of evaluation.

A number of people are coming to see that the rapid introduction of course management tools actually reduced e-learning's impact on the way most faculty teach. Blackboard and WebCT made it almost too easy for faculty to transfer their standard teaching materials to the Web. While Blackboard's promotional materials talked about enabling faculty to use a host of new applications, the software's up-front promises were less dramatic: the ability of faculty members "to manage their own Internet-based file space on a central system and to collect, share, discover and manage important materials from articles and research papers to presentations and multimedia files."

All the faculty really needed were the rudimentary electronic library skills that most have already mastered. When asked, "Are you involved in e-learning?" Blackboard and WebCT allowed the faculty users to respond, "Yes, my courses are already online!" The rapid introduction of PowerPoint as e-learning's principal course enhancement tells much the same story. As used by most faculty, PowerPoint became e-learning "clip art"—in the sense that it allowed the instructor to import graphics and graphs from other media, including the instructor's old lecture notes. Illustrated lectures did not constitute electronically mediated learning any more than courses that used Blackboard or WebCT to distribute learning materials.

Even the most adventurous and committed faculty members often approached the use of e-learning in ways that lessened its general impact on the curriculum. On most campuses seeking to spur interest in e-learning, faculty were promised technical support, summer salaries, and the ability to make their e-learning course on any subject of interest to them. Most courses were well-designed, technically sophisticated, and, given the faculty members' freedom to teach what they wanted, idiosyncratic. Once the course was offered for two or three years, the faculty member often moved on to other topics and different experiments, having satisfied his or her own interests and curiosity. Then the courses died, largely because no one wanted to teach someone else's e-learning syllabus. These universities began to discover that they constantly had to offer faculty extra incentives to involve them in e-learning—often to reinvent the wheel. When the expenditures of those funds became too expensive, the institutions dropped the incentive programs and witnessed a general flattening of e-learning adoptions and experiments. All but forgotten, by then, was the idea that e-learning might lead to a more general reformation of both teaching and learning styles.

By then most administrators responsible for technology and e-learning on their campuses had made their decisions. The best way to promote faculty use of technology was to ask the faculty to change as little as possible. Hence the major investments in e-learning came to be concentrated in infrastructures designed to promote traditional forms of instruction. Smart classrooms with a full panoply of devices for linking to the Internet as well as projecting slides and other instructional aids became the norm. Course management systems became not just the preferred but the expected mode for linking faculty and students for the purpose of distributing materials and exchanging messages.

Over time the amount of money invested in full-scale e-learning productions dwindled. While the more technologically adventuresome continued to experiment with learning objects, they too remained curiosities rather than standard elements of either a refashioned curricula or altered modes of instruction and learning.

Where's the Market—Where's the Beef?

The other assumptions to be jettisoned were the beliefs that e-learning would both pay for itself and, if an institution were clever and lucky enough, provide a revenue bonanza with which to underwrite other institutional projects. After the fact it is easy to suggest that higher education's fascination with the potential market for e-learning was but one more manifestation of the dot-com bubble and the market model embedded in e-commerce. No doubt the giddy optimism that underwrote so many of higher education's investments in dubious market schemes reflected a classic "bubble psychology" in which everybody worried about being left out by arriving at the party too late.

Higher education's early embrace of e-learning also reflected a kind of desperate hunger, particularly on the part of those without access to sponsored research and indirect cost recoveries, for a new, more robust source of revenue. While institutions of nearly every stripe went in search of this El Dorado, those first in line were some of our nation's most prestigious professional schools in general and business schools in particular. Among the first entrants into the market for online courses were a variety of high-cost, high-prestige programs of business education, usually leading to the MBA, involving some of the western world's best-known universities and business schools. Initially the most visible as well as the first to launch a well-conceived and well-financed set of products designed to serve a worldwide market for business education was Cardean University, a joint venture of five major business schools—Stanford, Columbia, Carnegie Mellon, Chicago, and the London School of Economics—and UNext, a major Internet education company. The problem was fundamental: the Web-based products, despite the prestige and visibility of Cardean's sponsors, never attracted the volume of students it required to be a successful business enterprise.

In the summer of 2003, Universitas 21 announced itself as the next venture seeking to make a Web-based, but nonetheless top-end, business education available to students online, promising to offer MBAs at roughly 20 percent of the price of the in-residence programs that the sponsoring universities provided. A different set of institutions—for the most part either present or former British Commonwealth universities—forged a joint venture with the Thomson Corporation, the single largest enterprise with major investments in programs of e-learning. In mid-2004, Universitas 21's educational offerings were just being announced and initial cohorts recruited. Without waiting for the results of these efforts, however, many of e-learning's experts and advocates, cast their votes. *The Chronicle of Higher Education* quoted Frank Mayadas, the program officer at the Sloan Foundation responsible for the most sustaining investments in e-learning and online-education, as saying Universitas 21 may have "set its expectations too high. 'What sells in education is price and name. . . . A new entity like Universitas 21 Global may not be needed . . . now that many well-known public and private universities offer distance-education degrees that students anywhere in the world can take.'" What Mayadas should have added is that, while readily available, such courses also have problems enrolling sufficient numbers of students to recoup their initial investment.

The simplest truth is that almost nobody made money. Some universities that invested heavily in online distance education programs found that upward of 80 percent of their online enrollments were in fact from resident students who were taking the online courses as a matter of convenience. As a result, a modest net growth in enrollments was often swamped by a substantial increase in delivery costs. The biggest losers were Columbia's Fathom and NYU.online. But nearly every institution that dabbled lost, some more than others, and then as quietly as possible reduced and in some cases closed out their online ventures.

There were, however, important successes. By mid-decade, the University of Maryland University College (UMUC), already an internationally recognized supplier of continuing education in this country and of distance education for military personnel serving overseas, had parlayed its successes with face-to-face and distributed education to become a major supplier of online education. In the summer of 2004 UMUC could boast of a host of national awards for online education, a projection from the Maryland Higher Education Commission that by 2010 UMUC would account for one-third of the total enrollments in the University System of Maryland, and with 110,423 online course enrollments, the claim that UMUC had "probably the largest number of online enrollments in the world" (one problem with tracking the market for e-learning is that nobody knows with much certainty how large or small that market is). UMUC succeeded because it knew—indeed helped create the market—for distance and distributed education; through its contract with the U.S. military, Maryland had created both infrastructure and brand recognition coupled with a real understanding of the economics involved. Its shift to online education was just that—an adaptation of a successful education and business model to a new means of delivery.

UMassOnline's successes were smaller, its story briefer, and its business model different. UMassOnline had the prescience to hire RPI's Jack Wilson as its first CEO. Wilson instituted a brokering and support function. All the courses offered by UMassOnline belonged to one or more of the system's five physical campuses. Because the campus grants the degree and provides a physical connection for the students who need or want one, the student must apply and gain admission to a specific campus. The tuition the student pays is the same as the tuition charged its other students—an arrangement that meant that UMassOnline students received the same level of state subsidy as did other students in the state system. UMassOnline worked because it supported rather than competed with the system's traditional campuses, kept a relatively low profile principally by not competing in the market for spot courses, provided reliable technology, and, perhaps most important, charged students a subsidized rather than a market price.

The scale of the enterprise remained relatively modest. In the Spring of 2004 UMassOnline granted 161 degrees, roughly divided between undergraduate and graduate. Equally important was the actual distribution of degrees. Just 2 undergraduate liberal arts degrees were granted. The other 77 undergraduate degrees were split between nursing (49) and information technology (28). The 72 graduate degrees had the same cast. Through a special program that offered a transitional doctorate in physical therapy, the UMass-Amherst campus granted 26 degrees. The balance was taken up with 19 masters of public health, 19 masters of education, and 8 MBAs.

The institution that pioneered the development of niche degrees was the University of Phoenix, which, by mid-2005, had the most robust and, by most accounts, the most successful online education program. Mention the University of Phoenix, and the response across higher education is almost uniform: "you mean *that* for-profit enterprise," and by extension that money-grubbing corruptor of higher education's mission and message. We neither endorse that view nor consider Phoenix's motives or corporate structure; rather, its business and delivery models became the basis for higher education's most successful investment in online delivery.

The University of Phoenix succeeded because it was well organized, well financed, knew what it wanted from its faculty, and knew how to exploit the market opportunities traditional higher education was creating largely by ignoring potential customers. In many ways, Phoenix's launch strategy can best be described as cherry-picking— looking for the pockets of demand that traditional higher education has come to treat as cash-cows. Education service courses were one such opportunity—most education schools had come to assume that teachers taking extra courses to satisfy state licensing requirement were a captive audience ripe for exploitation. Mounting competitive pro- grams was neither high cost nor high tech, the target audience was appreciative of the efforts Phoenix put into course design and quality control, and the value gap between what Phoenix was offering and what had traditionally been available was sufficient to command a higher price. The profits came easily once Phoenix's enrollments were sufficient to achieve modest economies of scale.

Business administration represented another ripe target. Little ini- tial investment was required, the market was looking for a quality pro- vider that knew how to design and deliver instruction effectively, and the demand was sufficient to make entry into this market relatively easy. In time, that became the Phoenix model. Look for a market that had been poorly served or underserved. Pay a lot of attention to design and quality control. Pick sites—really little more than educa- tional store fronts—that were convenient, safe, and pleasant. Price the product between the premiums charged by medallion, for the most part private institutions, and the tuitions charged by local public providers.

The Phoenix business and delivery model had one more feature. Its faculty did not own the courses they taught; the institution did. Working with a largely part-time and adjunct faculty whose benefits, ironically, were often paid by the colleges and universities that pro- vided Phoenix's instructors their day jobs. Phoenix's instructors are professionals, but they are also employees of a system designed to de- liver consistent educational products that are tested, evaluated, and modified on a regular basis.

That commitment to design and delivery, along with Phoenix's extraordinary brand recognition as a supplier of vocationally related higher education, allowed the institution to succeed with its online educational offerings. The presentation of the product was remarkable. In GOOGLE the first sponsored link under "online education" was the University of Phoenix promising "Real Degrees for Busy Adults." There was the same tight focus on earning "a degree in Business, Education, Nursing, or Technology." Interested shoppers were told: "Professionals holding an advanced degree earn up to 177% more than under-graduates." Phoenix offered plenty of human contact—via telephone and the Internet and in person. There was always the option of doing part of the degree in a traditional format at one of Phoenix's convenient locations—FLEXNET® Phoenix called it, though everywhere else it is more colloquially known as "bricks and clicks." As its online business grew, Phoenix added one further wrinkle—an admissions process designed to test whether the applicant would likely succeed in an Internet environment. Proud of the rate at which its students completed their degrees, Phoenix wanted to be sure its online product achieved the same results.

Each of these examples—the University of Phoenix, University of Maryland University College, and UMassOnline—provides a checklist of what it takes to earn one's way when providing e-learning products: an established brand; an emphasis on design and quality assurance; a product that is consistent and reliable; a capacity to readily serve an expanding number of learners; a physical network or presence to complement and support the online products. The technology made possible the rapid distribution of learning materials along with constant and immediate feedback, both from student to instructor and vice versa. The products themselves, however, were, for the most part, twenty-first century correspondence courses rather than technologically advanced learning environments. The market to be tapped consisted primarily of adults seeking midrange professional degrees that they could readily convert into higher pay. The really expensive aspects of higher education—most sciences, most engineering disciplines, and almost all the liberal arts that comprise the general education component of a traditional baccalaureate education—were left to others, and to other pocket books.

Who's the Customer?

The University of Phoenix's success, both online and on its campuses, teaches one last lesson about how and why traditional higher education institutions so often misread the market. Phoenix knows exactly whom it serves and why—it has customers! More than that, it expends considerable energy and resources querying and otherwise learning about its students—who they are, what they want, how they learn, how are they doing. It uses that information to shape products, to teach its students what they need, and to monitor their progress through the institution. In this sense, the University of

Phoenix provides a model for customer relations management that the rest of higher education might profitably emulate.

A large part of the problem traditional institutions encountered in trying to develop and grow the market for e-learning was that they neither knew nor could imagine the territory. In the fall of 2001 we asked a cross-section of faculty and staff at six representative colleges and universities whether their students would be able to utilize computer-based learning—as part of a course either on the Internet or in a classroom using an electronic course management system or learning objects. Those we talked to were nearly unanimous in answering in the affirmative. Indeed, they were often incredulous that we had even asked such a question: "Not a problem," we were told, "the kids take to e-learning like ducks take to water. After all, they love games and technology, are dismissive of professors who seem to have trouble navigating Blackboard."

Two years later when we returned to many of the same campuses, neither the faculty nor the staff reflected that previous certainty. When queried about this change of opinion, their answers reflected a growing appreciation of the fact that initial assumptions about e-learning were being modified by actual experience; apparently no one had ever asked the students whether they actually *liked* e-learning.

Several weeks after our visit to the University of Texas–Austin, there appeared in the *Daily Texan* an opinion piece by Laura Isensee, a University of Texas senior honor student. Her column is worth quoting in some detail, not because it proves in and of itself that students are becoming distrustful of what she called "teaching technology," but because it gives voice and language to those doubts.

> The fairy tale of e-learning assumes that classroom technology enhances the learning experience for both the professor and the students. The reality of such educational technology is far from ideal. Often poorly integrated into a course, its use skews the balance of content and technology and lessens dynamic interaction among students and between students and faculty. . . .
>
> The use of teaching technology can quickly transform into a pedagogical crutch. In an upper-division linguistics course last fall, the daily lecture consisted of no more than a PowerPoint presentation and printed handouts of the same display. This un-innovative approach reduces the role of the

teacher to a mere conduit that transmits ideas into student depositories.

Particularly troubling are the choices of lower-division language classes to implement technology that might allow for a greater quantity of students but lessens the quality of the education. . . .

A prime example of the increasing pervasiveness of classroom technology is the electronic textbook. The e-book makes technology the primary educational tool, even though many students seem to prefer to use technology as a secondary source. Consider the case of Management 320F last fall when the chosen text was electronic. Professor Victor Arnold initially ordered enough print copies of the textbook for less than a quarter of the class. Students could buy a download version of the e-book or purchase a password that would allow a page to be viewed a maximum of four times. Yet one-third of the class opposed the e-book and lobbied for more print copies to be ordered.

The University of Texas also provided an important clue as to why the students' interest in games and their quick adoption of most computer-based technologies did not translate into an interest in e-learning. One senior manager of the University CO-OP, the university's mega bookstore, told us to check out "the kind of software the kids were buying." We did by turning to *The Chronicle of Higher Education's* monthly tracking of the "Best-Selling Software at College Bookstores."

The results were fascinating. In June 2003, for example, basic Microsoft products accounted for five of the ten best-sellers. Number seven on the best-seller list was the leading anti-virus software, Norton, reflecting the heightened concern over a raft of viruses and worms then infecting machines worldwide. The remaining four? In order, they were: Adobe Photoshop, Adobe Acrobat, Macromedia Studio MX, and Macromedia Dreamweaver MX. Photoshop is used for editing, enhancing, and optimizing photographs. Acrobat allows the reader to read and prepare PDF files. Dreamweaver allows the user to construct sophisticated Websites. And Macromedia Studio MX, to quote the product's own Website, "provides professional functionality for every aspect of Web development and includes the newest versions of Dreamweaver, Flash, Fireworks and FreeHand." This last set of software products has a common denominator: their capacity allows the user to prepare and distribute complex presentations. Or, as the manager of the Texas CO-OP reminded us, this software is principally about showing off.

The implication, borne out in subsequent interviews, is that student fascination with computers and software has three major components: students want to be connected, principally to one another; they want to be entertained, principally by games, music, and movies; and they want to present themselves and their work. As most faculty in the United States have learned, students have become almost obsessively adroit at "souping-up" their papers, which they submit electronically and which they festoon with charts, animations, and pictures. One frustrated professor, who had just spent a half-hour downloading a student's term paper, was heard to remark, "All I wanted was a simple twenty-page paper—what I got looks suspiciously like the outline for a TV show."

Most promoters of e-learning simply missed all of this devotion on the part of students to complex presentations of self. The students they saw in their mind's eye were gamers who would love simulations, who would see in the computer a tool for problem-solving, who would take to e-learning like ducks take to water. And, in fact, some students are just like that, though, for the most part, they are concentrated in engineering schools.

In the summer of 2004 ECAR (the EDUCAUSE Center for Applied Research), the research arm of the organization to which most campus Chief Information Officers and their staffs belong, released a study that the *Chronicle of Higher Education* summarized under the headline, "Students Have Mixed Views of Technology's Impact on Teaching." Actually the results were not so mixed. The students surveyed were hardly Luddites—just 3.7 percent said the new technologies provided no benefits in the classroom. However, less than 15 percent said improved learning was the greatest benefit of the technologies, while nearly half (48.5 percent) said far and away the biggest advantage technology conferred was added convenience. Asked how much technology they wanted, 41.2 percent said they wanted "moderate use of IT," about a third said they wanted courses with "extensive IT," and slightly more than 20 percent said they preferred courses with "limited IT."

It turned out that students, e-learning's would-be customers, wanted pretty much what faculty wanted—a technology that increased personal convenience while, at the same time, not requiring any fundamental change in how lessons are either taught or learned.

Not the End of the Story

E-learning, particularly in the United States, attracted a host of skilled entrepreneurs and innovators who sought, as
their most immediate goal, to establish early prominence in an industry
that had yet to be defined. They sought to achieve market position
quickly, lest others get there sooner and close the door behind them.
In seeking that advantage, they were aided by two phenomena particular to postsecondary education and to the times. First, the boom
in commercial investments in e-learning enterprises followed more than
a decade of experimentation by faculty with the use of computers in
teaching. A few experiments had even flowered into commercially successful products such as Maple and Mathematica, applications designed
to teach students calculus using electronically mediated instruction.
Although such work involved only a minority of the faculty, it was
enough to advocate the new technology and assure university leaders
that the expertise needed for e-learning ventures was available. As it
turned out, that experimentation proved to be too narrow to feed the
e-learning boom that followed.

The dot-com boom provided a second major impetus. It spawned
rosy estimates of the market for Internet-based services—Michael Moe's
extrapolation of a trillion dollar market was only one of a dozen or
more highly publicized claims. Assured by the technology's advocates
that the necessary expertise was in hand or soon would be, entrepreneurs both inside and outside traditional postsecondary education
rushed to market with e-learning ventures. A veritable feeding frenzy
ensued, with large amounts of time, effort, and capital committed to
e-learning development and marketing.

In retrospect, the rush to e-learning produced more capacity than
any rational analysis would have said was needed. In a fundamental
way, the boom-bust cycle in e-learning stemmed from an attempt to
compress the process of innovation itself. The entrepreneurs' enthusiasm produced too many new ventures pushing too many untested
products—products that, in their initial form, turned out not to deliver as much value as promised.

There were many aftereffects to e-learning's inevitable crash; perhaps most dangerous, the experience jaundiced the academy's view
concerning the actual value of technologies promising electronically
mediated instruction and the market's willingness to accept new learning modalities. The hard fact is that e-learning took off before people
really knew how to use it—before anything like dominant designs for

learning objects or new course/program configurations were even on the horizon. Missing, in the first instance, was a proven knowledge base of sufficient breadth to persuade faculty that adaptation was necessary. As a result, e-learning entrepreneurs assumed a much higher level of risk than they bargained for—and not surprisingly, most ended up paying the price.

Despite the travails of the last several years, e-learning has retained a core of true believers who argue, still forcefully and occasionally persuasively, that a revolution is at hand; the computer will do for learning today what printing did for scholarship in the fifteenth century. Don't be fooled by the failures and false steps, they proclaim. The best is yet to come.

More quiet, and also more numerous, are the pragmatists who point out that e-learning is alive and has in fact spurred a host of important educational changes, probably best symbolized by the widespread adoption of course management tools, such as BlackBoard and WebCT. We count ourselves among the pragmatists. We believe the story of e-learning is still unfolding; no one really knows what tomorrow will bring, although we suspect that computer-based learning technologies will continue to serve as a major catalyst of innovation. The underlying information technologies on which e-learning depends are themselves too ubiquitous, and the people attracted to having them serve as learning platforms are too smart for us not to take seriously the prospect that major changes will flow from their efforts.

Equally important, we see e-learning as an invaluable lesson on the dynamics of the market—what traditional colleges and universities need to learn if they are to become truly market-smart, as say, the University of Phoenix already has.

8 Who Owns Teaching?

It is a perfectly simple question, almost childlike in its innocence. It is also a question to which there is a host of classic answers. Teaching is an activity that belongs to everyone and to no one. Its origins are as deep as a parent's instinct to provide for a child and as powerful as a child's desire to learn. It is Mark Hopkins and his student on the log where both are learners and hence both are owners of the learning that links them. Teaching is perhaps the strongest and most central bond linking one generation to another.

In a world of markets, copyrights, and digital entrepreneurs, however, the question is almost Marxian. To ask who owns teaching is to ask, "Who owns the means of production?" Teaching and learning are integral parts of the processes by which societal benefit are apportioned: who learns what largely determines who advances in what degree to a life of economic security and professional fulfillment. In a society that is as competitive as it is complex, the stakeholders of teaching are many, and the question of ownership becomes harder to define with certainty in a digital age in which the means to reproduce and distribute intellectual content or expression have become ubiquitous.

Teaching, particularly at the collegiate level, is also big business, with higher education now accounting for some $225 billion in annual expenditures. More than ever, the badges of successful learning—degrees, certificates, and course credits—have become the currency of success; they transform teachers and their institutions into suppliers of essential goods and services. If an earlier tendency was to observe that "those who can't do, teach," today the more apt observation is that "those who teach, empower." Where once, as Clark Kerr taught, the key questions for higher education were "Who pays?" and "Who benefits?" The size of the collegiate market along with its capacity for social transformation makes answering, "Who owns it?" equally important.

Within every academic community, almost regardless of discipline and institution, a core of faculty members shares a deep and passionate commitment to teaching. Although teaching remains central to the educational mission, it now, however, lacks a sense of common engagement within the academy. Across American higher education surprisingly little sense of community centers around the act of teaching itself; no collective voice from within defines what teaching seeks to achieve and how to evaluate and improve its effectiveness. The absence of a sustained and purposeful dialogue about teaching in most institutions has allowed the forces of commercial competition and public accountability to become the main drivers of educational quality. For-profit enterprise along with public agencies have appropriated increasingly powerful roles in defining teaching, measuring its success, and identifying the beneficiaries of the teaching. Accompanying the rise of commercial interests are the growing challenges to the traditions of attribution, synthesis, and knowledge development that have informed the environment of open inquiry in college and university classrooms.

Freedom, Community, and Markets

Really good teaching can be said to resist the boundaries of ownership whenever it emphasizes unfettered inquiry and derives its authority from the autonomy, legal as well as intellectual, of the academy. Most faculty regard the singular benefit of a faculty career as the academic freedom it confers. In turn, that freedom provides the context in which both teaching and scholarly exploration take place. Although no faculty member ignores matters of compensation and financial well-being, for many the intrinsic rewards of teaching become equally if not more important parts of the equation. In this sense, teaching is something more than a job or even a profession. It is a calling—an activity undertaken from a passionate, often intensely personal commitment to explore knowledge and ideas and to engage others in this process of discovery.

Because teaching is an activity that incorporates within itself the purposes of academic freedom, in today's academy teaching is largely private, left to individual faculty members to define and undertake. In shutting the classroom door a faculty member creates a domain, not just of his or her own choosing, but also of his or her own design. Having the freedom to teach in one's own style has contributed immeasurably to the vitality of American higher education. Institutional flexibility has allowed the emergence of different teaching conceptions and styles, accompanied by the recognition that effective teaching can take a variety of forms, which range from theatrical performance to the most subdued and low-key interactions with students.

At the same time, this mantle of freedom provides the necessary cover to explain both how and why most faculty and nearly all institutions have avoided almost all systematic explorations of the meaning and nature of teaching itself. Ask most young professors just starting out in their careers, and they will repeat the ideas and ideals that helped persuade them to pursue an academic career: teaching is an activity carried out by people with shared commitments.

In reality, younger faculty quickly discover that the community of discourse that ought to derive from this sense of shared commitments is all but impossible to find. The absence of a common basis for understanding and evaluating teaching makes it more difficult for members of the academy to agree on what good teaching is. As a result, the teaching dossier is likely to make more of a symbolic than a substantive contribution to the decisions reached by tenure and promotion committees. Even in settings where most faculty care deeply about their own teaching, universities and colleges lack both a strong culture of evidence for defining good teaching and a highly developed community that is itself based on teaching.

It's the Market

The larger truth remains: in most institutions almost anything goes when it comes to teaching and the curriculum, as long as the faculty member meets his or her classes, provides orderly assignments and fair tests, and turns in his or her grades on time— this last requirement being the most tenuous. In the 1980s the shapeless and ill-defined nature of the collegiate curriculum became the focus of a series of sharp, and to many within the academy, hostile critiques. *A Nation at Risk* decried a "rising tide of mediocrity" across all of American education that it said was eroding the "educational foundations of our society." William Bennett, when not excoriating higher education for its profligate ways, was arguing for a return to an old-fashioned core curriculum that placed the humanities at the center of collegiate teaching. Ernest Boyer in *College* sketched a dismal landscape of colleges that had become purposeless, of faculty who too often felt trapped and out of place, and of students and families who saw less and less value in an increasingly necessary as well as expensive product.

The most sustained as well as serious critiques came in three volumes, each produced by different sensitivities as well as for differing purposes. Allan Bloom's *The Closing of the American Mind,* E. D. Hirsch's *Cultural Literacy,* and from the Association of American Colleges a major report with the ironic title *Integrity in the College Curriculum.* Largely the work of Williams College's Frederick Rudolph, *Integrity* was an indictment that minced few words. "As for what passes as a college curriculum, almost anything goes. We have reached a point at which we are more confident of the length of a college education than its content and purpose."

Integrity also thought it knew the culprit. "The curriculum has given way to a marketplace philosophy: it is a supermarket where students are shoppers and professors are merchants of learning. Fads and fashions, the demands of popularity and success, enter where wisdom and experience should prevail." It was the market and its dreaded companion, commodification—a term of reproach not yet in vogue when *Integrity* was issued—that explained the near-absence of both structure and coherence from the American collegiate curriculum.

The explanation worked until the University of Phoenix, in its embrace of the market, produced some of the most structured as well as coherent curricula in higher education. The irony was obvious: among institutions with large numbers of students, the for-profit University of Phoenix made the most sustained commitment to curricular structure and coherence. Phoenix made clear that teaching was a product to be owned, invested in, and supervised by the institution itself. Courses required management as well as design and then evaluation on a continuing basis. Consistency, borne of acknowledged standards, constituted successful teaching.

Traditional institutions, however, lacked a sustained commitment to managed instruction and evaluation, although they increasingly did not lack for students who saw themselves as customers. As colleges and universities came to educate a larger share of the population and encompass a broader range of purposes, students began exerting a stronger influence on what was taught—principally through their increasingly vocal desire to learn only what was needed for an immediate career goal. In the fractured world of teaching that then prevailed, parts of the academy sought the economic advantages that came with satisfying their students' pragmatic demands. Because these accommodations brought extra funds into the institution, the questions asked, but seldom answered, centered on whether the institution was being changed: is the definition of a college education itself being altered? A visible demarcation emerged between two conceptions of teaching, which might otherwise have evolved as points on a continuum.

The older, more traditional conception, based primarily in the arts and sciences, sought to engage students in a broad range of human thought and achievement and to foster the habits of inquiry that lead to both heightened understanding and the creation and refinement of knowledge. Underlying this approach were two central convictions: the academy itself was the natural arbiter of knowledge by evaluating what was known and determining what should be taught; and the ultimate purpose of teaching was to foster intellectual curiosity for a life of continued learning and engaged citizenship.

In this conception, the individual faculty member served as an independent broker, if not the sole owner, of his or her teaching. Even as they reserved the power to shape the circumstance and dynamic of learning, most faculty members in the arts and sciences taught from a conviction that knowledge itself was a shared public domain, freely available for consideration by any who sought to explore.

The second, increasingly pervasive conception of teaching shifted the focus from the pursuit and discovery of knowledge to the acquisition of applied skills and competencies for entry or advancement in specific careers. From the 1980s onward, the weight of public attention centered increasingly on the practical economic benefits that successful teaching conferred on students. Unable either to draw on a strong consensus defining good teaching or even to sustain an institutionwide conversation about what ought to be taught and how, those who favored the older, traditional view lost out. The intellectual control—and in that sense, the ownership—of teaching shifted from the faculty to the market that defined both what was taught and how that teaching was evaluated.

The justification for any course of study in any given field now had less to do with the inherent reward of discovery than with the contribution that such a course made to students' success in their careers. The definitional high ground had also shifted from the arts and sciences to the professions.

How much had things changed? Two signs of the time told most of the story. First, was the increasing number of for-profit educational providers openly competing with traditional two- and four-year institutions. Second, student goals and motivation notably shifted. Three decades ago, faculty members could reasonably expect their very best students to continue beyond their undergraduate majors, earning graduate degrees and becoming faculty members themselves. Three decades later, the prospect of attracting the best and brightest into faculty careers had become the exception more than the rule.

An Array of Stakeholders

Given the changes in society and institutions during the past three decades, the answers to "Who owns teaching?" become just as multifaceted as the answers to "Who owns intercollegiate athletics?" Both cases demonstrate how institutions can stray from a primary educational purpose to pursue other, more achievable and remunerative goals along the way.

Like intercollegiate sports, teaching became an activity in which a host of vested interests exerted a shaping or even distorting influence on both mission and performance. Within a particular college or university, one could say that the individual faculty member had primary ownership of the course. Individual departments were, in turn, owners of the academic programs students pursue in fulfillment of the major. And the institution itself, through the collective action of its faculty, owned the curriculum. Although these circles of ownership overlap, they nonetheless represented what nearly anyone within higher education recognized as a territorial mapping.

At the same time, an array of forces both inside and outside the academy were exerting new claims on teaching and its purposes. On a near-daily basis, religious, ethnic, and gender interests proclaimed what should be taught and by whom. In the public arena, what colleges and universities did and did not teach—and what the faculty did and did not do—became potent public symbols often defining what the public felt was wrong with higher education. Most state governments launched their initiatives to make public institutions, at least, more accountable; in the process, state legislatures demonstrated a new willingness to mandate that colleges and universities measure the impact of their teaching in the name of achieving tangible results. Some states implemented testing programs designed to measure student learning progress without any substantial consultation with state higher education institutions or their faculty. Although the drive toward standardized testing was almost universally decried within the academy as a caricature of teaching and learning, high-stakes testing nonetheless became a central fixture in the landscape of many states.

Potentially the biggest winners in this market-driven redistribution of intellectual control over teaching are the students. They become the educational owners—not just heirs of the knowledge and scholarly traditions they encounter, but consumers of the services higher education institutions provide. The choices that students make among institutions and programs of study determine the financial health of all but a handful of super-endowed private colleges and universities. The internal distributions of enrollments play the same role in determining which schools are winners, which departments are secure, and which courses are available. It was, after all, the very size and financial power of the student market for postsecondary education that gave rise to commercial enterprises ranging from for-profit educational providers to the annual published rankings of colleges and universities. In an educational world dominated by an admissions arms race, the media rankings exemplify how even an indirect stakeholder can subject teaching and other activities of higher education to distraction, in a sense appropriating a portion of the ownership of teaching away from higher education institutions and their faculty.

Pay-per-view and Napster

Many issues surrounding the question of who owns teaching are as old as the academy itself. New, however, is the political and commercial context in which the questions are now being answered. Because colleges and universities, both individually and as a whole, have not engaged the question broadly in terms of roles or responsibilities or values, the scenarios of ownership and definitions of property rights now coming into vogue have been cast almost exclusively in the legalese to which the realms of publishing and entertainment are devoted. Higher education is discovering that, because it has not pursued a more forthright definition of the ownership of teaching and learning, what happens in the world of mass entertainment could well play a bigger role in defining teaching's commercial formats than what happens in the classroom or the faculty lounge.

From the perspective of big media, teaching potentially becomes a performance and hence just another commodity to be developed and sold as an article of commerce. At its height, the dot-com boom and its offshoots in e-learning sent a near-army of for-profit vendors to administrative offices everywhere, pitching the idea of forming partnerships that could design and deliver instruction in a host of new formats and settings. In more than a few cases, parallel pitches were made to faculty, particularly those with reputations as spellbinding instructors, to offer instruction as free agents operating outside their home institutions. Among the more successful of these ventures was The Teaching Company, which promoted learning principally as enrichment and, if not entertainment, at least as leisure-time activity. Today its Website boldly proclaims, "The Teaching Company brings engaging professors into your home or car through courses on DVD, audio CD, and other formats. Since 1990, great teachers from the Ivy League, Stanford, Georgetown, and other leading colleges and universities have crafted 175 courses for lifelong learners. We provide the adventure of learning, without the homework or exams." It was but a short jump to having nationally recognized experts teaching specific skills and offering to certify that the learner had successfully completed the course—or even learned the material. Much of the boom in e-learning was initially fueled by these hopes and promises.

Teaching as Object

Only in this context did universities come at last to confront the growing number of financial questions surrounding the ownership of teaching. If one conceived of teaching as an outgrowth of an academic community, what kind of claim did that community have on the teaching of individual faculty? If a university or college provided the physical and academic infrastructure that supported the faculty member's teaching—in the form of salary, classroom, laboratory, and office space, as well as opportunities for interaction with other colleagues—where did the responsibility for and ownership of teaching ultimately lie?

Those with fiduciary responsibility for an institution—principally boards of trustees and executive officers—were the most likely to believe that what a faculty member produced while being paid by an institution, from classroom teaching to published work, belonged to the institution. Neither salaries nor offices nor libraries and labs were to be free goods—not when the use of those assets produced financial gain. After all, the institution bore legal responsibility and the obligation to defend both the faculty member and itself when a disgruntled student filed suit for wrongful instruction.

While welcoming and even demanding such legal protection, few faculty championed such a definition of institutional rights and prerogatives. From the faculty perspective, intellectual property vested in one's teaching and academic freedom were but two sides of the same coin. Teaching in the classroom belonged to the institution—but individual lecture notes, PowerPoint presentations, computer simulations, slides and photographs belonged to the faculty member regardless of whose equipment or space was used to produce them.

Prior to the 1980s few institutions had pressed to resolve the inherent conflict between these executive and collegial views of who owned teaching. There was no reason to—the potential financial rewards, except for the occasional best-selling text book, were never enough to fight about. But patent rights to scientific discoveries were another matter. Pushed by the federal government's interest in the commercialization of research its grants had supported, most universities put in place well-staffed offices of "technology transfer," a fancy label describing offices charged with finding buyers for university patents. These new initiatives worked because the universities had collectively made certain that it was they, and not their faculty, who owned the patents. Most faculty researchers acquiesced in this arrangement, partly because they lacked the skill and resources to complete the patent process, and in part because most universities developed policies that made the researcher a direct beneficiary of the financial deals the university was striking with its new, for-profit partners.

There were few parallels in the world of teaching, largely because the universities had already given away their claim to what faculty produced in the form or scholarly publications or textbooks. When asked, and few ever were, faculty responded that their teaching was theirs to do with as they saw fit. After all, faculty could readily teach in another institution's summer school, for example, using the same notes, slides, and demonstrations as they used on their own campuses, and no one asked faculty members to share their extra salary with their home institutions. But again, the larger point is that almost no one asked, no one told, and no one paid much attention to the commercial potential of teaching.

Nor was much attention paid to the steady erosion of that sense of common purpose that had traditionally informed teaching and academic inquiry. Until confronted with the legal and financial questions that suddenly swirled about the academy, few had thought that what was once conceived as a common domain of human knowledge could be apportioned as just another commercial product. However, once the questions were asked, once the digital entrepreneurs descended upon campuses everywhere, the cost of inattentiveness became clear: fenced and gated precincts quickly sprang up in a landscape of formerly open access and attribution. The new battleground was not the world of ideas or philosophies, but rather the narrow confines imposed by the legal battles being fought in the broader world of publishing and entertainment, where the unit of copyright was becoming smaller and smaller. The concept of fair use, which was a central component of academic inquiry, was being whittled away in a legal process to which higher education was not a party, but a likely victim.

Wanting to maximize their control over the intellectual properties they bought, sold, and bartered, the major commercial players in both entertainment and publishing were being driven toward a world of information and performance financed by the tolls of pay-per-view. It was a world in which the presumptive owner of a piece of intellectual property exacted a usage fee for each unit of knowledge and performance, no matter how small and contextual that unit might be. As never before, colleges and universities encountered the specter of a steady reduction of space available for the open sharing of knowledge and ideas, even in the once-general domains of teaching and learning. In a world of absolute commodification, higher education would be shorn of that free-wheeling sense of learning that comes from the often unplanned interaction between professor and student, as well as from the interaction among students themselves.

While the business model based on pay-per-view was defining one end of the continuum that described higher education's emerging confrontation with the commercialization of its products, the other end was conforming to the realities of a digital technology that allowed almost anyone to copy and distribute intellectual content or artistic expression through the Internet or other means. Enter Napster. Before it was constrained by legal action in 2001, Napster had attracted some 80 million users freely exchanging files of copyrighted music through the Internet. While pay-per-view threatens to make all knowledge proprietary, the Napster phenomenon held out the prospect of rendering all human knowledge and expression absolutely free, thus removing many, if not all, financial incentives for intellectual or artistic creativity.

In many ways the more fitting analogy to the question of who owns a faculty member's intellectual and creative expression can be seen in the aftermath of Napster's injunction for copyright infringement. The legal and financial debates concern the division of revenues from the sale of music through the Internet among record companies, recording artists, and the Internet providers that make recordings available to the public for a fee. Thus far these discussions have left recording artists feeling alienated from and even victimized by the recording industry. Most observers agree that the record companies have positioned themselves to reap a far greater share of the profits from Internet distribution of music than that of the recording artists themselves. In this sense, the deals being struck differ very little from the earlier Napster scenario of widespread copying and distribution of music files, which yielded no financial benefit to the recording artists.

In education as in entertainment, the new medium was creating new opportunities, which in turn raised new questions about the ownership and rewards of creative and productive activity. From the faculty's perspective, whenever an institution claims ownership of all or even most aspects of teaching and intellectual property, then teaching and knowledge creation have few, if any, direct financial rewards for those who actually provide the instruction. Although indirect rewards, in the form of salary for example, remain, the new system effectively removes some important incentives for faculty to achieve excellence, not just in teaching but also in other forms of scholarly activity.

Somewhat belatedly, higher education is learning that the preservation of conditions that allow teaching and learning to take place in an environment of vital and open inquiry requires the kind of open and frank conversations that most institutions have successfully avoided. As in the case of athletics and quality, such conversations must necessarily deal with values and commitments, and at their outset they focus on questions of where the lines of ownership overlap between an individual faculty member and the institution of which he or she is part. Questions abound, for example: Do the teaching materials that a faculty member posts to a Web site on the institution's server belong to the faculty member exclusively? Does a faculty member's home institution have the right to make use of recorded lectures in contexts other than his or her own course? Does a full-time, tenure-line faculty member who "moonlights" by providing educational services to a for-profit proprietary institution violate the terms—or the spirit—of the faculty appointment at his or her home institution? If higher education does not build a stronger sense of community around teaching, then the question of who owns teaching and the knowledge it helps to create and perpetuate will increasingly be decided by others.

Even the most preliminary attempts to sketch answers to these questions make clear, however, that a policy requiring faculty members to relinquish all claims to financial gain from teaching, research, or creative expression effectively removes a set of important drivers of faculty achievement. Remaining are the intrinsic motivations that faculty have to teach well, to conduct research and scholarship, and to write articles and books that contribute to the state of knowledge—and those extrinsic rewards associated with research in particular: tenure, salary increases, market power.

Structuring the Deals

The challenge that colleges and universities face—to give extended meaning to the phrase we have used often enough—is to learn what it means to be market-smart in a world of commercial performance. Probably the first lesson is not to impose a single fixed model on the act of teaching or the concept of intellectual property. Required, instead, is a set of flexible definitions that recognizes where both individual and shared responsibilities for teaching lie. Framing working as well as workable definitions will likely require institutions to build, often from the ground up, communities that center on teaching itself—its goals, its methods and outcomes, and on the conventions of fair use that make knowledge openly accessible to present and future generations. One important result of creating more active and purposeful communities around teaching would be a strengthened understanding that teaching is in fact a shared undertaking—and that, as such, the responsibility and ownership of teaching is widely distributed among all members of an academic community. The more teaching itself comes to be defined as a community responsibility, the more likely that faculty will focus more of their attention on improving the quality of the educational products and services they deliver.

Although it does, in fact, matter who owns teaching, it turns out that what matters more are the deals that both institutions and individuals make when defining the distribution of revenues that might derive from teaching and its associated activities. In negotiating such deals, the goal should be to preserve the conditions that support inquiry and discovery—in classrooms, libraries, laboratories, dormitories, and other settings where learning can occur. Colleges and universities must act in concert to preserve that environment in an age when commercial and regulatory forces are beginning to erode not just the edges but the very foundations of knowledge as a common domain and heritage of humanity.

One promising example of an institutional framework for deciding how the rewards of faculty creativity should be apportioned in a digital age is the work of the Standing Committee on Copyright of the University of California—though we hasten to add that the University's Berkeley campus has also been chastened by what turned out to be bad policy governing its preferred vender contract with the drug maker Novartis. The University's new policy on the ownership of course materials made tangible in a digital form vests ownership in the originators of such materials, unless exceptional institutional resources have been used in their creation, in which case a deal must be struck defining the share. The determination of what constitutes "exceptional" at any particular time is vested in a committee of faculty peers. In drafting this arrangement, which some have characterized as a compromise, the Standing Committee argued that such a group would be best suited to find a balance that maintains the incentives for individual creativity, the values and financial support of the collegial community, and service to society as a whole. From our perspective the arrangement should result from an explicit discussion of the issues as well as the values involved.

Two simple lessons have emerged from drafting this and similar policy statements. First, the more clearly property rights are defined, the better things work. Second, never enter negotiations without knowing what you want or understanding the objectives of the other parties. To be market-smart, then, begins with defining clear goals of what teaching seeks to achieve. Too often in the past, colleges and universities did not understand the deal because they lacked a forceful conception of what, as institutions, they wanted. To a considerable degree, universities and colleges instead allowed the definition, and in that sense the ownership, of teaching to become the province of for-profit interests and public regulatory forces (and on occasion their faculty's private interests); as a result, the academy lacked a widely shared internal understanding of the purposes and goals of teaching. To be effective negotiators—to get the deals they need and want—colleges and universities, again as institutions, must develop policies that clarify both the individual and the collective responsibilities of teaching.

Once an institution knows what it wants, the next task becomes structuring the deals intended to achieve those institutional purposes. An effort to preserve the middle ground that inhabits the space between the open source movement and pay-per-view is necessary. In a world of markets and entrepreneurship, digital and otherwise, it neither pays nor proves possible to remove all financial incentives for innovation and discovery. All the more important, therefore, to strike deals that, while incorporating targeted financial incentives, are structured to remind everyone that effective teaching, learning, and discovery require an environment that allows a free space for the exchange of knowledge and ideas.

To preserve the free space that fair use defines as essential likely requires colleges and universities to establish consortia, replete with the necessary legal and financial trappings. Their principal purpose is creating and operating various collegiate arenas dedicated to the open exchange and use of information and ideas. We recognize that barriers must be surmounted in creating such coalitions, for colleges and universities have always consisted of both shared and competing interests. But the absence of common resolve and activity now results in higher education's being carried down the same path toward pay-per-view that is coming to characterize the world of popular culture.

Again, the larger truth is that no strategy or tactic will prove successful unless most colleges and universities succeed in building and sustaining a more active and visible community and culture of evidence around good teaching. For all the centrality of teaching to their missions, higher education institutions continue to lack a compelling language and metric for describing the responsibilities and attributes of successful teaching—to either themselves or the public in general. The popularity of the media's institutional rankings and the willingness of state policymakers to assert ownership of teaching are signs of a vacuum in higher education's internal dialogue about teaching. Although there is widespread agreement about conventions of evidence and modes of discourse within the academic disciplines, there is remarkably little consensus about how to recognize and describe good teaching—to either those within the academy or higher education's external stakeholders. Colleges and universities must concentrate on the business of explicitly building communities and cultures of evidence centered on teaching and learning. Put another way, a college or university negotiates the ownership of teaching from a much stronger position if it can first say with conviction, "We have made educational quality job one."

Strengthening the Fabric

Colleges and universities have always found themselves occupying the often tenuous middle ground between different conceptions of human productivity and livelihood. Colleges and universities are mission-centered. Their primary goals have less to do with making money than with creating social capital through the discovery and perpetuation of knowledge as well as the development of an educated and productive citizenry. However, these institutions cannot afford to ignore the workings of markets that combine with other societal and political forces to provide the context in which they perform their missions.

Teaching is ultimately a fabric of interwoven threads supplied in part by an individual faculty member, in part by students, and in part by the traditions and repositories of knowledge that inform all human inquiry. The institutional setting provides the framework, the warp and weft that allows this interweaving to take place. As such, universities and colleges need to uphold the tenets of academic freedom that define the faculty role and make possible both the open inquiry of knowledge and the public expression of thought and ideas. At the same time, these institutions need to foster continued dialogue about the responsibilities that accompany the faculty role—including the shared responsibility and ownership of teaching that link together the faculty, not just of a single institution, but ultimately of all universities and colleges.

A central question to be resolved in the years ahead is the extent to which college teaching is an entrepreneurial activity carried out by individuals in search of personal gain or a community activity carried out by people with shared commitments who are in conversation with one another. Henry Rosovsky would be among the first to observe that any scenario in which faculty come to regard themselves as free agents, able to pursue any remunerative opportunity for teaching while retaining full faculty status in their home institutions, is unlikely to strengthen communities of teaching within their institutions. Rather, those practices of free agency accelerate the societal forces that transform teaching, and knowledge itself, into commodities, accessible only through the restrictive lens of pay-per-view. At the same time, a scenario in which faculty members were forced to relinquish all personal reward from teaching and scholarly activity—specifically in the form of monetary rewards—dramatically lessens an important set of incentives for achieving excellence.

The last two decades provide a critical lesson that sustaining the fabric of teaching will require a more deliberate effort than ever before. No longer can colleges and universities take for granted that the space allowing open inquiry—freedom of exploration and the common domain of knowledge and ideas—will be preserved as either a matter of course or a matter of virtue. Required instead is a persistence of institutional will and the application of individual leadership—and, in the final analysis, a conscious building of communities devoted to an explicit exploration of what it means to be both teacher and learner in a world forever changed by markets and technologies and by the competing passions spawned by institutions themselves. Who owns teaching? We all do, for at least a little while longer.

9 | Making Educational Quality Job One

The Ford Motor Company once exemplified how skillful management could use the workings of the market and questions of quality to achieve and then sustain a competitive advantage. In the mid-1980s Ford confronted a double task: differentiating its products from those produced by other American manufacturers while at the same time developing a product of sufficient quality to stem the tide of Japanese imports—what Detroit was calling openly, if somewhat inelegantly, the Japanese invasion. To win in the American market, Ford needed to persuade U.S. consumers that quality was important; and to win against the exports, Ford needed to in fact produce a demonstrably better product.

Ford's solution was an ingenious fusing of advertising moxie and human resource management, all neatly packaged in the slogan "At Ford Quality is Job One." The first task was to teach a skeptical workforce that quality really mattered—to them, in terms of better job security and more opportunity. But if the public did not buy quality, then it mattered little what the workers produced. Gambling that its workers and engineers could produce what the advertisements promised, Ford set about the task of teaching the car-buying public what to look for in a quality automobile.

We have already argued that half of Ford's equation has not worked for higher education. Market forces have neither limited prices nor promoted quality. In most states, making "no new taxes" a political imperative has yielded higher tuitions at both public and private institutions. The absence, for now and well into the foreseeable future, of a higher education consumer movement has meant that colleges and universities have been free to define quality largely in terms of what they already deliver.

What about the other half of Ford's equation—the proposition that quality is a function of effective human resource management, provided the product is well designed and efficiently engineered? Were there a good definition of quality, were educational products designed and engineered, and if the academic workforce understood its role in achieving a quality product, would the result be a better educational product?

Our answer is at best tentative, largely because we are just now beginning to see evidence suggesting that a sustained focus on both the definition and the practice of quality has the potential to change higher education. Among us, Bill Massy would go further, arguing, as he did in *Honoring the Trust,* that there is a growing body of examples and pilot projects demonstrating that quality processes do in fact work, that they neither increase costs nor undermine the academy's traditional commitment to research and scholarship, and that they can be implemented to reinforce rather than conflict with faculty concerns about mission and autonomy. But it won't be easy.

Clearing Some Underbrush

Ask a president or trustee about educational quality, and eventually the answer revolves around the question of how the institution ranks in *U.S. News.* If the institution ranks high, the answer is accompanied by a set of caveats and just a little false modesty. If the rankings are low, the caveats become more pointed—"Rankings aren't about quality"—and the claims to being one of higher education's "best kept secrets" more persistent. Push further, for example, by requesting a definition of quality, and the answers become calibrated in terms of endowments and expenditures per student, class sizes, faculty-student ratios, and the quality of the freshman class as measured by test scores, high-school class ranks, and grade-point averages. The faculty likely gives much the same answer to the quality question, all the while noting that what really counts is research and scholarship—the hiring and retaining of a research-productive faculty drives both prestige and educational quality. When pressed about how they might improve educational quality, professors likely turn to the curriculum and concede that they might rethink the content of their educational offerings to better reflect their fields' latest research results; they probably add that it would be a good idea to get more undergraduates involved in research.

These elements have pretty much defined educational quality on most American campuses—a focus on inputs, market power, and the central role of research and scholarship. Quality is about money and the resources money can buy, like libraries, recreational facilities, and lower faculty-to-student ratios. Quality is about credentials, those of the students as well as the faculty. And quality is about the primacy of research and scholarship.

Those responsible for achieving quality products elsewhere would define each of these attributes as necessary but insufficient. For them, quality is more a function of what the enterprise does with its resources than it is a product of their scale or magnitude. Making quality job one means getting the most out of the resources you have. Quality means adding as much value as possible for enrolled students—transforming every student to the maximum extent possible given his or her talent and preparation. Quality means focusing on education as a primary institutional outcome, not an adjunct to knowledge creation. Quality means focusing on people as much as ideas.

Ford's efforts to make quality job one went far beyond getting good workers and supporting them with effective training, modern production facilities and equipment, and well-designed and engineered products. The campaign focused on the people at Ford—not just who they were, but what they did. By characterizing quality as a "job," Ford shifted the focus from inputs to the production processes themselves and the roles the workforce played in converting raw materials into high-quality products. Making "Quality Job One" required everyone in the organization to care about quality and its improvement—for every product and each customer.

Throughout the last two decades, American businesses have learned a lot about quality. Whereas quality was once either taken for granted or dismissed with the aphorism "you know it when you see it," successful firms acknowledged that systematized processes were necessary for producing quality. Such firms acknowledged that quality pioneer W. Edwards Deming was right when he stressed that meeting user needs represented the defining criterion for quality and that all members of the organization needed to participate actively in constant and continuous quality improvement. The new mantra became "good enough isn't."

American businesses also learned that any dimension of quality that could not be measured and assessed, even judgmentally, could not be systematically improved. Assessment provided the feedback an organization needed to monitor its performance over time. Data from assessment made it possible to diagnose difficulties and pinpoint improvement opportunities. Arraying the measurements in time series helped identify the improvements that still needed to be made along with trends that needed reversing. Comparing time series across similar enterprises or operating units allowed an organization and its people to benchmark their progress and gauge what might be accomplished with different approaches.

The problems inherent in making these ideas relevant for colleges and universities begin with the bewilderment most outside observers confront when the subject is educational quality. Upbeat images of record numbers of students crowding college campuses and America's continued leadership in higher education and science reinforce the view that U.S. institutions are the best in the world. And in some sense they are. However, the traditional university's core competency lies in knowledge creation, not in educating large numbers of students at the highest quality possible given available resources. Most faculty care about educational quality less passionately than they care about knowledge creation.

What's Missing and Why?

"What's missing and why?" The one-paragraph answer to that question underscores that relatively few faculty understand how their students learn. Most have at best a passing knowledge of quality processes, and very few have the training to implement such knowledge. Most faculty equate quality with content—with the design specifications for the finished product, so to speak. Few are trained in the art and science of pedagogy. Great teaching is viewed mainly as classroom performance, which is discounted by saying that some professors have more standup-talent than others. Many professors think that little can be done to improve classroom performance; after all, good teachers are born, not made. Moreover, the traditional methods of teaching have been in place for decades or even centuries and are almost never the subject of either research or development.

Aside from spurring research, most universities behave as if the only way to boost educational quality is to improve faculty-student ratios and spend more on educational support functions. Almost no one sees paradigm-changing pedagogical innovations as realistic alternatives.

The lack of self-conscious reflection about teaching and learning processes limits the academy's ability to improve educational quality. Most faculty want to do a good job on their teaching, but they simply have not considered that there might be well-documented processes for either identifying improvement opportunities or marshalling resources for innovation. Instead, they experiment with changing their own courses, provided their efforts don't cost too much in terms of discretionary time. Most of these experiments are undertaken in isolation, given the difficulty to persuade one's colleagues to join in a concerted effort. Then there is the problem of balancing the risk that an experiment will fail, which could result in a poor course evaluation against the near-certainty that success brings rewards that are largely—and often exclusively—intangible.

Younger faculty in particular find themselves caught between wanting to do a better job in the classroom and pursuing what it will take to further their own careers; the incentive to publish and get grants is stronger than ever. Unable to compensate by cutting back on teaching effort, some faculty feel overwhelmed. Others reach an accommodation that avoids the necessity of trying to maximize two contradictory goals simultaneously. They put enough effort into teaching to achieve acceptable performance and then turn their attention to their research.

Economists call this practice "satisficing": doing enough to reach a performance threshold and then turning one's attention elsewhere once the threshold has been achieved. Rather than trying to do the best job possible, a satisficer commits only enough effort to attain what he or she perceives to be an acceptable result. Satisficing is a fancy way of saying, "good enough is okay."

Assessment as Accountability

After noting the quality movement that had become ubiquitous across much of the world of business, state agencies, including budget offices and legislative committees, in the 1990s began asking why educational institutions weren't following suit. Why were colleges and universities, in particular, seemingly immune to both internal and external examination? Initially much of this unwanted attention was little more than ill-disguised institution bashing.

Commentaries often began by asking why faculty didn't teach more, and by implication talk and travel less? Why did so many students fail to graduate? Why, for that matter, should the public be expected to underwrite research that was of interest only to the researcher?

Imbedded within the rhetoric, however, was the notion that higher education needed to be more accountable to both its customers and the public agencies that directly and indirectly footed much of the bill. In a host of states a variety of state officials began calling for colleges and universities to focus more attention on their core business, principally the teaching of undergraduates. Working from the idea that in education, as in industry, measurement held the key to quality improvement, most states began calling upon their colleges and universities to measure student learning and make the results available in efforts to improve market information and, where applicable, to provide a basis for oversight. In a few states these calls for greater accountability were accompanied by the promise that measurable improvements in performance resulted in additional public appropriations—something that came to be known as performance-based budgeting. Specific requirements varied, but institutions were usually obligated to demonstrate that they had an organized assessment program capable of producing results. These state initiatives intended to make clear that in the future colleges and universities would be judged by the outcomes they and their students achieved.

This new interest in outcomes as opposed to inputs was often shared by the agencies that accredited colleges and universities. Accreditation requirements introduced in the 1990s told institutions to document their student outcomes, to analyze the resulting data, and to demonstrate that they had the capacity to act on the basis of that analysis. The language varied, but the thrust was remarkably consistent. The North Central Association required measures of student "proficiency in skills and competencies essential for all college-educated adults; completion of an identifiable and coherent undergraduate level general education component, and mastery of the level of knowledge appropriate to the degree attained." The Western Association of Schools and Colleges, responsible for accrediting institutions in California and Hawaii, asked for the inclusion of measurements covering the "effective communication, quantitative reasoning, critical thinking, and other competencies judged essential by the institutions." The Middle States Association, responsible for the middle third of the Atlantic seaboard, listed "cognitive abilities, content literacy, competence in information management skills, and value awareness" as measures of student achievement. Increasingly, institutions sought definable benchmarks of educational quality.

The accrediting associations, precisely because they were in fact member organizations consisting principally of the institutions they accredited, also argued that the distinct and diverse purposes and goals of their member colleges and universities demanded equally diverse assessment approaches. Hence they did not require specific processes or measurement instruments. The state assessment initiatives also reflected considerable variation. In 1997, for example, of the forty-six states with assessment initiatives, only seventeen used common performance indicators for all colleges and universities, and only eight used common measurement instruments. Twenty-nine states allowed the institutions themselves to define the indicators and instruments. Some tests measured student performance during the college experience rather than at exit. Other programs measured proficiency at graduation. Tennessee and South Dakota, for example, used a standardized test developed by the American College Testing program or ACT, Inc., as it now chooses to be known. Although there was a slight trend toward the use of standardized indicators to provide comparability among institutions, the issue proved sufficiently controversial that colleges and universities came to oppose commonality.

The institutions need not have worried, for in the end most state initiatives promising greater institutional accountability produced stormy press but few results. In the late 1990s the National Center for Postsecondary Improvement (NCPI) surveyed 1,393 chief academic officers about how their institutions "support, promote, and use student-assessment data to improve student learning and institutional performance." The results were not encouraging. Provosts and academic vice presidents in public universities, those most directly subject to state-initiated assessment regimens, reported that resistance from the faculty had essentially nullified most publicly mandated efforts. At smaller institutions, the obstacles included the "limited sophistication of personnel." Everybody chimed in as most academic officers, along with the scholars of the assessment within their own faculties, argued that assessment policies were problematic because of the difficulties associated with perfecting valid measures of learning outcomes.

Chief academic offers from private institutions included in the survey made much the same point. Their institutions had learned to meet accreditation requirements, but efforts to embed assessment in faculty quality regimens had come to little. Charles Cook, director of the New England Association of Schools and Colleges' Commission on Institutions of Higher Education, that region's accrediting agency, summed up his own and others' frustrations by observing that "millions have been spent by thousands going to hundreds of assessment workshops, and you need a microscope to find the stuff"—or, we would add, the results.

As the chief academic officers reported, much of the problem stemmed from the mistrust of available assessment measures. But there were more fundamental issues as well. On too many campuses, the use of assessment data to guide academic planning was being undermined by a lack of corresponding commitment to faculty accountability for student performance. Faculty expected to be the graders, not the graded.

Given the strength of faculty resistance, not surprisingly few institutions were willing, able, or ready to link the results of assessment to budget decisions or faculty rewards. For example, only 4 percent of the surveyed institutions used assessment results to inform resource allocation among departments—which was and is the best way to get the chairs' and hence the faculty's attention. Although no data are available, the percentage using assessment results to inform routine salary and promotion decisions was probably low as well. Assessment as concept and slogan remained focused on improving academic outcomes. However, there was simply no broadly accepted way of defining the faculty's classroom responsibilities to include being held accountable for student performance.

The problem was compounded because most state or otherwise externally mandated assessment programs were developed in isolation from grass-roots academic work. There was, to be sure, an assessment movement within higher education, though it too was better on crafting slogans—the oft-quoted mantra that a faculty member should not be "a sage on the stage but rather a guide on the side"—than it was at getting institutions to change. Too much time, as Charles Cook noted, was spent going to meetings and workshops, too little on finding ways to convince skeptical colleagues that assessment worked. Like e-learning's early adopters, those on assessment's front lines simply assumed that others would follow. Too often these early adopters were located—some might say isolated—in schools of education, not part of their institution's core research or educational programs.

Faced with the need to get the process started, most presidents and provosts sought to minimize conflict and debate by shielding their faculty from assessment-related tasks. Much of the mandatory work specified by the accrediting and state oversight agencies was assigned to administrative staff or to members of that limited circle of faculty committed to pushing assessment. The result was a repetitive cycle, which largely went nowhere. Little effort went into developing and perfecting the assessment measures external agencies were seeking. With most of the institution's faculty leaders on the sidelines, the institution's product was neither very interesting nor very likely to add to the effort's credibility, which in turn further limited faculty as well as institutional investment.

The ultimate problem was positioning assessment as the instrument of external accountability. Faculty everywhere began asking the obvious question: Is assessment about making us better or making us accountable? Who is to say what constitutes better—those of us who have given our lives to the academy, or some ad hoc group of outsiders with little appreciation for or faith in institutional autonomy? Was the assessment agenda really about improvement, or was it about control?

Universities and their faculties expend considerable energy protecting their sense of autonomy: for instance, their ability to define their own standards and set their own policies defining educational and research standards, degree requirements, and the rules governing faculty appointments. Both the states' and the accrediting agencies' assessment initiatives faltered because universities defended their autonomy against the efforts of "outsiders" to define academic policies and procedures.

Accountability v. Improvement

To a large extent, making quality job one in higher education will depend on the extent to which universities and oversight bodies can combine their accountability and improvement agendas. This idea goes against the conventional wisdom in higher education, but it is familiar in other contexts. Executives in for-profit enterprises frequently combine improvement and accountability when they assign responsibility to subordinates or agents. "Let me help you be the best you can be," they say, "and I will reward you for good performance. But I will also apply sanctions if you fail." While this use of the carrot and the stick may seem like common sense to people outside the academy, many academics insist that any element of accountability creates an impenetrable resistance to improvement in general and its measurement in particular.

Martin Trow, long an educational stalwart at UC–Berkeley, developed a fourfold typology to demonstrate what he saw as the inherent conflict between improvement and accountability. His schema first differentiated between *internal reviews*—those by deans or provosts as part of an institutional quality process—and *external reviews*—those by governmental bodies, governing boards, and oversight agencies as part of a quality oversight. Next he distinguished between reviews oriented toward *improvement,* which he labeled as "supportive," and those oriented toward *accountability,* which bore the "evaluative" label. Trow argued that no review could be both supportive and evaluative and that supportive internal reviews tap intrinsic motivation and produce the greatest improvements in teaching and learning. Conversely, he claimed, externally driven evaluative reviews trigger evasive strategies and produce much noise but little improvement.

Trow's arguments offered comfort to those wishing to resist accountability, but they frustrated would-be change agents. Most oversight boards and systemwide administrations, even governmental bodies, do in fact want to help universities improve educational quality. Many are prepared to fund initiatives that promise such action. The sticking point remains: what happens if improvements are not forthcoming? Can or should these agencies be proactive, or must one wait until people who subscribe to their quality agenda become ascendant within the university, campus, or department? Most public stewards have now chosen the proactive route, which means they are looking for ways to stimulate change without triggering resistance.

Intrinsic motivations are especially powerful in academe, but that does not mean rewards and sanctions are irrelevant. It is clear, for example, that a confluence of intrinsic and extrinsic factors drives faculty attention toward research, and that most faculty expect to be held accountable for their research productivity. The irony is that banning accountability from educational quality improvement only perpetuates the asymmetry that favors research over teaching.

In the 1990s Peter Ewell of the National Center for Higher Education Management Systems (NCHEMS) evolved a useful model for quality evaluation; he focused on processes that "add value to institutional-level management and quality-improvement efforts" as well as fulfilling an accountability function. Such processes, Ewell argued, were consciously informed by "theories of institutional development" that consciously distinguished compliance from the "deep engagement" functions associated with self-study. Effective processes, in Ewell's terms, included review criteria that focus on broadly defined institutional functions and results, not on the specific structures or activities used to achieve them. Effective processes emphasized existing evidence and documentation, not the commissioning of one-off reports. Finally, the institutions and their departments required processes that allowed them to raise and address their own problems within the context of evaluation.

Those who sought to make higher education more publicly accountable had ignored—some would say trampled on—the need to embed their evaluations within a comprehensive program of improvement that benefited faculty and the institution as much as, if not more than, external agencies. Those pushing for accountability simply did not comprehend that faculty would take assessment seriously only when they saw it as helping them achieve their own goals. The lesson of the 1990s was that assessment would become salient only when the faculty, for their own purposes, sought to continuously improve educational quality—in short, once the faculty made quality job one.

Bootstrapping Faculty Involvement

As in the case of e-learning, we are pragmatists when it comes to higher education's progress in embedding quality processes within educational programs. We discount the hype while taking note of what now works and why. From our perspective, the way forward begins with the same step necessary for resolving the conflicts surrounding intercollegiate athletics: the convening of sustained and structured conversations with faculty and others about educational values, educational quality, and their role in defining the former and achieving the latter. The conversations need to be sustained because they are aimed at changing behavior—an outcome that will not occur quickly. They must be structured because academics without structure are likely to wander away from issues, like learning and assessment, on which there is substantial discomfort and a practice of avoidance.

First, a logical reason for convening the conversations and an agreed focal point toward which they should aim are required. Most kinds of conversations about quality and its attributes have taken place outside the United States—in the United Kingdom, Hong Kong, New Zealand, Australia, Sweden, Denmark, and the Netherlands—all nations with strong traditions of centrally mandated oversight. In those places an invitation to participate is sufficient inducement in itself. In the United States, the conversations are just beginning—more ad hoc, less structured, and hence more tentative. Probably the most systematic experiments melding assessment, accountability, and improvement are taking place at the University of Missouri system. In the spring of 2003 a department at each of Missouri's four campuses volunteered—with a little push from the system's academic vice president—to study their quality processes, describe them in a short paper, and then discuss the paper with a team of colleagues from other departments and campuses across the system. The invitation had come accompanied by the promise that volunteering departments would be excused from the mandatory cycle of program reviews that hitherto every department was to engage in every five years. Their experiences over the course of more than a year of intensive focusing on educational quality have become a primer in quality processes. A second round of conversations, involving new departments, is now taking place in Missouri, and similar conversations are being convened in Tennessee on twelve of the nineteen campuses overseen by the Tennessee Board of Regents.

The Missouri departments began their conversations by identifying a limited number of accomplishments that members of each department believed fit the definition of a quality process or attribute. As examples, the faculty were asked, "Do you have a well-informed statement of purpose defining the major, the coherence of your curriculum, your use of technology, and your ability to assess student learning?" Each department had at least one success it wanted to talk about, which ensured that the process got off on the right foot. The next step was to ask why the accomplishments were exemplary, how they had come into being, and whether the lessons learned could be applied to other aspects of educational quality.

At this point structure became important. The program had to avoid the tendency to drift, to mimic the past laissez faire experiments focusing on educational issues that had produced largely unmonitored individual initiatives. The answer was to define quality processes as a set of ordered activities, self-directed inquiries really, that could provide what higher education quality pioneers David Dill and Frans van Vught have called "a framework for quality management in higher education . . . drawn from insights in Deming's approach, but grounded in the context of academic operations."

In their pilot project the Missouri departments drew heavily on the experience of other universities pursuing educational quality. One important lesson they internalized was that a well–ordered set of inquiries—what are coming to be called quality focal areas—came in five basic flavors or clusters. The first focal area centers questions on *learning objectives.* What should the students the department has taught know and be able to do? How would the students' educational experiences contribute to their employment success, their capacities as citizens, and their quality of life? Were the specified learning objectives based on the needs of enrolled students rather than the ideal student most faculties wanted to teach?

The next set of questions focused on *the curriculum and cocurriculum.* How did the curriculum relate to the program's learning objectives? What was being taught, in what order, and from what perspective? Did the curriculum build cumulatively on the students' prior knowledge and capacity? To what extent did the cocurriculum, those organized experiences outside the classroom, support the curriculum?

The third focal area centered on *teaching and learning.* What teaching and learning methods were being used across the department? For example, what methods were employed for introducing students to new materials, for interpreting those materials and answering student questions, for stimulating student involvement, and for providing feedback on each student's work? Was learning active? Was technology being used, and if so, was it being exploited effectively?

The fourth area focused on *the assessment of student learning.* What measures were the departments using to assess student learning? Were they aligned with the learning objectives? Did they compare beginning and ending performance to ascertain value added? Who within the department was actually responsible for student learning assessment—each individual faculty member? A department committee? Members of the administrative staff, either within or without the department?

The fifth and final set of questions the Missouri departments asked focused on the process of *assuring educational quality.* Could they assure first themselves and subsequently their colleagues on the review team that their designs for curricula, teaching and learning activities, and student assessments were being implemented as intended? Could they be certain, in short, that their teaching was the subject of robust evaluations?

As they went about answering these five sets of questions, the

Missouri faculty came to understand that they had seldom, if ever, addressed all five dimensions in a systematic way. When confronting questions of quality their first impulse had been to assign the topic to a curriculum committee that would spend little if any time talking about educational objectives. Technology innovation might spark teaching and learning improvements, but the technology was usually just bolted onto existing methods. Learning assessment too often reflected the requirements of outside agencies instead of an intrinsic interest in better understanding "how we're doing." Across the four departments, indeed across the University, student course evaluations had become ubiquitous, while more powerful quality assurance methods like peer review of teaching were conspicuous mainly by their absence.

Having embraced the idea that quality processes required a systematic inquiry into departmental practices across the five focal areas, the Missouri departments next came to understand that providing answers would be easier if there were in fact a set of acknowledged principles to help guide their deliberations. Here they drew on the work of the National Center for Postsecondary Improvement (NCPI), which had identified seven common-sense principles that could help a department or institution systematize its pursuit of educational quality. The principles had their roots in business, government, and health care, but they had also been adapted and tested in academe.

1. Define educational quality in terms of outcomes. The most obvious goal most clearly parallels the kind of quality assurance standards then holding sway in the world of markets and margins: The quality of student learning, not teaching per se, ultimately mattered. The outcomes should pertain to what is or will become important for the students enrolled in the program.

2. A focus on process. It becomes important to know, in some detail, how teachers teach, how students learn, and how each approaches the task of assessment.

3. Quality is everyone's business. Faculty needed to demonstrate collegiality in teaching, just as they did in research. The department, as the organizing unit, needed to encourage faculty members to work together, to hold one another accountable, and to bring a broad array of talent to bear on difficult problems. Such teamwork sought to make the department a learning organization with respect to teaching and education as well as disciplinary content.

4. Base decisions on evidence. Departments should collect data on

student preparation, learning styles, and, where relevant, probable requirements for employment. The data—testimonies by current and former students, and perhaps by employers or the faculty members who taught them in graduate or professional school, along with the numeric data culled from the institution's student record system—must be analyzed carefully in light of disciplinary standards along with the faculty's own professional experiences. The results then must have a direct and demonstrable impact on the department's curricula, learning processes, and assessment methods.

5. View coherence as a virtue. As a goal, departments must see learning through the lens of the student's entire educational experience. In an ideal curriculum, courses build upon one another to provide the desired depth and breadth, and the students' educational portfolios should reflect the same coherence.

6. Identify and learn from best practice. The departments were instructed to seek out examples of good practice and adapt the best to their own circumstances. They were to compare well against both average and poor performing methods and students, assess the causes of the differences, and seek ways to minimize the variation.

7. Continuous improvement is not only important but also attainable. Quality had to be everybody's business all the time. While the faculty should continue to place strong emphasis on research, they should spend sufficient discretionary time on educational quality to keep the improvement process moving. The department's as well as the institution's personnel committees needed to make the results of such work, along with teaching and research performance, a criterion for promotion and tenure.

The faculty across the Missouri departments also understood that, while primarily intended to improve practice, the departments' adherence to these seven principles allowed the central administration as well as others to mark each department's progress toward systemizing its quality processes. Progress could be defined and measured in terms of whether the department was focusing on outcomes— whether it had at its disposal a rich array of facts attesting to the nature and effectiveness of its curriculum as well as its teaching. Similarly, anyone observing the department from the outside could easily determine whether it had actually collected examples of best practices or if it was addressing issues of quality, not only collegially but collectively. The departments came to understand that a relatively straightforward process could distinguish between the good, the bad, and the ugly when applying these principles.

Quality Process Maturity

By the time that higher education was beginning its experiments with quality processes, Carnegie Mellon University had already developed its capability maturity model for tracking the prowess of software development teams. Somewhat unexpectedly, the categories and definitions, along with the model's conceptual approach, had helped Hong Kong gauge the relative maturity and hence systematization of the quality processes in its eight universities.

The zero point was *no effort* at all. The department being evaluated did not have organized educational quality processes. Quality and quality assurance remained in the hands of individual professors. Next came *firefighting*. The department responded to problems, but mostly with ad hoc methods. The five focal areas described above were not covered systematically, and the quality and evidentiary principles received little attention.

Midpoint on the scale was occupied by *informal effort*. The department could report individual initiatives and experimentation with the principles in one or more focal areas. Coverage remained spotty, however, and the department had yet to become a learning organization with respect to its educational quality processes.

The fourth point on the scale was reached when the department's quality process showed evidence of *organized effort*. The department planned and tracked quality process initiatives in all five focal areas. Emergent norms were encouraging departmental investment in the quality and evidentiary principles. Methods for gauging performance were under development.

The true winners were departments that had reached the scale's terminus: *mature effort*. The quality principles became embedded in the departmental culture, and the idea of regular improvement in all five focal areas became an accepted way of life. The department recognized the planning, tracking, and performance evaluation of quality processes as important elements of peer accountability and collegiality, and it would have developed appropriate and feasible performance indicators.

The experience in Hong Kong showed that almost anyone and certainly most chairs, deans, and provosts could use the scale to evaluate the maturity of each unit's quality processes. It is but a small step to say that quality has become job one when a department or school reaches the mature end of the scale.

In Pursuit of Educational Quality

Demonstrating that it is possible to introduce effective quality processes combining both assessment and improvement—as in the cases of the University of Missouri and the eight institutions presided over by Hong Kong's University Grants Committee (UGC)—makes it all the more salient to ask once more, "What happens if, for a given university or department, quality is not job one?" Can academics be held accountable? Should they be? Should the nation, a state, an individual institution, or department be concerned that most higher educational quality processes fall substantially short of maturity? Should higher education's stakeholders be concerned that the term that fits most quality efforts is *firefighting* or at most *informal effort*, or that too many institutions are still at the zero point on the maturity scale?

Most university communities, when they bother to confront the issue, are likely to note the inconsistencies between calls for punitive accountability and the heavy demand for college degrees. "Why," in the words of the Spencer Foundation's 1995 study report on accountability, "is American higher education the subject of such high regard and consumer demand and at the same time the subject of escalating, sometimes vitriolic, criticism and calls for greater accountability?" Why don't the pundits and politicians just leave colleges and universities alone? Why force these institutions to use scarce resources to fend off endless queries about what they're doing and why they're doing it?

Part of the answer lies in the ready embrace of accountability by for-profit universities like the University of Phoenix. That institution not only accepts but embeds accountability from top to bottom—from senior management to individual teachers—as a matter of principle. Phoenix uses the results of its quality assurance processes to change what it teaches, how it is taught, and, not just occasionally, who does the teaching. Traditional universities, however, suggest and on occasion openly assert that market forces and oversight initiatives by external agencies impinge on their autonomy and, by extension, their academic freedoms. Most faculty feel that this impingement, real and spreading, hence is now an ever-present danger. Most presidents, provosts, and deans, rather than take on this fight, actively work to shield faculty from the impact of markets and oversight initiatives.

Audits of Quality Processes

To understand the full ramifications of the problem, it helps to return to the bootstrapping example. This time we look at the processes put in place at the University of Missouri from the point of view of the system's central administration and the state's quality oversight agency. If the agencies, both governmental and accrediting, were actually to believe that the quality processes the University of Missouri system was putting in place for their own purposes would also provide sufficient management and oversight information to certify their accountability, then the question becomes, "How does an institution or a state system jump-start a structured conversation about quality?" Such conversations seldom start spontaneously, and requesting them in a speech or memo is also unlikely to be effective. Some kind of stimulus is needed—one that may well have to come from a change agent.

Enter the academic audit. One purpose of audit is to stimulate just such structured conversations. A related and fully compatible purpose is to check on whether the conversations are probing deeply enough to develop mature quality processes.

An academic audit program involves five steps.

- *Workshops.* Daylong sessions to introduce prospective participants to the principles of educational quality processes and the mechanics of the audit methodology. The agenda includes presentations, role-playing demonstrations, and breakout discussions. Advance interviews may provide examples of existing good practice and areas that need improvement.
- *Self-Studies.* Participants, principally faculty, start by identifying areas of good performance and asking how the quality and evidentiary principles contributed to their success in these areas. Then they apply the lessons learned to other quality improvement areas. The self-studies are short, action-oriented documents rather than long essays or encyclopedic descriptions. The goal is straightforward: participants commit to addressing the highest priority issues identified in their self-studies.
- *Auditors.* Audit teams of five to seven members are drawn from other departments on campus, other campuses in the system, and/or other universities. Because the auditors look at educational quality processes rather than educational quality itself, they need not come from the same discipline as the department being examined.

(Having one or two auditors from cognate disciplines is helpful, however.) The auditors receive a day of training on educational quality processes and the audit methodology.

- *Audits.* The audit team visits the department or program for the better part of a day. (The visit may be longer for departments with multiple programs.) The team engages groups of faculty and students in conversations about the self-study and offers constructive criticism. Then the team scores the department in terms of the maturity of its quality process and offers suggestions for improvement. The product or deliverable is a written report addressed to the department, with copies to the dean and other academic officers, and where appropriate, the relevant external agencies. Ideally the report should be made public.
- *Debriefing.* Representative auditors and participants get together with the program's sponsors to evaluate the exercise, discuss lessons learned, and share best practice. This should lead to an ongoing system for sharing best practice and a commitment to continue as well as expand the audit program.

Audits start from the view that faculty want to improve the quality of the programs they deliver—to in fact make quality job one. The approach is constructive first and evaluative second. The mantra is, "Trust but check." Accountability enters the picture only when the department or school or even campus collectively appears uninterested in the process of quality improvement.

Educational quality processes are not limited to the departmental level. The system can also include school and university quality committees, deans, chief academic officers, presidents, trustees and regents, and governmental oversight boards. Quality committees should provide leadership and set policies. Deans should make sure their departments follow the policies, attend to all five quality focal areas, and apply the requisite principles. Chief academic officers should ensure that the deans are discharging their quality-related responsibilities. Governing and oversight boards should not micro-manage, but they should assure themselves that the university's senior administration is continuously strengthening the deans' and departments' quality processes.

Impetus for quality process improvement can be initiated at any level. In Hong Kong, for example, the oversight board was the initiator, while in Missouri it was the systemwide academic vice president. The beauty of audit is that it provides such impetus without requiring higher-level approval or disempowering the lower organizational levels.

Advantages of Academic Audit

An academic audit's fundamental advantage is that it elicits the structured conversations about educational quality on which *both* improvement and accountability depend. These conversations occur first within the department or school itself and are then broadened to include the members of the audit team. Use of quality and evidentiary principles focus the conversations on good practice and on questions that spur improvement. The capability maturity categories provide a language for self-evaluating the unit's of progress up the quality-process scale.

The United Kingdom, New Zealand, Sweden, Hong Kong, and Missouri systems have all completed one or more cycles of academic audits, and each experience has been evaluated in terms of the audit methodology's advantages and disadvantages. Reviewers generally agree that the academic audits they observed have made improving teaching and learning an institutional priority. They lead to active discussion by and cooperation among the members of individual departments and schools concerning how best to improve teaching and learning. The audits generally help clarify to whom responsibility for improving teaching and learning belong at the program, department, school, and institutional level. Finally, the audit process itself is reported to have provided new venues for sharing best practices within and across institutions.

Missouri's evaluation process also yielded a host of interesting observations from participating faculty:

> We all learned a lot. People on both sides of the table were thinking outside their disciplines. . . . We identified some real problems. For example, the curriculum is haphazard— "chaotic" as one department member put it, and we generated some good, tangible, ideas for improvement. . . . In retrospect, as a result of the process, we collectively learned more about what we actually do (indeed, some members learned for the first time what some of their colleagues do), and because students were included in the audit process, we received some valuable perspective on how they view our attempts to provide a quality education. . . . Even if no one beyond ourselves

reads the final report, we are a better department for having stepped back to ask fundamental questions. . . . As a result of our participation in the audit process, the department now has a clearer vision of the changes it needs to make in order to improve what is generally regarded on campus as an effective educational program serving the needs of a diverse body of students.

Stephen W. Lehmkuhle, Missouri's vice president of academic affairs, summed the experience up this way: "Sharing experiences among faculty from all four campuses as well as working together on this unique audit . . . builds bridges in many ways, . . . some related to the audit, . . . others just come up as they talk." Missouri is extending its audit initiative to include research and other subjects now covered in program review, but the essential focus on educational quality processes will be retained.

First, it is important that the process itself involves matters of direct consequence to faculty, not lofty abstractions or requirements sent down by some remote oversight body. University administrations and external agencies can evaluate educational quality processes more easily than educational quality itself. Furthermore, because the audit data are easy to interpret and difficult to fake, it is not hard for auditors to determine whether respondents have embraced the quality process and evidentiary principles.

Focusing on principles that transcend academic disciplines eases the selection of auditors. Auditors should be familiar with or be willing to learn about quality processes, but they need no particular disciplinary or institutional knowledge. An academic audit respects institutional and departmental diversity. Centrally determined standards for teaching or student assessment are not needed because the auditors evaluate what is happening on the ground against broad, generally applicable principles.

In sum, an academic audit provides the light but firm touch needed to improve quality without constricting regulation or micromanagement. In the words of David Dill, an audit stimulates universities to "more closely approximate academic 'learning organizations'—building their capacity for developing and transferring knowledge for the improvement of their core academic processes."

Here then is the countermarket example. The audit demonstrates that universities and oversight agencies can both draw upon and learn from how quality processes work in the larger world of for-profit enterprises. But they cannot expect the market to be the same driving force for quality that it has become in the private sector. Rather, quality in education remains an intrinsic goal—something that deliverers of education need to believe in and practice for their own reasons and purposes. It can be encouraged, but not imposed.

The pursuit of quality is a tough master—promising but failing to deliver is worse than never having promised in the first place. That certainly is the lesson the Ford Motor Company learned. As the number of SUV rollover lawsuits against the company escalated, "At Ford Quality is Job One" became a slogan ripe for deadly parody. Its replacement, announced in the fall of 2002, had all the safety of a sound bite minted on a college campus. "At Ford, the Future is Now."

10 | Not Good Enough

They are like the banks of a river, forever separated, stretching across decades, and seemingly going nowhere. They are the statistical markers of a nation in which a span of river defines two distinct banks, running in parallel, forever separating majority and minority experiences as do the graphs of median family income, college participation, and college degree attainment.

The problem of the river is one that has been defined largely in terms of the economic barriers that have historically discouraged students of lesser means from pursuing a college education. All the basic policy options for reducing the price of a college education have been tried: direct grants to needy students, guaranteed student loans, subsidized student loans, externally funded student jobs, and grants to encourage institutions to invest more of their own resources in their programs of student financial assistance.

Although access has been expanded, the gap remains and in some cases has actually become wider. Some argue that the federal government, in particular, has not done enough—that the purchasing power of a Pell Grant, the principal program for distributing federal student financial aid, has not kept pace with inflation. Others, pointing fingers at the states, observe that their disinclination to raise taxes has been a prime factor in the rapidly escalating prices public institutions have been forced to charge—prices that effectively shut out of the market substantial numbers of students of lesser economic means.

We have argued elsewhere, principally as part of our work with Patti Gumport and the National Center for Postsecondary Improvement (NCPI), that the access agenda, like the *U.S. News* rankings of institutions, places inordinate weight on the front end of the equation—on the number and types of students enrolling—without considering the content and quality of education provided or the subsequent institutional impact on students' learning and later achievements. Rather than simply counting numbers and calculating initial participation rates, we thought it equally important to ask, "Access to what?" realizing that to answer these questions is to discover anew that higher education's core practices have remained largely unchanged. Many items heading the agenda for change in 1970 are still pertinent today— or as the National Center's final report put it:

> Critics regularly question the learning exhibited by college graduates. Moreover, achievement gaps in higher education persist between students of lower and higher socio-economic status, and across ethnic and racial groups. Despite repeated calls to recast the preparation of future faculty, no substantial reform of graduate education has occurred. Colleges and universities have made little headway in building a faculty that reflects the increased diversity of the students they educate. Moreover, while everyone agrees that improving educational performance entails more concerted interactions with primary and secondary schools, the linkages between them remain weak.

What has not diminished, of course, is the importance of a college education for substantially greater numbers of disadvantaged students—not as privilege, but as a necessity for raising their prospects. A college education has become a key to personal economic success. Although colleges and universities have changed little, the import attached to their basic products has undergone a radical transformation. Like merit badges sewn on a sash of green, a progression of degrees— from associate to bachelor to master and doctorate—have become signals of achievement and hence access to the pathways of personal success. In many ways what the NCPI report called "this disjunction between societal necessity and institutional inertia" has itself become a powerful driver reshaping colleges and universities, often by limiting their capacity "to respond to the growing forces of markets and to fulfill the terms of the social charter that has historically linked American higher education to the nation it serves."

This focus on a social charter linking higher education and the body politic harkens back to Henry Rosovsky's notion of a social contract binding faculty members and the institutions that appoint them; each conception assumes that the ties that bind are real, though increasingly they are being worn away by market forces. The other point each makes, at least implicitly, is that the way forward requires not just an accommodation with the market, but an actual blending of social and commercial purposes, such that the latter come to reinforce the former. The social charter affirms that colleges and universities have a vital role in ensuring the economic strength and competitiveness of the nation through the production of skilled workers. Beyond this practical function, however, colleges and universities serve the public interest by creating an educated citizenry, preserving and advancing knowledge in all fields regardless of their market currency, and fulfilling the public expectation that a higher education should be accessible to any student who exhibits a desire and commitment to learn. Citizens have historically understood public investment in higher education, through state support of public institutions and federal funding of student financial aid and research, as a fitting means of achieving such societal purposes.

A Market-Driven Public Policy

At this point one encounters another of those ironies that underlie much of our fascination with markets and institutional responses. Historically, the federal government was seen as having only a limited role in providing access to American colleges and universities. Not until the 1970s did higher education's advocates succeed in having federal appropriations help underwrite the cost of a college education—all in the name of making certain that limited financial means did not translate into limited educational opportunities.

The initial impulse had been to channel federal funds to colleges and universities that would then be used to underwrite institutional programs of student financial aid. That idea, though energetically supported by higher education's Washington lobbyists, never made it past mark-up. Even in the 1970s, Congress was in no mood to give what looked suspiciously like a blank check to higher education. What emerged instead was a plan to fund students who would then "vote with their feet" in deciding where to take their student financial aid vouchers.

The market—rather than any government agency—would decide the actual distribution of public monies. In the years that followed, this largely unspoken commitment to the market was augmented by the introduction of federally guaranteed and subsidized student loans, the benefits of which flowed first to students and only subsequently to the institutions in which they chose to enroll. The only concession to institutional sensibilities were modestly funded programs of supplemental grants and student work-study, both of which benefited institutions first and their enrolled students second.

What governmental agencies at neither the federal nor the state level have been able to do in the realm of K–12 education, Pell Grants along with guaranteed and subsidized student loans have accomplished for higher education—the introduction of a federally funded voucher system. By almost any measure the funding was insufficient to make every college and university affordable for every student, but the scale of the program was extraordinary—in recent years more than $11 billion annually going to more than 4.5 million enrolled students.

Because Pell Grants provided stipends as well as tuitions, the program afforded substantial cash assistance to students with limited financial means. The U.S. Department of Education's *Student Guide* for Pell Grants responded to the frequently asked question, "How will I be paid?" by telling eligible beneficiaries, "Your school can either credit the Pell Grant funds to your school account, pay you directly (usually by check), or combine these methods." For low-cost proprietary schools, the federal grant and loan proved a bonanza once their students became eligible. In the 1980s higher education was rife with stories of agents for storefront trade schools walking through poor neighborhoods pushing grocery carts filled with the necessary applications for the federal vouchers.

Apocryphal or not, stories about students who enrolled in colleges and universities as well as trade schools simply for the cash have been commonplace since the program's inception. Initially high default rates on guaranteed student loans and low completion rates for students receiving Pell grants gave these tales prima-facie credibility, though there was never much of a push to abandon the market as the principal distributor of federal student assistance.

The question as to whether the federal student aid programs also benefited institutions by allowing them to charge higher prices was more complex, leading to a lively though occasionally vitriolic debate among a handful of economists focusing on education. Had the Pell Grants in particular really made a college education more affordable? Had they expanded economic as well as educational opportunity in the United States? Or had the institutions' higher prices simply soaked up the federal funds, yielding little additional opportunity or relief?

As often in the cases of markets and market mechanisms, the answer is not altogether clear. The net increase in tuition revenue certainly exceeded several times over the federal funds made available through Pell Grants and related federal programs. Those who raised their prices the most—the nation's private and public medallion colleges and universities—could do so simply because the demand for their degrees had increased dramatically while the supply of places in their freshmen classes had only inched up slowly. These institutions were the most likely to spend generously of their own funds to underwrite programs of student financial aid. No doubt institutions in the middle used the availability of the federal dollars to soften the impact of their increased prices—but for the most part, those increases were necessitated first by the inflationary spiral of the 1970s and later, for public institutions, by the absence of additional state funds. For low-cost institutions—community colleges and some proprietary schools—the federal bonanza meant increased enrollments and hence revenues, rather than increased prices per se. Those enrollment increases were exactly what the federal funds were designed to spur— more students, more opportunity at reasonable prices.

But the federal programs did change higher education in one important, though still too seldom acknowledged, way. In retrospect, what mattered most were not the direct grants but the loans. In the 1970s, the Middle Income Assistance Act made subsidized as well as federally guaranteed loans available to almost everyone. Given that decade's hyperinflation, some of the most adroit users of the federal loan programs were upper-income families who had discovered that they could borrow to pay for their children's education, taking advantage of the fact that as long as the child was in college, there was no interest on the loan. The loans could then be repaid shortly after the child graduated with substantially cheaper dollars.

By the mid-1980s borrowing to pay for college had become standard practice for almost everyone. Federal guaranteed loans at market rates were brokered by most institutions—while at most institutions student loans became part of the standard, need-based financial aid packages of almost all aided students. Saving for college became something of an anachronism—and in the cases of middle-income families with children interested in moderate- to high-priced institutions, a mistake. Because the basic formulas used to calculate need defined available savings as assets, any family that had saved to pay college costs would be awarded that much less student financial aid. Parental responsibility was further reduced in the 1990s as the need formulas stopped counting home equity as an asset that could be converted into cash to pay college tuition bills.

To Clark Kerr's query, "Who pays?" the answer was becoming the students themselves. Their tuitions were increasing faster than the rate of inflation. They were being required to assume truly awesome levels of personal indebtedness, and, not surprisingly, they were finding themselves working to pay for college while in college. It was not uncommon to find young and sometimes not-so-young people both working and going to college full time. Not surprisingly, what most students—whether they borrowed or worked or both—wanted from their college years was the prospect of economic advancement.

Dual Purposes

Often lost in the evolution of this tale is the quest with which it all began. Were there public policies or institutional programs that once in place and fully funded would make a college education affordable for everyone? In part it was a quest for economic neutrality where one's own or family's personal means would not be a barrier to college attendance. Just as important, however, was the quest for equity. A world in which college students were for the most part white, for the most part from families of at least some means, had to change.

Inevitably the question of access became entwined with—some would suggest inseparable from—the question of whether programs of affirmative action were needed to redress two centuries of treating African-Americans as less than full citizens of the republic. If a college education or even college attendance created personal advantage, and if identifiable segments of the population had been historically denied access to a higher education, then there was a public responsibility to right that wrong by all available means. For Americans of color in general and African-Americans in particular, righting that wrong meant both more student financial aid and preferential admissions.

Through most of the 1960s and well into the 1970s this policy with its twin thrusts held center stage. But it was always a policy on thin ice, dependent on a willingness of institutions to make race an explicit element in the admissions process and on the government's willingness to supply the necessary funding. Then in the late 1970s the case of Adam Bakke came before the Supreme Court. Bakke had been denied admission to the Medical School at the University of California–Davis. In court, Bakke's lawyers had demonstrated that minority students with lower grades and test scores had been admitted, while their client had been denied admission in what Bakke and his supporters called a clear case of reverse discrimination. In 1978 the Supreme Court rendered a confusing as well as split verdict: Bakke was granted admission, but the ability of institutions to use the tools of affirmative action to shape their incoming classes was also upheld.

The Bakke decision and the controversy it evoked marked the zenith of affirmative action as a national policy designed to address questions of access and race. Thereafter the justification for granting African-Americans enhanced or special access to colleges and universities as a means of redressing an historical wrong became a less dominant feature of both policy and rationale. Federal student financial aid programs were instead refocused to target more of their aid to those who were economically disadvantaged—a group that included substantial numbers of students and families of color—as part of a larger effort to broaden support for the awarding of federal student financial aid.

Diminished Prospects

In the early 1990s, as the United States girded for a presidential election amidst a recession that was sapping America's self-confidence, the question of access was transformed into one of economic opportunity, for both individuals and the nation as a whole. Though the insight was painful, most Americans were coming to believe that their country's standing in the world economy had perceptibly diminished. The new America was a net importer of automobiles, machine tools, steel, textiles, consumer electronics, and computer semiconductors. Even in the service sector, which was once all but an American invention, U.S. firms were losing their once-dominant places in banking, telecommunications, and even advertising.

Candidate causes for this slippage were rife: bad management; too much attention to short-term profits at the expense of long-term investments; drastically low savings rates; the failure of public agencies

to make strategic investments in American competitiveness; the decline in the relative productivity of American workers. This last realization really stung. Americans were coming to believe that there was
a growing disparity between their education and skills and those of
their principal competitors abroad.

This decline in American competitiveness paralleled a marked
increase in the number of youngsters who were educationally and economically at risk in the United States. For all the politically correct
discourse one heard on the subject, the real story was the lack of any
substantial progress in increasing the number of at-risk students who
succeeded educationally and then economically. It was a population
that too often did not graduate from high school, too seldom attended
college, even for a year, and, as a consequence, too frequently was absent from the workplace.

The irony was that all sectors of the nation's educational system,
including colleges and universities, were convinced that they had
"done their part" to open the doors of opportunity to the nation's at-
risk population. Most institutions, again including colleges and universities, were substantially more successful in delivering symbolic
victories than in providing access to programs that empowered at-risk
youngsters. In this context, "doing one's part" became a code language
for a public show of broad-mindedness that all too often masked the
more narrow and parochial routine of business as usual.

In part the problem was that most educators, along with most
policymakers and public officials, had traditionally defined educational
achievement as progress through an education "pipeline," from which
those who lose their places can never return. Compounding this notion of "once a loser, always a loser," was a failure of American colleges and universities to cultivate K–12 institutions for what they were:
higher education's principal suppliers of new students and as consumers, in the form of teachers and administrators, of an important portion of higher education's own products. Finally, colleges and
universities frequently made the problem worse by failing to explore,
let alone invest in, alternate instructional methodologies specifically
designed to meet the learning needs of at-risk students.

Investing in Productivity

One key political message deriving from the 1992
elections was that reversing the ebb of American achievement meant
increasing worker productivity. The United States needed to make bet-

ter use of the productive capacities of that substantial portion of American society that too often had been excluded from the most remunerative and demanding jobs. In practical terms, that meant bringing more people of color into the nation's economic and educational mainstream.

Initially most attention was focused on secondary schools, vo-techs, and community colleges. Four-year institutions were largely left out, in part, at least, because of their own resistance to being lumped with institutions whose primary function was vocational training. But most four-year colleges and universities seemed tangential to the problem because most students of color they were enrolling had not come from at-risk backgrounds, but rather shared the same middle-income attributes as their white counterparts: they came predominantly from families that placed a value on education; and they attended schools that encouraged enrollment in college-preparation courses. If higher education had opened its doors to greater numbers of African-American and Hispanic students during the 1970s and 1980s, outside of a limited number of regional and community colleges that historically served at-risk and minority populations, it had done comparatively little either to attract those who might truly be called at-risk or to enable them to succeed once they arrived on campus. Colleges and universities generally had taken few steps beyond the threshold of their own doorways to see for themselves the educational needs of these students and the kinds of programs they required.

The success of the military in recruiting and training at-risk young men and women stood in stark contrast to what was not happening on college campuses. By 1990, African Americans accounted for 31.9 percent of enlisted personnel in the Army, 20.5 percent in the Marines, 17.7 percent in the Navy, and 17.5 percent in the Air Force. The basic elements of the armed forces' success began with a fundamental commitment to training and the systematic testing of outcomes. They had a demonstrable ability to instill structure in the lives of the recruits by having them on-site twenty-four hours a day. Recruits came quickly to understand both the immediate and the long-range benefits of the educational programs the armed services offered. There was an eagerness to work directly with secondary schools as an integral part of recruitment programs that stressed job skills as well as educational opportunities. And certainly not least was the military's nearly unfettered ability to discipline and dismiss recruits who could not be taught or who rejected the standards of military life.

The military was making clear that when public policy explicitly linked the nation's needs for skilled and educated workers to individual opportunities for self-improvement, there was a demonstrable increase in both educational performance and workforce productivity. The nation in general and American schools and colleges in particular were failing to make that very linkage on behalf of most at-risk students.

Alas, the linkage also lost its edge when the economy boomed despite little if any immediate improvement in the nation's educational system. The boost that technology was at last providing to productivity changed the dynamics of the labor market and made it less necessary to upgrade the skills of the nation's most at-risk populations. Once again a new wave of immigration brought to the United States a host of skilled as well as ready-to-learn workers. By the end of the decade, American firms were discovering just how easy it was to solve its labor problems by shipping jobs overseas. As the 1990s drew to a close, it was no longer possible to argue that the nation's economic prosperity depended on providing at-risk populations with access to a newly efficient education system ready, willing, and able to turn them into learners and workers.

Changing the Metaphor

But the gap remained, continuing to mark the persistence of diminished futures historically tied to race and economic circumstance. Now the Pew Higher Education Roundtable, often pushed by Alfredo de los Santos, Jr., began asking with greater persistence, "What will it take to reverse the pattern?" Alfredo answered, "You might start by abandoning the notion of an educational pipeline." An education pipeline inevitably suggested a continuum for those students who are "in the flow," while connoting the exclusion of any student who has somehow leaked out. The concept of the education pipeline did not allow for what Alfredo saw as the "swirling" of students over time within and about the educational system.

In fact, it was becoming increasingly common for students to interrupt or combine schooling with work, proceeding intermittently from high school to part-time enrollment in a community college, through several phases of education and employment before completing a postsecondary degree. The notion of the pipeline did nothing to accommodate that kind of student. Alfredo and his colleagues on the Roundtable cared less about the language than about the cast of mind that considered students who had stepped out of the flow to have lost their places.

"Swirling" brought to mind not just a pipeline but an entire system devoted to the intelligent deployment of resources for the vitality of a population. From an airplane it is often possible to observe the systems of water catchments, canals, and pumping stations that make life possible for a major city located in a desert—like Alfredo's Phoenix. The source or destination of a given unit of water is less important than the maintenance of the supply in sufficient quantity and quality to sustain life.

Alfredo was inviting everyone to think about the nation's education system in terms of its ability to harbor and channel the learning resources of the entire population. In a truly integrated educational system, schools, colleges, and universities, as well as training programs and other forms of postsecondary education, ought to provide social and economic benefits substantially greater than those possible when each unit separately draws from its own pool of students.

Both water and educational systems, to be effective, require a variety of points of entry and linked passageways. In the kind of educational system the Roundtable came to envision and promote, students would proceed by differing routes through primary and secondary schools, some continuing to four-year colleges, others to community colleges, still others proceeding directly to work or to service in the military. None of these latter would be considered as having foregone further education. They could return at any time or often, becoming adult learners in search of degrees and more specific workplace skills. It was a model describing a network with a variety of points of entry, transition, and passage, and with each node or institution serving as both an entry point and a pumping station, providing a steady supply of students to other nodes in the system.

A Managed Market?

Water systems are also managed markets—there is substantial freedom as to when and where individuals and businesses can use water, but always within a system that requires balanced flows. Educational systems can also be productively thought of in terms suggested by the notion of a managed market, particularly if the role of the associated system, as opposed to the market, is to ensure balanced flows.

In pursuing both the water catchment metaphor and the notion of treating the nation's educational system as a managed market, the first step is to identify the specific flows of students. The largest flow consists predominantly of students from middle-income families, who, upon immediately graduating from high school, account for the largest share of enrollments in the nation's public and private four-year colleges and universities. Most of these students grow up in family environments that presume the value of education.

A second flow of students exhibits starkly different characteristics. These youth experience traumas and adversity from birth or even conception onward, suffering from the effects of physical and mental abuse, malnutrition, and the debilitation of substance abuse. The needs of this population extend beyond the ordinary means of educational institutions. Higher education, along with employers and secondary schools, have a role to play in addressing the needs of this population, but it is largely a participatory role, in conjunction with public and social service agencies; here, colleges and universities can contribute most by educating the primary providers of care and assistance, conducting research, and providing public service.

It is the third flow of students who historically have been the focus of public policies designed to promote access: at-risk youngsters who have, on the average, come from families of lesser economic means; many are members of ethnic populations that traditionally have been underrepresented in higher education and in the more skilled and remunerative occupations. These students are most often at the borderline of educational achievement. Possessing the ability to succeed educationally and in the workplace, many nonetheless find little reason to persist through school onto work lives in which their capacities will be fully realized. But many do succeed, an outcome that suggests it is a pool half empty, half full. Their biographies and anecdotal accounts almost always associate individual success with the presence of someone—parent, teacher, friend, mentor—who saw the potential in the person and provided guidance and assurance along the way.

Ensuring access means providing this group of students and prospective workers with more sustaining opportunities for education and training. One way to think about how to meet this challenge is to imagine adopting the strategies that the nation's most successful firms have developed in forging profitable relationships with their principal suppliers. The managers of these firms no longer consider their role in a supplier relationship to be fulfilled simply by providing specifications for components of the final product. Effective management recognizes the necessity—and the payoff—of investing extensively and directly in their suppliers, becoming familiar with the details of the design and the production of the products and services they require prior to bringing their own products to market. In that competitive realm, the enterprise that understands what is entailed in meeting its own specifications can, in turn, be a far more effective producer of products someone else will use.

The lesson to be drawn from the business analogy would have colleges and universities contribute substantially to the prospects of at-risk students by developing better supplier relationships with the elementary, middle, and secondary schools that first teach these students. To engage in interactive design with suppliers means that colleges and universities in general, and their faculties in particular, would work with supplier schools—and their faculties—to design and implement more effective learning programs that better prepare their students for both college and productive employment. It means abandoning the defensive posture that says, "We can't teach these students because they did not learn anything in the years before they came to us."

This complaint is employed all too often by educational institutions of every stripe: each blames its predecessor and absolves itself of responsibility for the failure to teach, while the at-risk student becomes less and less attached and ultimately drops out, often becoming a net liability to society. This phenomenon provides one account of the educational deficit in America—the number of traditional-aged black and Hispanic students from at-risk environments for whom a college or university education could well make the difference.

Calibrating the System

Balanced systems—as well as managed markets— are possible only if the flows and exchanges can be calibrated. Expanding the prospects of at-risk youth means creating flows that are subject to the metrics of success. It means moving beyond educational process to focus explicitly on standards of achievement in schools and in college. Not "time on task" but "lessons learned" become the focus of attention. It is cruel and misleading to reward as satisfactory, or even exemplary, a performance that later shrivels in the face of real competition.

In a balanced system, accepted standards of achievement exist. Education researchers—too often maligned and too seldom read—have documented a host of applicable metrics. Students who cannot read at a third-grade level in the third grade when the curriculum shifts from learning to read to reading to learn are at a substantial disadvantage for the rest of their school years and for much of their working lives. The College Board's *Changing the Odds* documented that mastering high school geometry and algebra courses is a second of those gateways through which most college-bound students successfully pass. Being able to write a cogent essay in high school is a third, and some believe that being computer literate is a fourth. The rates at which groups of students flow though these gateways become important meters for judging the system's efficiency as well as its fairness.

The mechanics of a system that features successful interventions have also been described largely by detailing what has worked in the past. The Pew Roundtable argued that the most successful programs of interactive collaboration between schools and institutions of higher education have been those specifically targeted to improving the preparation, access, retention, and achievement of all at-risk students, whether or not they express a specific commitment to pursuing college after high school. Such interventions pay particular attention to disrupting the cycle of low motivation and low achievement; they involve full-time collegiate faculty in an ongoing way; they result in improved teaching at both the K–12 and collegiate levels; they are sufficiently funded; and they embody a long-range approach to helping students establish college as a goal.

It is also easier to maintain balances across the system when those responsible for particular flows—the engineers responsible for the individual pumping stations in our analogy—know how the system works as a whole. Thus it becomes important that college faculty know firsthand the atmosphere of a middle school or a high school that enrolls at-risk students. Too often it is left to the education school faculty to absorb and carry the message of the challenges K–12 institutions encounter in reaching at-risk youth—whether urban or rural, African-American, white, or Hispanic. Other collegiate faculty need to gain a fuller understanding of the growing pool of youth from poorer settings who acquire too little of the educational preparation or the self-confidence needed to succeed in college or work. A better understanding of this student supply must inevitably promote a greater willingness to experiment with curricular and teaching methods among faculty in K–12 and collegiate institutions, leading to programs that enable more at-risk students to succeed in both higher education and the workforce.

However tidy and optimistic the above principles may sound in the abstract, the voice of experience says that there will always be powerful impediments to change. Most of the current rewards and incentives in higher education point in a direction 180 degrees from the course of heightened educational achievement we have outlined. Not least among the obstacles to change is the resentment that primary and secondary school faculty often feel toward college and university faculty, whose practice has too often been to adopt lofty and patronizing attitudes toward those who ought to be their natural partners. To work successfully, the concept of interactive design must presume the equal importance of each point in the educational system and the equal stake that each partner has in the achievement of students at the borderline of success.

The Role of States

Establishing the requisite system of flows and partnerships is largely a people-to-people endeavor—teacher-to-teacher, administrator-to-administrator, school to college, university system to school system. When talking about how the system might work, the pumping station analogy with its image of channels and pipelines and reservoirs provides the apt metaphor. When it comes to the system's funding and regulation, however, the world of markets and their management provides the better perspective.

For the most part, public agencies have largely proceeded on the assumption that, not one system, but a pair of educational systems have minimal need for communication or interaction. In most states managing and funding K-12 education is as separate as it is distinct from the governance and funding of the state's public colleges and universities. Often the responsible executive departments and legislative committees are different, while the formulas and procedures for funding are as little alike as Mars and Venus.

Public schools are funded through school districts that supplement state grants with revenues derived from local property and business taxes. State agencies, however, both set standards and bear principal responsibility for regulating school activities and monitoring school outcomes. State-mandated testing, though often contentious, is nonetheless a well-ingrained feature of the landscape. While funding formulas often include a strong component based on average attendance, little reflects the market for education in how states fund their public schools.

For colleges and universities, public as well as private, the market distributes funds. Most states use modified enrollment formulas to establish the necessary funding baselines. In many of the nation's larger states, state-funded student financial aid, like most federal student financial aid, is distributed in the form of vouchers. Even when the funds come to public—and in some states, to private—institutions based on a funding formula, the monies actually come as a block grant. There are regulations, for the most part intended to prevent fraud and abuse, but to date there is still very little monitoring of student outcomes. High-stakes testing is something that happens to schools and not to colleges or universities.

These very differences are so maddening to those who would have their state's educational system be structurally integrated and capable of pursuing common goals—like access and economic empowerment—in consistent as well as coordinated ways. They are also differences on which the leaders of public higher education, sometimes in concert with the leaders of a state's K–12 schools, have insisted. Keeping the two enterprises separate has meant that the no one had to answer for the foibles of the other. There was no joint product, no sense of mutual responsibility—just two parties, each going its own way.

How well this separateness has served the public interest lies in the eye of the beholder. From the perspective of institutional self-interest, the bargain seems to have served higher education well. Colleges and universities are almost uniformly better funded than primary and secondary schools. College faculty are better paid than schoolteachers. Higher education has more autonomy as well as more money, along with the possibility of turning to the market whenever public monies appear to wane. In exaggerated cases—California being the prime example—it has allowed a state's colleges and universities to rank among the nation's best, while its primary and secondary schools are among the worst.

A Managed Market

We come at last to the crux of our argument. The fundamental fact remains that in modern America, access and hence opportunity remain too closely tied to race and initial economic status. It is too easy to predict which group will succeed and which will lag. Thirty years ago, in their study of the collegiate market, Bob Zemsky and Penny Oedel observed that the structure of college choice was stitched deeply into the nation's social fabric. That observation is as true today as it was then—and that's the problem.

Nothing has really worked to change the circumstances that make race and economic circumstances a principal distributor of educational and hence economic opportunity. The assumption on the part of many in the 1960s—that historical wrongs needed to be redressed—could not be sustained. The argument that programs promoting broad access, even affirmative action, were integral tools the nation could use to yield a more skilled and hence productive workforce lost traction once the economy righted itself in the 1990s. Federal programs and policies that used market mechanisms to distribute student financial aid helped secure the primacy of market forces in the shaping of American higher education, but they were insufficient to address the fundamental issues associated with at-risk students. Despite the extraordinary investment of federal dollars in Pell grants and associated programs, those who were at risk remained at risk and in the process became more disadvantaged. While solving the challenges of access and empowerment required an integrated, systems approach, the reality was a growing chasm separating the nation's public schools from its institutions and systems of higher education.

The persistent question is, "Does it have to be this way?" Accepting that the market in higher education is here to stay and that it is unlikely that a similar voucher-based market will be used to fund primary and secondary education, might there be ways to manage the system—and the higher education market—to increase the probability that more of the nation's at-risk population succeeds, first educationally and then economically?

Increasing that probability likely depends on a number of difficult—many will argue impossible—changes. First and foremost, there must be a recognition that the problem is not tied primarily to the price of a higher education—that providing more and better-targeted federal student financial aid dollars is not the answer.

Second, there must be a recognition that solving the problem involves an entire education system—as a system—rather than any particular part or parts of the system. That recognition requires state policy makers and leaders of public higher education to abandon the idea that higher education is somehow separate—or worse, somehow above the fray. It is not good enough to have colleges and universities simply admit those at-risk students that the high schools salvage. Rather colleges and universities, as institutions of public purpose, must act out of a sense of shared responsibility—a responsibility that, in system terms, includes increasing the supply of at-risk students ready to enroll in their institutions.

Primary responsibility, however, will reside with each state's political leaders, whether they like it or not. The public agencies with the most direct stake in designing a systems solution to the twin challenges of access and empowerment are also those with the clearest mandate and resources for making the system access ready. As the primary funders of K–16 education in the nation, state governments have the means to effect change almost immediately. States are the principal suppliers of what schools and colleges need most—adequate funding. In the game of school reform, money is the key player. A state that seeks to make real headway on the access agenda, for example, could aggressively offer high schools real bonuses for improving the rates at which their graduates attend college and gain sustaining employment. High schools with the lowest college participation rates would have the most to gain, though they would also face the toughest challenges.

But more money, even awarded as targeted bonuses, is not a sufficient answer. Instead, progress is likely to require state policy makers to better use the levers that markets have afforded them to push colleges and universities, as well as primary and secondary schools, toward the kind of integrated educational system imagined in our pumping stations analogy.

A real example may help explain. The Pew Roundtable meeting at which Alfredo de los Santos argued against the constraining image of an educational pipeline, was also attended by Ray Cortines, who was then superintendent of schools for San Francisco and about to become chancellor of the New York City Public Schools. Later he became the architect of the reorganization of the Los Angeles Public Schools. For most of Roundtable's day-long discussion he had been quiet, seemingly content to let others talk passionately about the need to expand access despite the lack of new ideas for getting the job done. Late in the day, he told the Roundtable that there was an eminently practical way of encouraging a sense of mutual dependency among school systems and universities. What would happen, he asked, if the governor proposed converting 10 percent of a state's appropriation for higher education into a scrip that school districts could use to buy services and expertise from the state's public universities? Why not make the school systems the universities' customers? With 10 percent of the monies that hitherto had gone to the universities set aside for this purpose, no one in the room doubted that the universities would pay attention—would in fact compete for the dollars the scrip represented.

Cortines was proposing to use the market to shape reform: first, attract the attention of the universities; then, focus that interest on the challenges of access and empowerment. He has made that proposal to a variety of groups and always, apparently, with the same response: a shudder on the part of university leaders, a bemused sense of "you can't be serious" on the part of legislators and governor's aides, and eagerness on the part of almost everyone to move on to the next item on the agenda.

But why not take advantage of higher education's hard-won experience with markets and market forces to manage the system's capacity for expanding access and opportunity? Imagine, for the moment, if a state became a true purchaser of educational services for at-risk students. Instead of giving grants to students or institutions, why not have the state ask for integrated proposals linking schools and universities to deliver an expanded supply of formerly at-risk youngsters complete with college educations and relevant job skills? To fund the experiment, why not take Cortines's 10 percent of the state's current higher education appropriations and give it to one or more agencies charged with making the requisite purchases? Why not open up the market to private institutions and for-profit colleges like the University of Phoenix?

We are under no illusions—none of this is likely to happen any time soon. Too many vested interests would be threatened. Those who worry most about at-risk students are often those with the greatest aversion to using market mechanisms to achieve public aims. There is too much inertia, too strong a belief that access is a matter of price rather than preparation. Finally, there is too much willingness on the part of higher education to believe its responsibilities begin where those of the primary and secondary schools leave off. But the questions are worth posing if for no other reason than to spark a debate—to ask once more, does the nation have to settle for a system that asks too many at-risk students to succeed while constantly swimming against the current?

11 | Crafting a Public Agenda

Not so long ago everyone in higher education was a policy expert, or so it seemed. For much of the twentieth century, colleges and universities looked to their capitals—local, state, and national—to help set institutional agendas as well as to provide the funds, both operating and capital, that sustained their missions. America's colleges and universities were in turn grateful, angry, even frightened—but they were seldom disengaged from the workings of public policy.

That mostly comfortable bundling of institutional ambition and public purpose has now been worn away. The worlds of both public policy and higher education have changed. Today fewer issues are capable of rallying public support, and institutions are even less willing to trust their futures to the process of public deliberation. As colleges and universities have become market enterprises, their sources of funding have become more diverse and more diffuse. The workings of increasingly competitive markets for enrollments and research support now determine the financial health of most colleges and universities. The competition is real, its discipline exacting, its capacity to reward those who most directly satisfy consumer demand readily apparent. The emergence of an aggressively financed, rapidly expanding network of for-profit providers has helped demonstrate just how much a college education has come to be regarded more as consumer good and less as a public good.

We began this volume by observing that historically the strength of American higher education was vested in its very public nature. America's colleges and universities—both public and private—wanted to be and were seen as public assets providing public services, and as such they conceived themselves as an integral part of the nation's agenda. All that has changed, and that change has left a host of questions to be answered by those who lead colleges and universities in concert with those charged with the making of public policy.

What role is left for public policy? What courses of action—expedient, practical, in fulfillment of the public good—should those who direct the levers of civic purpose consider now and in the future? What kinds of public objectives can the forces of policy bring about most effectively? What objectives can the workings of the market best fulfill? How should the tools of regulation, resource allocation, assessment, and quality assurance be applied to ensure that American higher education fulfills broad public purposes, serves the particular aspirations of individual students, and supports the aspirations of public and private institutions as both creators and conveyors of knowledge? How can policy help these institutions adapt effectively to change, rather than being overwhelmed by it?

The New Reality

The necessity of asking these questions makes clear just how much the context for public policy has changed. Largely discarded is that sense of an all-embracing public agenda capable of determining the missions of institutions and the distribution of students and research support across them. There is a diminished sense that policy in itself can satisfy the public's appetite for high-quality educational programs made available at low cost to consumers. Diminished as well is that commitment to a broad social agenda that characterized public discourse in the 1960s, beginning with civil rights and equal employment opportunity and culminating in local, state, and federal programs of affirmative action.

In recounting the history of federal student financial aid we have already observed how the makers of public policy came to use market mechanisms to distribute the program's funds and define its public purposes. Thereafter public policy for higher education became more narrowly focused on vouchers and student loans to promote access and on the markets for sponsored research that reshaped how the nation invested in discovery. While the federal government continued to monitor whether colleges and universities promoted equal opportunity, the two most important changes in this arena involved eliminating mandatory retirement and making sure that women's intercollegiate athletics was funded on a par with men's sports. Where policy was once the trigger for finance, finance had become the trigger for policy.

Within both institutions and legislatures, there was a growing sense of "getting policy without making policy," which allowed what was once a clear, guiding framework for public initiative to be nibbled away by both budgetary constraints and doses of self-interest. Making student loans more important than grants in the 1990s was not the result of a major policy change in Washington; rather, it was a consequence of successive years of responding to budgetary limitations at the margin, each of which transferred a little more of the cost burden to the students themselves. The evolution of a near-open market for federal research funds followed a similar pattern; out of the daily need to balance priorities and resources, new rules were adopted that led most of the nation's research universities to alter faculty incentives as well as change their responses to federal initiatives.

The cumulative action of higher education's markets more than filled the void left by this retreat from policy: consumers of higher education's services, including students and their families, powered some; the federal government's procurement of sponsored research funded some; and firms ready to pay for the research talents vested in university faculty created still others.

These markets, to reprise an earlier observation, also accorded new importance to outcomes—not, to be sure, those defined by public agencies or educational researchers, but rather the kind that fueled the admissions arms race. Matching this push for competitive advantage are the combined effects of a growing as well as changing technological presence that may still alter institutional definitions as well as recast the form and content of a college education.

It also helps to remember that acquiring a college education is not like purchasing a new car, despite the proclivity of university presidents to compare the prices their institutions charge to that of a Ford or a Chevy. To a considerable degree, higher education's markets owe their current shape to the substantial price subsidies that federal, state, and local governments provide in the form of direct appropriations, student financial aid, local tax levies, and tax laws that both allow individual deductions for gifts to colleges and universities and decline to tax the assets of those institutions. One perplexity facing institutions and public agencies alike is that the public expects both the range of choice that markets provide and the subsidies that make the price of a public college education less than the cost of its provision.

Primacy of Access

Assuring personal opportunity through access to postsecondary education was once the rock on which almost all higher education policy stood. It was the one tenet that every public initiative shared, including the GI Bill, the growth and development of community colleges, the creation of Pell Grants, and the provision of federally guaranteed loans. At one level, the nation, its individual states, and its citizens have every right to declare victory in this achievement: no other nation has succeeded in creating a system of higher education that offers greater access to a college, a university, or any other provider of postsecondary education.

But this policy, as we noted in the last chapter, has also failed to narrow the gap, largely because the policy assumed that the provision of sufficient financial resources allowing students to enter the front door of a college or university was tantamount to success. As budgeting concerns came to displace explicit policy as the driver of institutional goals and incentives, the nation as a whole drifted closer to a practice of educational triage: the most likely survivors are known in advance and accorded a lion's share of the resources the public makes available in support of public higher education. Triage invokes scenarios of battlefield medicine, where time and supplies are short and the likelihood of catastrophic failure is alarmingly real. In those settings it makes practical sense to divide the wounded into roughly thirds—those with a fighting chance for survival, those with more modest odds, and those whose survival at best depends on the application of extraordinary means simply not available on a field of battle. Triage distributes scarce medical resources according to the wounded's statistical probability of survival.

What is successful on a battlefield, however, is not acceptable, for example, in an emergency room. In that setting the extraordinary measures are expected to be applied, given the value our society places on every human life. The probability of survival in higher education increasingly resembles the battlefield model. Even today in the United States, the majority of publicly provided educational resources are spent on those deemed most likely to succeed; the public and private expenditures for higher education on behalf of students at the higher end of the socioeconomic spectrum are nearly twice those made in behalf of students at the lower end. It is as if the nation as a whole, through its policies and practices, has not yet fully answered the question, "How much of an investment in educational opportunity should be made on behalf of a population that has a higher statistical probability of failure?" Left to its own devices, the market's answer to this question will be unequivocal: "Less and less."

Mission-Centered, Market-Smart

Hence the central tenet challenges higher education policy in an age of markets. How best can local, state, and federal agencies ensure that the subsidies they provide secure sustained educational opportunity for a broad cross-section of the population?

In sorting through this challenge, among the more salient elements is the fact that the market for higher education is projected to more than double in size during the next twenty years. It will, however, be a different mix of students and aspirations from that which produced higher education's expansion in the 1950s and 1960s. That era of growth was brought about almost entirely by public funding, publicly proclaimed and allocated as investments in common pursuits. Today those investments will more likely be private: venture capital, gifts and bequests, and tuitions, all in pursuit of more personal agendas.

Because the funding that made possible higher education's last expansion was predominantly public, the institutions those funds created or helped to expand were almost entirely mission-centered: traditionally organized two-year and four-year universities and colleges. Although their individual missions differed and then evolved over time, these new institutions had most in common the mission of expanding academic access to an array of programs that collectively cost the institutions substantially more to operate than the revenues they generated through tuition.

In contrast, a considerable share of the investment that will create the next wave of growth will come from private sources, and many, if not most, of the institutions and programs either created or expanded will be more explicitly market centered: targeting the most pressing educational demands, as determined by individual consumers, that promise the greatest return on investment. Many initiatives will be decidedly commercial, frequently combining the energies and ambitions of for-profit vendors with the skill, prestige, and educational savvy of traditionally configured colleges and universities.

The workings of these higher education markets always achieve some elements of the public good—providing more options to students with clear educational goals and more efficiency in serving particular fields characterized by rapid growth and change. Likely to be lost in that mix, however, are those mission-centered programs and initiatives that, in an earlier era, embodied the public's commitment to access and opportunity. Moreover, the values of inquiry and discovery that motivate traditional institutions and their faculty—the pursuit and conveyance of knowledge beyond what the market itself demands— could easily become lost in all but the best-endowed institutions.

For this reason alone, good public policy necessarily means something different from what it has meant in the past. Where public policy in the past created institutions largely separate from market forces, advancing the public good in the future requires policies that work with—or even through—these markets. We have already suggested how market mechanisms—whether they allow school systems to purchase services from colleges or universities or create public agencies to purchase places in programs jointly operated by universities and school systems—might be used to make colleges and universities, in particular, take more seriously the challenge of developing programs that actually help at-risk young people to succeed educationally and economically. Using these and other market mechanisms requires a substantial departure from the status quo—in legislatures as well as institutions. The result just might be a public policy that induced colleges and universities to use skills honed in the marketplace to pursue public purposes more explicitly.

What remains constant is the importance of money and the centrality of the questions first posed by Clark Kerr and the Carnegie Commission three decades ago—"Who benefits? Who pays? Who should pay?" In more modern dress, these questions become: How can the investment of public funds best ensure that the markets for post-secondary education deliver public as well as personal advantage? Can the leverage that such public appropriations provide purchase educational attainment as well as institutional access? What public objectives require the explicit action of policy to achieve, and what objectives are best achieved through the workings of the market? What incentives and processes are available to public agencies for encouraging—perhaps even requiring—colleges and universities to be mission-centered as well as market-smart?

Renewal of Public Discourse

The first step to answering such questions is renewed public discourse about the public purposes of higher education. The conversations we have in mind would necessarily begin with a broad, explicit reconsideration of the relationship between the individual return and the larger good that results from public investments in higher education. In the nation at large and within individual states, what would hopefully emerge is a new focus on the steps policy makers and institutional leaders might take together to make educational outcomes at least as important as the politics of budget balancing. The goal reconsiders the who, the what, and the how of higher education in a time of markets and changing horizons.

These conversations might also ask, "What happened in the 1990s in particular to make the federal government channel so much of its funding for higher education through the agency of the market?" During that decade the issues of access and quality lost traction. Higher education preserved its federal funding not because it was capable of reminding Washington of the importance of public purpose, but largely because those responsible for protecting the industry's interests understood just how much the game had changed. Out of necessity, the academy's associations—or at least their Washington arms—had learned to apply the leverage accruing from the economic benefit that colleges and universities confer to every congressional district in America.

One of the more important lessons brought back from higher education's legislative battles of that decade was that official Washington was all but vendor neutral. While it remained mindful of the unscrupulous practices of proprietary institutions in the late 1980s, the federal government was increasingly disposed to consider for-profit and traditional institutions as interchangeable. What mattered were the educational or research services delivered, not who delivered them. This attitude was found increasingly in state capitols as well. Roy Romer, former governor of Colorado and former chair of the Education Commission of the States, would regularly tease higher education audiences by claiming he was ready to take the money his state spent on its colleges and universities and see if some other provider, like the University of Phoenix, wouldn't give him a better deal—less talk about educational process, more promise about immediate outcomes, and a greater willingness, even eagerness, to talk frankly about what things actually cost.

The willingness of policymakers to consider the University of Phoenix and a host of lesser ventures as just another set of vendors played a critical role in allowing the for-profits to enter student markets that universities and colleges had claimed as their own. Students enrolled in for-profit institutions became eligible for the federal government's student financial aid programs, which in turn provided an augmented revenue stream to the vendors. Any organization that captured part of that market could turn a significant profit as long as it also succeeded in containing its instructional costs.

At the same time, traditional universities and colleges carried on business as usual, having largely misunderstood the impact their new competitors were having on the shape of American higher education. Being purely market-driven, for-profit education targeted only those parts of the postsecondary education market that offered the promise of greatest financial return. Moreover, these institutions competed with traditional colleges and universities not so much on the basis of price as on convenience, service, and even quality of teaching. Lacking the patina of a traditional institution, for-profit institutions knew that they must rise or fall on their ability to serve the needs of the market more effectively. Not surprisingly, they exhibited a greater willingness to teach at times and in places that met the needs of working adults; and because their instructors were paid and evaluated on the basis of teaching effectiveness, the quality of instruction was often superior to that of traditional institutions, which reward faculty for an array of activities often tangential to teaching.

Traditional institutions of higher education were finding themselves in a situation like the nation's railroads in the early twentieth century: those enterprises considered themselves in the railroad business, though they were in fact only one of several contenders for the nation's transportation business. As for-profit providers of postsecondary education came to gain greater societal acceptance along with regional accreditation, they became enterprises poised to capture an ever-larger share of the student market in many fields seeking both baccalaureate and post-baccalaureate degrees. Some believe this increased competition for the dollars that the federal, state, and local governments make available through their programs of student financial aid, sponsored research, and service purchase will make traditional higher education more susceptible to change, more adaptive and flexible. We are not so sure. Immunity to change is so much a part of the history of higher education, that stagnation can become as likely an outcome as adaptation. One principal challenge of public policy is to manage the market such that adaptation in fact becomes the pre-ferred choice of even the most hide-bound institutions.

Up for Grabs

Probably the most lasting as well as troubling ef-fect of the nation's retreat from policy is the erosion of the guiding purposes that once shaped most colleges and universities. The lines of demarcation that once distinguished colleges and universities from one another are becoming increasingly blurred, as the differences that had previously defined institutions become all but irrelevant. In a host of now documented cases, the markets for both research and student enrollments have seduced institutions into impulsive, even contradic-tory ventures, putting institutional purpose up for grabs.

Every institution needs the ability to innovate and evolve within the guiding frame of its mission. In recent years, while seeking out new sources of revenue, however, too many institutions have surren-dered to the temptation to divert their energies away from their core strengths and toward ventures like e-learning, which promise a false bonanza from programs of research or education that are beyond their capacity to deliver. More than one aspiring university has been drawn to the dazzling light of opportunity that markets for sponsored research seem to offer. The push within such institutions has been to strengthen graduate programs, develop more research capacity, and make research and publication more central to their value and reward systems—regardless of how well these ambitions fit the institution's mission, its financial resources, or the most of the students it serves. Other in-stitutions have distorted their purpose in the pursuit of new student markets, by developing new programs more in the hope of revenue enhancement than from any deeper conviction about the contribution these programs would make to an institution's educational offerings.

Lacking a sense of unified mission, no longer certain of where their real strengths lie, such institutions have often found themselves con-sumed with internal discord about their central purpose. We conducted focus groups on behalf of the National Center for Postsecondary Im-provement that documented just how this absence of clear direction derived from a lack of communication and trust between the faculty and the institution's principal executives—presidents, provosts, even

deans. Often, these feelings had yielded a prolonged sense of contentiousness that prevented the institution from moving purposefully in
any direction. Having lost sight of the bearings that had earlier guided
them, many of these institutions had found themselves at a loss for
how to resume course.

The Erosion of Trust

One enduring achievement of federal policy immediately following the Second World War was that near-simultaneous
launching of the two initiatives that made American higher education
a world leader in two important domains. The GI Bill made a college
education a benefit for service to the country; that principle throughout the next half-century evolved into a conviction that a college education ought to be within the grasp of all the nation's citizenry. The
establishment of the National Science Foundation and the rapid expansion of the National Institutes of Health, as called for by Vannevar
Bush's *Science, the Endless Frontier*, made the nation's universities
and their faculties the drivers of scientific research in America and
the world. The federal government's dual commitment to educational
opportunity and unfettered scientific research helped make possible
a uniquely American system of higher education.

It is equally important, however, to remember why the mindset
that gave rise to these policy commitments and their accompanying
investments in higher education no longer holds sway, in either Washington or state capitals. Once federal and state investments in support
of higher education constituted an act of trust in the ability of the
nation's colleges and universities to fulfill societal objectives through
their own processes, in accordance with their own academic values.
Vannevar Bush trusted the nation's universities to pursue science for
its own sake, letting the act of discovery and the inquisitiveness of
university researchers be the principal guides as to what was relevant
and hence important. From that perspective, the research grants the
federal government awarded were seen as investments rather than as
purchases. The nation's top universities were often awarded large block
grants—more or less akin to getting money in a brown paper bag—to
establish research centers and institutes to pursue important, though
still largely undefined areas of research. No one talked about pork or
earmarking or Golden Fleece awards in an era of mutual trust.

With its more mundane launching the GI Bill, however, relied more
on the idea that individuals could be encouraged to pursue personal

advantage in ways both directly and indirectly beneficial to the nation. The original impetus for giving veterans tuition benefits was to keep them out of the labor market at least for a while. The fact that the rush of returning soldiers to college campuses would also help restart many universities whose programs had been reduced during the war was a welcome, though secondary consideration. Few doubted that a college campus would be a good place for a returning veteran to begin his transition to a civilian economy that many in Washington thought still too fragile, too close to the brink of the Great Depression.

None of that would be likely, maybe not even possible, today. Part of what has changed is the nation's faith in governments and their ability to allocate resources either fairly or efficiently. Among many, the notion of a smaller government that takes less from its citizens in taxes and spends less trying to level the educational playing field now has great attraction. Even among those who support a more active government, there is a kind of contagious cynicism that holds that those vested with the public trust are often the same office holders who pursue personal advantage at the expense of the public weal.

Part of what has changed as well, however, is the faith the public has in its colleges and universities. In good times, when the economy is booming and personal incomes are on the rise, colleges and universities remain in the public's good graces. Near the end of the boom cycle of the 1990s, a National Center for Postsecondary Improvement Heads of Household Survey asked a random sample of one thousand adults, "Overall, how good a job are the colleges in your state doing?" Twenty percent rated higher education's performance as excellent, 59 percent thought it good, and 21 percent considered it just fair or poor. If "A" is excellent, "B" is good, "C" is fair, and "D-F" is poor, then colleges and universities were earning a respectable "B" in the public's opinion—but not much more.

When the economy stalls or inflation takes off or the unemployment rate rises, colleges and universities are viewed with the same crankiness as other major entities—businesses, hospitals, even governments themselves. For higher education that crankiness takes the form of complaints about high prices, professors who can't and don't teach, students who can't get the classes they need to graduate, athletic programs run amok, crazy research projects that benefit no one save the researchers, and college and university presidents more interested in the trappings and remuneration of their offices than in their public responsibilities. Whether true or false, these and similar charges have been leveled often enough during the last thirty years that they have helped erode the sense that colleges and universities are special places fundamentally devoted to the pursuit of public purposes.

Keeping Traction

It was not so much that markets were wonderful as that the alternative of trusting governments and institutions was becoming less and less attractive. As a nation, the United States was saying that henceforth policy would in fact matter less. But should it? Our answer, which may surprise some, is that the making of policy ought to remain an important enterprise precisely because time and circumstance have made the market the arbiter of public choice. In a world of markets, the role of public policy becomes one of providing the necessary checks to unbridled competition—through regulation, through price subsidies when necessary, and through public investments in institutions.

To have public policy and public agency fulfill these functions requires more of the body politic coming again to understand that public choice and market behavior are not always synonymous. And it requires a careful, at times painfully slow, restoring of public trust in both the means of government and the purposes of institutions.

In the case of the nation's colleges and universities, progress likely depends on the readiness of institutions to require both their leaders and their faculty to recalibrate their political rhetoric by taking into account that articulated public policies no longer sustain their institutions or define their academic values. Frankly, what is required is a willingness to acknowledge that they, as colleges and universities, have changed and not necessarily for the better.

That acknowledgment helps those within the academy understand how and why governments on every level are making less of a distinction between nonprofit and for-profit enterprises. Then and probably only then will the lessons of privatization sink in. What matters today is how well the student is served, not who does the serving. It matters less and less to Washington whether a student spends a Pell Grant attending a for-profit trade school or a traditionally configured institution. Moreover, the widespread increase in federal earmarking suggests that it is an open question in Washington whether a limited number of major research universities should remain the locus of the nation's basic research as determined by academic peer review.

Public agencies need to be equally frank in acknowledging that markets can distort public choice. If the increased power of markets has helped the nation to achieve some aspects of the public good more expeditiously, then experience has also taught that markets alone cannot accomplish major societal objectives. Nor will the market alone assure that the college educations provided by publicly funded institutions are either low cost or high quality.

Framing a Market Policy

It would also help if state legislatures better understood the interplay between markets and the provision of public subsidy. Given the clamor for both lower taxes and more affordable college tuitions, there will always be the temptation to mandate that result by legislative fiat. This temptation needs to be resisted. In most regions of the country the independent sector in combination with for-profit providers sets the market price for higher education. When a state sets public tuitions below that market price, it essentially faces two choices: first, to provide public appropriations on a per-student basis roughly equal to the difference between the market price and legislated price; or second, to curtail all appropriations.

When a state occasionally limits *both* tuition *and* appropriations, it assumes that, as a result, public institutions will become more efficient simply through the expedient of having less money to spend. That result never happens. Instead, institutions, denied both tuition revenue and public appropriation, pour more of their energies into those activities that do not have legislated tuitions—special courses and contracted services to businesses being two of the most popular—while achieving the necessary budget reductions by squeezing resources out of their core programs. The result has been public institutions that are less competitive, less shaped by their core missions, and, ironically, more subject to the vicissitudes of the market.

In setting levels for public tuitions that take account of the market, a state legislature needs to ask three fundamental questions: How much of its appropriation should go to providing general price subsidies, and how much should be targeted, either in support of specific classes of individuals or specific classes of programs? How important is the notion that all public institutions charge the same tuition, regardless of the demand for their programs? What would be the consequences of establishing a per-student appropriation and then letting the state's public institutions set tuitions in accord with their own sense of mission and market position?

Again it would help if public agencies in general developed more effective strategies for ensuring a broader mix of publicly supported institutions. What is required is a mindset, one that shares Alfredo de los Santos's notion of educational swirl, that pushes for a substantially expanded range of learners and educational needs, including but not limited to the traditional undergraduate proceeding directly from high school. Equally important are the twenty-nine-year-old parent who is completing a baccalaureate degree at night, the forty-year-old Ph.D. who needs retooling in mediated instruction, the thirty-five-year-old software engineer who is six months behind and needs an upgrade, and the high school dropout who, having struggled to earn a GED, now sees in further education a real prospect for financial security.

Some will be tempted to let the market solve the problem of program diversity, relying on demand to attract the necessary capital— the entrepreneur's version of "where there's a will there's a way!" In this case, the most likely result will be more specialty vendors— either for-profit firms or subsidiaries attached to traditional institutions—focusing on educational programs yielding high margins for the vendor and better salaries for the graduate.

The alternative is for a state to use the power of public subsidy and price support to encourage its more traditionally configured institutions to be less set in their ways, more willing and able to develop, test, and then market new programs. Part of the answer lies in reducing the levels of bureaucracy the state itself imposes on its institutions. Part of the answer lies in encouraging publicly funded institutions to reconsider how they recruit, assign, and reward faculty.

Public agencies need to admit that they distort as well as strengthen institutions when deciding the rules governing the use of public subsidies. State policies that have prohibited the granting of student aid to part-time students or the use of state funds to underwrite the cost of continuing education programs, for example, have often resulted in reduced enrollments on the part of at-risk students as well as institutional programs that cater principally to those with sufficient discretionary income to pay for evening and weekend classes. If a state wants a more diversified set of postsecondary programs—without letting the market be the sole determinant of who and what is taught— then the state must become an active partner in those new ventures, frequently supplying much of the necessary venture capital.

In this world of commingled markets and public purposes, the nation's colleges and universities also have the opportunity to help shape the policies and market interventions pursued by public agencies. Probably the clearest example of this sense of shared responsibility involves the market for sponsored research that is largely underwritten by federal agencies. Research-intensive universities, in particular, need to find a way of working with policy makers to ensure that academic peer review continues to be the principal method for allocating federal financial support of university-based research. The movement in Congress to award sponsored research contracts and earmarked funds in pursuit of "research equity" threatens to undermine both the quality and the impact of scientific, medical, and educational research. Transforming the national government's investment in research into a public works program to benefit regional economies can only diminish the quality of research conducted in university settings. For their part, research universities must focus on the quality and utility of research conducted under their auspices; if peer review is to hold its ground against political influence, research universities must be able to demonstrate that research funded on the basis of peer review in fact sets the standard for quality.

It is another of those truisms to say that colleges and universities ought to be better at defining and then adhering to their missions. They ought to resist the impulse to pursue every new opportunity that presents itself as new markets evolve in response to societal needs. In considering its options for developing new educational and research programs, an institution must be certain that the requirements for successful competition in a given field match the skills of its faculty and staff. It may seem perfectly obvious to state that institutional mission should determine which new opportunities a college or university chooses to pursue. But too many institutions have inverted the syntax of that statement; they distort their missions beyond recognition in pursuit of unfocused and even disparate ambitions. This lack of definition harms individual institutions and contributes to the larger sense that "anything goes" in higher education. The point is not that institutions should remain static but that their decisions for new programmatic development should derive from their core values, as well as from understanding their real strengths and capacities as honed by market competition.

At the same time, colleges and universities need to make educational results a defining element of their programs. Given the disposition—in Washington, in state capitals, and in the public mind—that now stresses accountability above virtually all other objectives, no institution can ignore the need to develop a culture of positive results. It is in the interest of every university or college, for example, to ensure that its students' undergraduate learning experiences are characterized by rigor and coherence, not just in the major but in its program of general education. Even more particularly, no institution can neglect the task of ensuring that its future K–12 teachers receive substantive grounding from their baccalaureate educations to become both knowledgeable and effective in their primary and secondary school classrooms.

The Third Imperative

We have argued that for colleges and universities to succeed they must become both mission-centered and market-smart. To this we would now add a third imperative. For higher education to sustain public support it must become politically savvy as well.

Being politically savvy means accepting the fact that most of the time most governments will be persuaded to let market forces shape public choice. Railing against the inevitable only lessens the possibility that colleges and universities will be listened to on that handful of issues of paramount importance to higher education as the nation sets its public agenda. Being politically savvy means understanding how changing societal values have recast both the context and style of political exchange. Colleges and universities must find new ways to convey their collective purpose and value to the public in general— and to state and federal policy makers in particular. In many ways, universities and colleges have reached a point at which they can no longer expect the public or its political leadership to be particularly moved by the fact that higher education's mission is to educate and conduct research. Simply to satisfy their markets, most colleges and universities must demonstrate the impact they have on their graduates. Those institutions interested in or dependent on government funding must learn better how to mobilize the rhythms of contemporary politics for the deeper, perhaps even self-serving, purpose of fostering a lasting public understanding of the social products they supply to the nation.

Higher education's experience with state and federal politics through the 1990s taught three fundamental lessons. First, higher education needed to choose carefully the issues it brings to the political arena. A complex array of issues and needs is not likely to leave a lasting impression in a field where flashes and sound bites clamor for public attention. Higher education needs to delineate its upper-case objectives from its lower-case objectives; it must focus its agenda on those matters that have greatest importance and the potential for greatest societal benefit, and it must leave other items to be resolved in other ways. The difficulty of doing so stems from the fact that higher education is a large and diffuse industry; the greater the range of missions it embraces and populations it serves, the greater the difficulty of speaking in a single voice to which policymakers and the media-minded public might best respond.

Second, universities and colleges must communicate that agenda in terms that have currency in an image-driven environment. In many ways, policymakers appear to have lost connection with the values and commitments that were the underpinnings of the nation's substantial investments in higher education at midcentury. Reestablishing that connection requires learning the new boundaries and images that have come to define the political playing field. A cynical view of this field might suggest that any astute institution should immediately retain the services of a K Street firm to make sure it wins its own share of pork—and many have done just that. To the extent that traditional higher education institutions convince themselves that intensive lobbying in pursuit of their individual interests is the answer, however, they become part of the problem, and they contribute to the perception that higher education is, after all, no more highly principled than any other industry seeking to advance its fortunes.

Third, when responding to changed circumstances, in Washington as well as in state capitals, colleges and universities must resist the temptation to suppose that, by their very nature, they will receive special regard and treatment. To assume that the federal government or any other interest holds higher education in abeyance from market forces on the basis of recent memory or longer tradition is to turn a blind eye to the reality of contemporary politics.

The irony, perhaps, is that the resolution of these tensions lies in having colleges and universities, both singularly and collectively, reaffirm higher education's historic sense of itself as a special calling with a coherent set of concerns and goals. The market has already introduced too much fragmentation into the process by substituting short-term success for longer-term values and commitments. In the lingo of the modern political campaign, higher education must first develop a message and then learn to stay on it. To the question, "What's the mission?" there must be a more compelling answer than "All things to all people." In those areas where higher education claims to deserve some insulation from or correction of market forces, the argument must be grounded in a disciplined and empirically supported case that the unaided market will lead society astray. The case cannot be based on vague claims of virtue or intellectual superiority or historical privilege.

Being mission-centered means finding and keeping that central weight of academic values and missions. Being market-smart entails using the nature and forces of the market to promote coherence and cohesion. Being politically savvy means understanding the changed nature of a political process in which only a limited number of goals can be achieved, and even then for only a limited time. There is no forever, however compelling the argument or however virtuous its claimants may be.

Being politically savvy also entails a kind of Machiavellian stubbornness. Fundamentally, what colleges and universities need—and they should not forget or abandon—is more public funding as opposed to market funding. And here we need to be clear. We believe an effective public policy requires greater public underwriting of institutions in pursuit of public purposes. Without a sufficient level of public funding, higher education effectively ceases to be a public good. Or, to put the matter more directly, without the public underwriting of a substantial portion of the cost of providing an educated citizenry, it becomes more difficult to conceive, much less achieve, a truly public agenda for higher education.

12 | Dancing with Change

In February 1993 the members of the Pew Higher Education Roundtable invited all 1,800 plus presidents of American colleges and universities to meet in St. Louis. The invitation made clear that we expected everyone to pay their own way and that we intended to focus on the three issues we had begun discussing in *Policy Perspectives*: costs, learning, and access. Important as those issues had been to the Pew Roundtable in the previous five years, we were cautious enough to suspect that in themselves they would not inspire a massive migration of presidents to the banks of the Mississippi. The most important draw was the fact that the letter of invitation had been signed by Tom Langfitt, the head of The Pew Charitable Trusts. We had purposely chosen one of Lambert Field's smaller hotels with an absolute limit, or so they told us, of 450 people in the hotel's only ballroom—and that was OK; at best, we hoped to attract 200 skeptical presidents.

We were wrong. Our initial mailing drew seven hundred acceptances. We checked with the hotel; the fire marshal would actually shut the meeting down if he even guessed there were more than five hundred people in the ballroom. We sent out a second mailing, which made explicit that The Pew Charitable Trusts would *not* be announcing a new program of grants. There was some melt, but not enough. In the end all that saved us was the decision of the flight attendants for American Airlines to go on strike, and even then more than a dozen presidents from Texas rode Greyhound buses to St. Louis to attend the meeting. When the sessions began, we had just a whisker under five hundred presidents in attendance.

The meeting was unusual in another way as well. Knowing the habits and attention spans of college and university presidents, we brought in extra banks of telephones (cell phones being still over the horizon). No one used them. Instead, the presidents came—on time, attentive, ready to listen, and consider. The question we kept asking was why?

Setting the Agenda

In the end we concluded that most presidents had come to St. Louis because *Policy Perspectives*, by tapping a wellspring of urgency, had gotten it right. The agenda for the meeting had been set in the inaugural issue of *Policy Perspectives* under the somewhat perplexing title, "Seeing Straight Through a Muddle." The first peril facing higher education we had proclaimed was the escalating costs associated with a college education. Second was the widening gap between the teaching that colleges and universities liked to talk about and the learning their students needed as well as wanted. Third was the persistence of economic status along with race and ethnicity as the dominant markers of educational and economic advantage in America.

The prevailing sense then was that colleges and universities knew what needed to be done: control costs, focus on learning, and make sure a college education was within the reach of all Americans. The challenge was to muster the will and energy to make good on each promise. The problem was that nothing really seemed to be working. Prices were continuing to spiral upward. While the number of conferences and speeches devoted to assessment and learning proliferated, hardly any change was actually occurring in the classroom. An admissions arms race was being launched that would, over the next decade, further stratify the nation's system of higher education—a system in which those who were economically disadvantaged or had been historically excluded were too often clustered on the bottom layers, or not present at all.

In taking on the challenge of reform, we understood not just the enormity of the tasks but the inherent contradictions to be overcome in achieving a more purposeful, more effective system of higher education. Our concluding paragraph in "Seeing Straight through a Muddle" was telling:

The agenda for higher education that we have laid out is not an easy one: control costs, pay greater attention to quality teaching and learning, ask colleges and universities to play major roles in reforming American schools and reaching out to the educationally and economically disadvantaged. The first priority is clearly in direct conflict with the latter two. It is one thing to ask colleges and universities to be more prudent, to learn to manage better, to use technology and other means to achieve increased productivity as well as enhanced quality. It is quite another to ask those institutions to invest those savings in what many within the academy will see as social rather than scholarly priorities. But it is clear that if advances in scholarship are to have a wide-ranging and democratic effect—if indeed scholarship is to make advances in areas vital to the interests of all parts of society—then all parts of society need to participate in higher education. Above all, *Policy Perspectives* recommends that the broad issues of educational quality and social equity be considered in tandem and recognized as truly interdependent.

Turning Point

The meeting in the fall of 1993 in St. Louis sharpened these concerns. "To Dance with Change," which summarized the message of the St. Louis sessions, became the most influential of all *Policy Perspectives*, in part, at least, because it offered such a chilling portrait of changing external circumstances and their impact on colleges and universities across the United States. Vocationalism, technology, privatization, and increasing legislative and public anger at a faculty lifestyle perceived as self-indulgent and beyond accountability—together these spelled a fundamentally different future for both public and private higher education. In their stead we offered ideas simple enough in outline:

> Make institutions less labor-intensive; simplify the curriculum; transform departments into instructional collectives. Together these actions would help to bring about institutions that are more nimble, more capable of responding collectively to shifts in markets and public attitudes as well as to changes in technology and the competition of alternative suppliers of postsecondary education. None of these changes can be com-

manded, legislated, or regulated. They must instead come from the sense of internal discontent that, when combined with external inducements, yields a purposeful recasting of institutional function.

From this point forward, both the pages of *Policy Perspectives* and our own research efforts, principally for the National Center for Postsecondary Improvement, came to portray a different, less independent system of American higher education. "To Dance with Change" had concluded with the observation:

> What is required now is a purposeful consideration of the alterations an institution can imagine itself making, as well as a real discussion of the consequences of not changing at all. To convene such a conversation is to dance with change, to enter into relation with a future not yet fully imagined. To demur, to respond, "I'm OK, just want to sit this one out," is to let someone else choose your partner as well as call the tune.

Too often, or so it seems to us, higher education has done just that—letting the market choose its partners and call the tune. A decade ago we were still prepared to argue that increased competition among institutions, coupled with a robust consumer movement, would yield either better products, lower prices, or—if the pressure on the competing institutions was intense enough—perhaps both. The ferociousness of the admissions arms race with its focus on competitive advantage has dampened our enthusiasm for this proposition. Although we continue to entertain the theoretical possibility that competition might hold prices in check, we have all but given up the idea that competition in today's terms promotes quality per se.

Make no mistake, however, the market is here to stay. No state has sufficient funds to operate a public system of higher education today that offers the same level of public subsidy per student that was provided in the 1950s and 1960s. In this century there are simply too many students in pursuit of a college education—upward of 70 percent of each graduating high school cohort. Nor is it likely that there will be any lessening of the demand for and hence the price of a medallion college education. In this world of markets, the competitive advantage derived from attending these institutions is only likely to increase.

Over the last dozen years colleges and universities have gotten much better at reading and responding to the market—at being market smart. In the years ahead they will have to prove even more adroit, more flexible, more nimble, and yes, more businesslike. Still, when the history of American higher education in the first quarter of the twenty-first century is written, we hope that becoming more market smart proves to be only part of the tale. The rest of the story ought to be about using market smarts to regain control of institutional mission—about the restoration of American colleges and universities as places of public purpose. Within this frame we offer a last, somewhat extended set of recommendations. Many were first set forth in the pages *Policy Perspectives*. Others derive from our working directly with institutions, as either consultants or members of The Learning Alliance for Higher Education. Some focus on how to manage colleges and universities more efficiently and effectively. Some focus on the kinds of learning environments necessary to recast colleges and universities as learning communities. Some focus on questions of access and the academy's role in shaping the nation's purposes. In each case the subtext is the same—how, in a world of markets and unbridled competition, can colleges and universities preserve and, where possible, strengthen their ability to pursue public purposes?

Changing Economics

In rereading the *Policy Perspectives* written before St. Louis and even immediately afterward, we were more than a little chagrined to find so much emphasis on getting smaller. The one recommendation that emerged repeatedly from the Roundtable—and one that caused most consternation—was our call for colleges and universities of every stripe to become smaller in size: leaner, more efficient, more capable of growth by substitution. We urged colleges and universities to plan actively for reduced levels of employment, and, when achieving the necessary reduction, to resist the temptation to make across-the-board cuts. We argued that no matter how well decisions to spread the austerity evenly might accord with the democratic notion of fairness, they in fact remained no decisions at all—evasions, really, of the need to choose among competing versions of the institution's future. Democratic cost-cutting represented not just a failure of will but a more significant failure to understand that maintaining quality in some areas necessarily required a reduction or elimination of others.

These were good management dictums that nonetheless ignored the fact that in a world of markets, real growth is the first imperative. Winning in the marketplace means that an enterprise requires more money every year to spend on truly good things. We have already cited the differing experiences of the University of Michigan and UC-Berkeley to exemplify the importance of being market smart. During the same time span, the experiences of Princeton teach the same lesson, though this time the focus is on a major private university.

Blessed with a highly focused set of undergraduate and graduate programs that included neither a school of medicine nor a school of law, Princeton enjoyed an enviable market position, a substantial endowment, and a long history of raising both operating and capital funds from friends and alumni. It was also an institution that had not allowed market revenue to increase faster than its other revenue sources. Princeton insulated itself from the hurly-burly of the market, principally by making sure that endowment income matched student/market income. But Princeton was also losing out in the race for new money, not as badly as UC–Berkeley, but in an increasingly apparent way. The gap in constant dollars between what Princeton had to spend and Harvard had to spend was widening year by year. Then in the spring of 2000, Princeton announced a 10-percent increase in the size of its undergraduate student body to be accomplished over three years. Princeton was about to do what Harvard and Michigan had done a decade earlier: make the university more dependent on student-generated revenues as a means of funding its ambitions. Princeton had decided to go to the market.

Getting smaller is not the answer—but getting more focused is. An enterprise wants to grow where and how it chooses to grow—with particular emphasis placed on the notion of making choices. It's what presidents and provosts ultimately do—make the choices or bets as to where the institution's next wave of growth and innovation are likely to originate and where they may lead. Sometimes enterprises get lucky, the growth comes from an unexpected quarter that encourages all those who distrust central decision-making to proclaim the virtue of "letting a thousand flowers bloom." Most of the time, however, those who believe in giving every contender a little bit of money and the opportunity to show its potential actually dissipate energies and thwart ambition. Winning in this market takes real money as well as real smarts and good ideas.

The Centrality of the Academic Department

Winning in this market also requires that institutions become more skilled at controlling if not actually reversing the academic ratchet. Entrepreneurial faculty, in particular, need to be reminded, forcibly at times, that they are not independent contractors attached to a university, which, for all intents and purposes, is nothing more than an academic holding company. In part, a more purposeful, more convincing rhetoric from higher education's academic leaders and principal scholars must define the responsibilities and obligations of a faculty appointment. More leaders need to sound like Henry Rosovsky, who argues that the academy works best when both institution and faculty proceed on the assumption that a social contract binds them together as a community of public purpose. That said, the larger question is whether, within the academy, agencies or organizations are still capable of calling the faculty to collective action.

Despite its often tattered reputation, we remain convinced that the academic department is best positioned to perform that collectivizing function. The way to reform lies not in the circumventing the structure endemic to academic institutions across the globe, but to enlist that structure in the reform itself. In most colleges and universities departments have primary responsibility for setting standards, conducting evaluations, monitoring quality, gauging the market, and, not incidentally, making sure that both they and the institutions to which they belong have a clear sense of their particular missions.

To serve the collective functions we have in mind requires substantial changes, which principally involve the executive power of the department and its chair. The power of the chair ought to derive from his or her ability to speak *to* as well as *for* the department. The chair needs to be both leader and manager. Though the position is likely to rotate, the chair needs to be a scholar-colleague who in fact has an agenda. It is common for presidential search committees to ask candidates, "What do you want to accomplish—and how will we know if you are being successful?" Would-be chairs must answer those same questions. Chairs ought to know that they will be judged and rewarded on the basis of departmental performance.

Chairs need to be held accountable for the quality of the leadership they provide; likewise, the department as a whole needs to be held responsible and rewarded for the quality of the programs its members provide, in terms of both instruction and research. As units expected to work as a team, departments need to be pushed to assign different roles to team members at different points in their careers. The next step, making the department the unit for reward and punishment, links individual faculty raises as well as discretionary departmental funds to the collective achievements of the department in both teaching and research. The few institutions that have begun experimenting with arrangements such as these are beginning to report that there is in fact the desired shift from "my work" to "our work."

The academic department also has the best chance of making effective teaching a subject of collective inquiry. Distinguishing most scholars is the relentlessness with which they pursue the objects of their curiosity—testing, challenging, asking new kinds of questions, exhibiting a willingness to consider the impossible as well as the unlikely. To the extent that teaching and learning become the focus of collective inquiry, the resulting sense of shared commitment enables individual faculty to visit one another's classes, to make effective teaching a regular subject of departmental discourse, and to make curricular and pedagogical experimentation a focus of departmental planning.

A host of questions needs to be answered if the department is to become an institutional agent for controlling the academic ratchet.

> Is it really possible to vest greater executive authority in the department chair? That is, can the chair ascend from a position of bureaucratic overseer or narrow advocate of faculty self-interest to one of real authority and leadership?
>
> How might departments enjoin their members to take collective responsibility for the quality of undergraduate instruction—to undertake internal quality review procedures that apply to all department members, regardless of individual rank and status?
>
> How might a recasting of departmental incentives and rewards bring about a more balanced distribution of faculty effort? What would be the effect, for instance, of departments according to all tenured faculty two-thirds of their current salary as the new base, leaving to annual negotiation the terms under which the final one-third is disbursed—in effect, granting to faculty tenure of rank but not of salary?

Managers as Leaders

Along with controlling the ratchet, there is a parallel need to pare back the administrative lattice, a process that best begins by reminding an institution's managers that they are not faculty: they are not independent contractors or even institutional entrepreneurs, but rather service providers. We were truly amazed to discover just how often administrative practice now mimics faculty processes. Even middle managers are being selected by hiring or search committees that become caricatures of the deliberative processes they are supposed to embody. At the same time, no administrative project or proposal is now too small to escape tedious scrutiny by a committee whose debates principally yield compromise decisions.

Unable "to get anything done," senior managers have begun aggressively seeking outside expertise to help them accomplish the practical tasks they confront. Sensing that a growing share of the most fulfilling work passes beyond them to external consultants, or is second-guessed by colleagues and committees, midlevel managers often feel stultified in their careers. Dilution of managerial functions and decisions makes it increasingly difficult to sustain an environment that allows an institution to feel effective in its mission or exhibit a sense of pride in its own identity.

The better-managed institution has become the one with a significant number of senior managers who, precisely because they have broad experience both within and beyond the academy, know what it means to be both mission centered and market smart. This institution has the capacity to make strategic decisions in keeping with its core values and market opportunities—decisions that allow it to enhance its distinctive strengths in the face of new and growing competition. Fundamental to acquiring that capacity is the reconceptualization of both the skills required of higher education managers and the kinds of experiences that qualify managers for the responsibilities they will assume; that process requires changes in the cultures and ultimately in the practices of most colleges and universities.

The key step in this transformation is to redefine the role of managers and the work they perform. Smart institutions provide their managers with incentives to be strategic. They develop purposeful strategies for attracting and retaining skilled professionals, including those whose training and background fall outside the traditional box. Institutions both public and private need to rethink career paths—trapping no one, that enables the institution to restructure itself in a planned way, rather than in response to crisis. Having vested executive authority in the president, effective boards make certain that the president's actions represent strategic steps to fulfill the broad policy objectives established by the board.

At the same time, trustees and regents need to make sure that they are not play-acting. One of the more interesting differences between public and private institutions is the prevailing mindset of their respective boards. In the case of public institutions, trustees and regents too often come to the table with their own agenda. They become "table pounders," good at expressing the "anger of the people" but not very effective at helping steer the institution. The trustees of private institutions are more likely to treat the institutions they superintend as ideal entities rather than the competitive enterprises they are. While seldom pounding the table, corporate executives who find themselves on the boards of the institutions they attended too often ask, "Why can't you be more like my corporation?" as if those entities can downsize at will, pick any executive they want, and convert to "mere employees" the professionals who are responsible for developing every new product the corporation brings to market. To be sure, corporations are more businesslike than colleges and universities, but the gap between the two sets of enterprises is not nearly as wide as these trustees would have one believe.

On Learning

For nearly two decades now, colleges and universities have been awash with recommendations for becoming learning organizations in the fullest sense. It is a torrent to which we have contributed mightily. Make teaching a central criterion in review for all hiring, promotion, and tenure decisions. Insist that faculty hired for their first teaching assignments have had a teaching apprenticeship as an integral part of their graduate training. Make the content, organization, and structure of the curriculum the first priority of academic planning. Invest discretionary revenue in programs that enable and encourage faculty to improve their teaching. Use technology to transform teaching and learning. Create programs that require collaborative teaching within and among departments to stress the importance of context and relation in the acts of learning, thinking, and knowing. Insist on effective criterion-weighted learning assessments. Make teaching count equally with research in the hiring of faculty, as well

but at the same time holding every manager truly accountable. Managers who fail need to lose their jobs more quickly, perhaps even more
publicly. Those who succeed will be managers with transferable skills
acquired through a broad range of experiences. Once recruited, they
require a certain license to take risks; they know that they will be re
warded if the innovations they sponsor are broadly seen as advanc
ing institutional goals.

Regardless of mission, size, or governance, paring back the lattice
requires a more purposeful definition of managerial roles and respon
sibilities, along with a stronger connection with the managerial skill
and savvy of the shop floor. But too much power residing in bottom
up processes makes executive officers, in effect, the employees of thei
employees, beholden to everyone who seeks involvement in the pro
cess of change. To the extent that top officials relinquish their leader
ship roles and regard themselves simply as players on a managemen
team, the institution will likely make bad decisions that proceed fror
fuzzy and contradictory images of the institution's mission, markets
and capacities.

The Role of Trustees

Trustees and members of boards of regents have
special role to play in this process of reinforcing executive initiativ
Primarily through the questions they ask of the president can boar
members best provide the spur that clarifies institutional mission. A
effective statement of institutional mission is one that knowingly strike
the balance between undergraduate and graduate education—betwee
teaching, research, and service. Trustees cannot allow a generic con
mitment to "excellence, quality, and access" to substitute for effecti\
design criteria capable of giving real shape and substance to th
institution's academic programs. Similarly, boards need to integra
their oversight of academic planning and budgeting processes to sa
isfy themselves that the institutional values as expressed in the mi
sion statement correspond to actual curriculum offerings ar
expenditures.

Although they are comprised of volunteers, most boards need
be more proactive in monitoring the health of their institutions. Bo
individually and collectively, trustees ought to be investing sufficie
time to become well informed about the workings of the institutic
They have a special obligation to insist on the kind of accountabili

as in tenure and promotion decisions. Make direct investments in teaching and curricular development that parallel the institution's direct investments in research and publication.

Amidst this welter two fundamental messages bear repeating. First, move learning to the center of the teaching enterprise. No one should blame members of a faculty for pursuing a vision of the academy that sustains the intellectual excitement and challenge that characterized their own training. The pursuit of knowledge and training of scholars are deep passions for anyone who would attain a place in the academy. These goals, however, create institutions whose conceptions of excellence are essentially all the same, cast largely in terms of disciplinary perspectives and best exemplified by the major research universities. This conception of excellence would be appropriate if the objective was only to prepare students for graduate school and ensure the continued well-being of the professoriate. But such a definition of faculty responsibility does little to ensure success among students who learn differently or who bring different experiences, expectations, and needs to the classroom and lab. Missing is the concept of "fitness for use," which is central to modern definitions of quality in the production of other goods and services. The challenge is to make fostering student learning a central "use" of faculty time and energy.

Second, make teaching and learning central subjects of discourse, where institutional leaders take primary responsibility for the quality of the discussion. There is a fundamental need to sustain and strengthen the practice of teaching as conversation. As a result institutional settings ought to reinforce a mentoring relationship best characterized by a willingness on the part of faculty to listen and respond to students in ways that generate an enduring passion for learning and discovery.

A third message, however, for the most part present only as a subtext in most discussions of teaching and learning, now needs to take center stage. To become learning-centered organizations, colleges and universities must learn, adapt, and then apply the discipline of quality assurance—they will at last have to learn the art of making quality job one. Good quality assurance programs will necessarily incorporate our first two messages; they will have to move learning to the center of the enterprise by first making teaching itself a subject of sustained conversation among faculty and students. But much more will be required. Higher education—forced to get over its squeamishness with measurement—will have to say, "If we know what we ought to be doing, then we can measure whether in fact we are doing it or not."

We have already laid out the basic architecture of quality assurance for higher education. We have no doubt that the specific mechanics and processes of calibrating quality will change over time. The key elements, however, will necessarily remain the same. Quality assurance is faculty work. The unit of analysis is the department except in those rare instances where the academic department is not responsible for instruction. Success depends on developing measurements that capture intuitively what both faculty and students mean by quality while at the same time providing enough precision to make comparisons over time genuinely useful.

Employ Data to
Achieve Strategic Purposes

This appeal to data-driven or evidentiary processes has important echoes for most of higher education's principal functions. Put simply, to have bearing on the circumstances of an institution, any conversation must be grounded in data. The key, however, lies in knowing when enough is enough. The danger inherent in any academic process is that those who disagree can hold any decision hostage by simply calling for more data.

College and university executives along with their faculty today manage enterprises that, for the most part, have come to have better control and understanding of the basic transactional data that track their operations. Virtually every institution has sharpened its attentiveness to these measures, largely in response to increased scrutiny and demands for accountability from without. Those responsible for the academic management of institutions are also finding that their strategic dashboards have increased in scope as well as in quality and reliability.

Yet most colleges and university are enterprises still lacking a culture of data in the fullest sense. A large part of the problem derives from the failure of most institutions to resolve their ambivalence about what data should tell and how they should be used in institutional decision making. Building a evidentiary culture requires that an institution become more willing to adopt shared conventions in data collection and analysis, even if that means initiating practices that differ from the past.

The academy must also improve at making data the instruments of prospective strategy, not weapons of turf defense and opposition. The very principles that define data of the latter sort often constitute nonanswers to the central strategic questions facing an institution, its schools and departments. Every institution could benefit from spending less time gathering data for proprietary purposes and more time identifying and analyzing data that genuinely speak to questions of institutional strategy.

One way to move forward is to have an institution's executive leadership demonstrate by example what it means to make effective use of data. Presidents, provosts, deans, department chairs, and senate chairs are in natural positions to show what it means to judiciously use information in pursuit of a well-conceived strategic course. They can convey to an academic community a responsible sense of what data do and do not tell; they can show when to draw upon quantitative measures and when to move beyond these indicators to make decisions on the basis of intuitive responses to a range of information. A leader who holds all decisions hostage to continual demands for more data very likely feeds a culture of defensiveness in an institution, which causes every unit to amass data like so many ramparts against any and all incursions. Making responsible use of data means knowing when it is time to act, even though it might be possible to attain more information; it means not sounding all alarms on the basis of a single early warning from a dashboard indicator; and it means not waiting until seawater is gushing into the captain's cabin before ordering all hands on deck.

Sorting

As in the case of learning, the prescriptions for fulfilling higher education's commitment to access are now ubiquitous. We have already argued that the way forward begins with a frank acknowledgment that the almost single-minded focus on making a college education more affordable through the provision of educational vouchers has not worked—and it not likely to work in the future, no matter how much money is distributed in Pell Grants or other forms of direct assistance. Required instead is a willingness to experiment with other market mechanisms to better tap institutional self-interest in pursuit of programs in which at-risk young people regularly succeed.

Here our sense of do's and don'ts should be abundantly clear by now. Do not reward institutions for recruiting and enrolling at-risk students that do not graduate—or, in the case of community colleges, do not complete their planned courses of study. Do not allow colleges and universities to remain above the fray. Instead, design market mechanisms to reward institutions that provide the structure and encouragement that help students succeed in completing their educations. Make sure that colleges and universities work with school systems as partners in joint ventures of public purpose.

We also conclude that it is important to expand the conversation about access to include a broader range of topics and groups. The result will be a richer, more nuanced definition of the kinds of exclusion that limit success and opportunity. The power of that lesson was brought home by a special roundtable convened at MIT under the joint auspices of the Knight Foundation and the American Association of University Women. The topic focused on the circumstances of women faculty members—in particular, women scientists—in the academy. Why were women scholars seen as less important contributors to the creation of new knowledge? Largely because of a mindset that too easily regarded such work as the exclusive domain of men. It was a disposition that, with embarrassing frequency, consigned women faculty members to the ranks of "permanent associates" who never quite attain the full recognition and reward of their male counterparts in terms of salary, research support, or assignment to important committees.

The recommendations that came from that special roundtable did not seek simply to advance more women to the senior ranks of the academy, though that could be one result. Neither did the roundtable seek different sets of standards for men and women. We sought instead institutional discussions that, by recognizing the deeply ingrained biases privileging one gender over another, provide the basis for reaching beyond gender blindness, beyond the screen that would hide the identity of the performer from the judicial panel. Higher education's next step must be toward a condition we came to call gender intelligence.

It is now time for access intelligence as well. American colleges and universities need to shoulder a greater share of the burden, even to the point of investing their own funds in providing a rich array of pathways to personal success. We once suggested to institutions in California that the truest measure of their success could be found in the strength of their public school systems. No longer should it be possible, as it then was in California, for a state's public universities to be ranked among the nation's best and its public schools among its worst. If the educational system as a whole was failing a significant portion of the population—then all its component parts were failing as well, no matter how illustrious its faculty or magnificent its facilities.

Seeing Straight through a Muddle

We close with a final irony. In an enterprise that is often caricatured as being obsessively devoted to talk, the larger truth is that today the members of academic communities do not talk enough. They do not talk to each other. They do not talk about values. When they do talk, they make speeches without first having listened to one another.

The topics requiring sustained conversation are many: athletics, teaching and learning, quality assurance, access, and the two topics that have been at the center of this volume—the increasing importance of markets and the diminishing of public purpose. More broadly, an environment is required that encourages continued dialogue and communication among higher education's many stakeholders. The foundation of an effective institution is a shared understanding of the enterprise and its challenges.

We have in mind two broad classes of dialogue. The first involves the continuing conversation between and among faculty and students: about the nature of learning, the subject to be learned, the roles and responsibilities each brings into the learning exchange. The second involves a continuing dialogue between an administration and its faculty: What steps can help an institution narrow the gap between faculty and administration in order to become more purposeful in defining and fulfilling its mission? How can these two groups of professionals work more effectively to reconceive—and as necessary redesign—the institution's learning environment, building from a shared vision that looks to the future as well as the past?

For many institutions, the first step that faculty and administration together must take is to overcome a history of distrust and animosity that may extend considerably beyond the tenure of the current president or provost. No one should imagine this to be an easy task because it is unlikely that the historical differences dividing an institution's faculty and administration can be effaced by simple appeals to enhanced community. A willingness of both parties to work together to bring about shared objectives is needed.

It will likely fall to the institution's executive leadership to take the first steps in convening the necessary conversations. But necessarily a joint faculty and administration process will give voice to the institution's mission by setting its plans and then translating those goals into tasks appropriate to the particular talents and expertise the different parties bring to the table. An institution's executive leadership—president, provost or academic vice president, executive vice president—must establish the groundwork for debate and decision in a way that makes clear the issues at stake and the tradeoffs involved. In taking these steps, institutional leaders must also work closely with elected faculty leaders, be they from faculty senates, bargaining units, or, as is increasingly the case, both.

The erosion of trust between administration and faculty was a theme repeatedly stressed during the 1993 meeting in St. Louis and a follow-up meeting of institutional leaders three years later. To that meeting came the senior executives—for the most part presidents and provosts—of the more than eighty institutions that had convened roundtables modeled after the original Pew Higher Education Roundtable. These leaders and the faculty who joined them talked about the processes they had used in conceiving a shared vision of their institutions and the resulting understanding of their institutions' capacities—the resources they had available matched against the resources required to remain mission centered.

What emerged was the description of a discourse that worked, facilitated by a set of simple exercises that could cumulatively yield a sense of shared purpose. The process began with a faculty-administrative team or roundtable focusing on the condition of the institution itself. The conversations started with definition, rather than data collection. The questions being asked, often guided by an external facilitator, were several: "What are we trying to accomplish? What problems do we face? Where is the market taking us? What kinds of information do we need and have available to answer these and related questions?"

Probably the most important result of this first round of guided conversations was a unique set of performance indicators to which faculty and administrators had mutually acceded, reflecting the health of the institution and its prospects for the future. Such indicators necessarily extended beyond standard input measures of endowment size and average SAT scores to include calibrations of institutional performance in pursuit of commonly defined goals. More than a few institutions came quickly to the realization that the kinds of records available to the community were simply not adequate to the task of calibrating either the present or the future.

As the process matured, the questions necessarily got tougher, focusing more explicitly on investments, tradeoffs, market performance, and priorities. When these became active topics, however, there was already in place an agreed-upon and mutually developed set of definitions—and, not so coincidentally, a climate of trust born of the sense that the data reasonably track what they purport to measure.

With a sense of trust established and a limited but pertinent set of data in hand, the next step was to engage the larger campus community in a continuing discussion of the institution's goals and plans. The development of a working document that seeks to articulate the choices before the institution—what one institution has called a "planning screed," and what might in more modern parlance be considered the product of an on-going electronic bulletin board—became an effective way of building common understanding and resolve. A first-draft planning paper, focused on key issues and simultaneously distributed for comment to the campus community, started the discussion as an invitation to question and think out loud as an institution. As each member of the community added his or her marks to the document, it became a medium for defining terms, for clarifying matters that have created confusion or disagreement, and for building accord for particular courses of action. As with sharing budgetary data, engagement in a continuing interactive planning dialogue enabled faculty and administration to develop an expectation of behavior that in itself contributed to developing institutional purpose.

In Search of Communitas

In a variety of contexts, roundtables and the *Policy Perspectives* that ensued have stressed the need for clearly articulated institutional values as the basis for particular actions taken. The best of them was convened in 2000 in conjunction with the National Center for Public Policy and Higher Education at the urging of Tom Ehrlich, former president of Indiana University and now a senior scholar of the Carnegie Foundation for the Advancement of Teaching. The stated subject was the obligation of colleges and universities to instill in students a more pronounced sense of their role as citizens. Tom and others perceived that the value of civic engagement had largely fallen off the agenda of most universities and colleges—a more specific example of the diminishing of public purpose across so much of American higher education.

The *Policy Perspectives* that derived from this roundtable appeared later that same year. Its two key recommendations offer an important coda to the themes we have woven together across the pages of this volume, starting with the importance of basing institutional action on a set of well-understood core values.

Convene broad-ranging institutional discussions of the meaning and importance of civic engagement in a democratic society. The logical first step is to convene broad-based institutional dialogues concerning the values central to a culture of civic engagement. Colleges and universities need to demonstrate, through both precept and practice, that the process works, that inclusion is a means as well as an end, and that the basis of a civic polity is shared values as well as shared responsibilities and tasks.

Productive discussions of human and societal values are never easy to convene—or to conclude. To discuss what citizens share in common is to become immersed in controversy. And yet, without those discussions and the confusion and pain they often entail, little beyond individual initiative is likely. The discussion of core values and civic responsibilities identifies the shared principles undergirding a democratic society; it is also the activity most likely to bring individual differences into sharpest form. But the difficulty of convening and sustaining such discussions cannot be an excuse for shirking the responsibility to get the process started.

Model responsible citizenship through the institution's own processes of academic governance as well as through engagement with its immediate neighbors. Beyond the dialogues they convene and the values and skills they impart through the curriculum and other learning experiences, colleges and universities must actively exemplify their commitment to promoting public purposes. Institutions willing to act publicly on the values they define will send a strong signal—to their students, their faculty and staff, their extended communities, in a word, to themselves—that those values are more than stylish rhetoric. One way an institution demonstrates its commitment to responsible citizenship is the manner in which it conducts its own affairs of governance. A tradition of academic decision making that encourages active, open debate on issues facing the institution underscores the strength of the democratic process and its potential for helping an institution align its values with the choices it makes.

No less important than ensuring the vitality and effectiveness of their own governance systems are the actions institutions take as citizens of an extended region. By involving themselves with their neighbors, colleges and universities model the kind of behavior they ultimately expect of their students. Becoming engaged in the workings of a community will mean different things to different institutions; even institutions of similar size and mission find that civic purpose derives from particular rhythms and purposes relevant to both themselves and their local communities. Often the key to effective partnerships is the realization by an institution and its stakeholders that their destinies are intrinsically bound to one another. When an institution achieves this perspective, engagement in community and civic life becomes something more than perfunctory obligation. The ties developed with society at large help to realize a vision of the institution as a genuine partner in creating a future of shared purposes.

There remains only one caution to add. The institutions that model civic engagement and pursue public purposes must also be those institutions that succeed in the market, in part because they and only they have sufficient resources to expend in pursuit of public purposes but, more important, because their embrace of civic engagement as well as markets sets a standard for the industry as a whole. In an era of unbridled competition, being mission-centered remains the principal reason for being market-smart. It is, as always, a question of both means and ends.

References

Association of American Colleges. 1985. *Integrity in the College Curriculum: A Report to the Academic Community*. Washington, D.C.: Association of American Colleges.

Bechtel, Louis. 1992. *United States vs. Brown University*. 805 F. Supp. 288 [E.D.,PA.1992].

Bloom, Allan. 1987. *The Closing of the American Mind*. New York: Simon & Schuster.

Boyer, Ernest L. 1987. *College: The Undergraduate Experience in America*. New York: HarperCollins.

Bush, Vannevar. 1945. *Science, The Endless Frontier: A Report to the President*. Washington, D.C.: United States Government Printing Office.

Chodorow, Stanley. 1997. "The Business of Universities: Foundations for the Relationship Between the University and Industry." Paper presented at the All-University of California Conference on the Relationship between Universities and Industry.

Dill, David D. 1992. "Quality by Design: Toward a Framework for Academic Quality Management," *Higher Education: Handbook of Theory and Research*. New York: Agathon Press, Inc.

Ewell, Peter T. 1999. "A Delicate Balance: The Role of Evaluation in Management." Paper presented at the Fifth Conference of the International Network of Quality Assurance Agencies in Higher Education (INQAAHE), Santiago, Chile.

Goldman, Charles A., and William F. Massy. 2001. *The PhD Factory: Training and Employment of Engineering Doctorates in the United States*. Bolton, Mass.: Anker Publishing Company, Inc.

Gumport, Patricia J. 2002. *Beyond Dead Reckoning—Research Priorities for Redirecting American Higher Education*. Palo Alto, Calif.: National Center for Postsecondary Improvement.

Hirsch, E. D., Jr., and James S. Trefi. 1987. *Cultural Literacy: What Every American Needs to Know*. Boston, Mass.: Houghton Mifflin.

Kerr, Clark. 1988. A General Perspective on Higher Education and Service to the Labor Market." Unpublished paper excerpted in "Distillations," *Policy Perspectives.* 1988. Philadelphia, Pa.: Institute for Research on Higher Education, University of Pennsylvania.

Knight Higher Education Collaborative. 1998. "To Publish and Perish." *Policy Perspectives.* Philadelphia: Institute for Research on Higher Education, University of Pennsylvania. March.

———. 1998. "A Very Public Agenda." *Policy Perspectives.* Philadelphia: Institute for Research on Higher Education, University of Pennsylvania. September.

———. 2000. "The Data Made Me Do It." *Policy Perspectives.* Philadelphia: Institute for Research on Higher Education, University of Pennsylvania. March.

———. 2002. "Who Owns Teaching?" *Policy Perspectives.* Philadelphia: Institute for Research on Higher Education, University of Pennsylvania. August.

———. 2002. "Of Precept, Policy, and Practice." *Policy Perspectives.* Philadelphia: Institute for Research on Higher Education, University of Pennsylvania. December.

———. 2003. "When Values Matter." *Policy Perspectives.* Philadelphia: Institute for Research on Higher Education, University of Pennsylvania. November.

Massy, William. 2003. *Honoring the Trust: Quality and Cost Containment in Higher Education.* Bolton, Mass.: Anker Publishing Company, Inc.

Moe, Michael. 2000. *The Knowledge Web.* New York: Merrill Lynch.

National Center for Public Policy and Higher Education. 2002. *Measuring Up: The State-by-State Report Card for Higher Education.* San Jose, Calif.: National Center for Public Policy and Higher Education.

National Commission on Excellence in Education. 1984. *A Nation at Risk: The Full Account.* Cambridge, Mass.: USA Research.

Pew Higher Education Roundtable. 1988. "Seeing Straight Through a Muddle." *Policy Perspectives.* Philadelphia: Institute for Research on Higher Education, University of Pennsylvania. September.

———. 1990. "The Lattice and the Ratchet." *Policy Perspectives.* Philadelphia: Institute for Research on Higher Education, University of Pennsylvania. June.

———. 1991. "Not Good Enough." *Policy Perspectives.* Philadelphia: Institute for Research on Higher Education, University of Pennsylvania. May.

———. 1992. "Testimony from the Belly of the Whale." *Policy Perspectives.* Philadelphia: Institute for Research on Higher Education, University of Pennsylvania. September.

———. 1993. "A Call to Meeting." *Policy Perspectives.* Philadelphia: Institute for Research on Higher Education, University of Pennsylvania. February.

———. 1994. "To Dance with Change." *Policy Perspectives.* Philadelphia: Institute for Research on Higher Education, University of Pennsylvania. April.

———. 1996. "Rumblings." *Policy Perspectives.* Philadelphia: Institute for Research on Higher Education, University of Pennsylvania. November

Rosovsky, Henry. 1991. *Annual Report of the Dean of the Faculty of Arts and Sciences, 1990–1991.* Cambridge: Harvard University.

Shulman, James, and William Bowen. 2001. *The Game of Life: College Sports and Educational Values.* Princeton, N.J.: Princeton University Press.

Utterback, James M. 1996. *Mastering the Dynamics of Innovation.* Boston: Harvard University Business School Press.

van Vught, Frans. 1994. "The New Context for Academic Quality." *Symposium: University and Society.* Enschede: University of Twente, the Netherlands.

Winston, Gordon C. 1997. "Why Can't a College Be More Like a Firm?" Discussion Paper DP-42. Williamstown, Mass.: Williams College, Williams College Project on the Economics of Higher Education.

Zemsky, Robert. 1989. *Structure and Coherence: Measuring the Undergraduate Curriculum*. Washington, D.C.: Association of American Colleges.

Zemsky, Robert, and William F. Massy. 2003. *Thwarted Innovation: What Happened to E-learning and Why*. West Chester, Pa.: The Learning Alliance for Higher Education, University of Pennsylvania.

Zemsky, Robert, and Penney Oedel. 1983. *The Structure of College Choice*. Princeton, N.J.: The College Board.

Zemsky, Robert, Susan Shaman, and Marcus Iannozzi. 1997. "The Landscape: In Search of Strategic Perspective: A Tool for Mapping the Market in Postsecondary Education." *Change*, December.

Zemsky, Robert, Susan Shaman, and Daniel B. Shapiro. 2001. *Higher Education as Competitive Enterprise: When Markets Matter*. San Francisco: Jossey-Bass.

Index

accountability: assessment as, 143–147; calls for, 144; external, 147; faculty, 15, 146; graduation rates as measure of, 42; higher education and, 144; improvement and, 147–149; institutional, 145; markets and, 38–40; price, 35–38; promises of, 145; for student performance, 146

admissions: alternative processes for, 32; budgets for, 34; consultants for, 34; effect of choices on students, 33–34; excess of applicants and, 54; for full-time students, 35, 36; influences on, 35, 36; marketing and, 34–35; need-blind, 54; for part-time students, 37; price fixing and, 47–48; selective, 47; for working students, 36–37

admissions arms race, 32–50, 199, 201; market and, 11; proposals for ameliorating, 46–50

affirmative action, 9, 166–167, 181

Alverno College, 44

American Association of Higher Education, 35

American Association of University Women, 212

American College Testing (ACT) program, 34, 145

Amherst College, 54

assessment: as accountability, 143–147; allocation of resources and, 146; budget decisions and, 146; external, 152; faculty resistance to, 145; learning, 152; of learning outcomes, 145; mandated, 146; mistrust of available measures, 146; organized programs of, 144; policies, 145; program structure, 150; standardized, 145; of student learning, 151; tasks assigned to administrative staff, 147; workshops, 146

athletics, intercollegiate: change in mission of, 58; commercialization of, 58; selective admissions and, 12; women's, 182

audits: advantages of, 158–160; auditors for, 156–157, 159; countermarket example, 159–160; debriefing and, 157; faculty involvement in, 159; of quality process, 156–160; respect for diversity and, 159; self-studies and, 156; steps for, 156–157; workshops and, 156

About the Authors

ROBERT ZEMSKY is a longtime professor at the University of Pennsylvania where he currently serves as the chair of The Learning Alliance. He has served as Penn's chief planning officer, as master of College House, as the founding director of the Institute for Research on Higher Education, and as the codirector of the federal government's National Center on the Educations Quality of the Workforce (EQW).

GREGORY R. WEGNER is director of program development at the Great Lakes Colleges Association. Prior to that he was associate director of the University of Pennsylvania's Institute for Research on Higher Education and managing editor of *Policy Perspectives,* the periodical publication of the Pew Higher Education Roundtable and the Knight Collaborative.

WILLIAM MASSY is president of the Jackson Hole Higher Education Group, Inc., and professor emeritus of higher education and business administration at Stanford University. He has served as Stanford's vice provost for research and vice president for business and finance and has published many books and articles on higher education.